LATIN AMERICA vs EAST ASIA

LATIN AMERICA
vs EAST ASIA

A Comparative Development Perspective

Ching-yuan Lin

An East Gate Book

M. E. Sharpe, Inc.
Armonk, New York
London, England

An East Gate Book

Copyright © 1989 by M. E. Sharpe, Inc.

Available in the United Kingdom and Europe from M. E. Sharpe, Publishers, 3 Henrietta Street, London WC2E 8LU.

Library of Congress Cataloging-in-Publication Data

Lin, Ching-yuan.
    Latin America versus East Asia : a comparative development perspective / by Ching-yuan Lin.

        p.   cm.
        Bibliography: p.
    Includes index.
ISBN 0-87332-526-5
    1. Latin America—Economic policy. 2. East Asia—Economic policy. 3. Chile—Economic policy. 4. Argentina—Economic policy. 5. Brazil—Economic policy. 6. Taiwan—Economic policy—1975– . 7. Korea (South)—Economic policy—1960–   . I. Title.
HC125.L556   1989
338.98—dc19   89-4128
                                                              CIP

Printed in the United States of America

To my dear wife, Fu-yun, for her strong support and loving care as I worked on this manuscript during a severe illness.

With a jug of wine among the flowers,
I drink alone, not a soul keeping me company.
I raise my cup and invite the moon to drink with me,
And together with my shadow we are three.
But the moon does not know the joy of drinking,
And my shadow only follows me about.
Nevertheless I shall have them as companions,
For one should enjoy life while there is time.
The moon lingers as I sing;
My shadow looks confused as I dance.
I drink with them while I am awake;
And part with them when I become drunk.
Let us keep a lasting companionship without emotional complications,
And together traverse the clouds in yonder sky!

—Li Po (A.D. 701–762)

Based on a translation by Tsang Bing-ching,
with some alterations. See Robert Payne (ed.),
The White Pony (New York: The New
American Library, 1947), pp. 172–173.

CONTENTS

CHARTS

TABLES

PREFACE

The idea for this study originated in my 1973 work on Taiwan, published as *Industrialization in Taiwan, 1946–1972: Trade and Import-Substitution Policies for Developing Countries* (New York: Praeger Publishers, 1973). There, in chapter 1, section 2, and in the concluding chapter, section 5, I briefly compared Taiwan's development experience with several countries (including Argentina, Brazil, and Mexico in Latin America) in a similar stage of import-substituting industrialization. I suggested causes for their divergence in economic performance at a more advanced stage of the development process. I have only recently pursued this subject further, at a time when the recurrent nature of Latin American economic problems have again caught the attention of our profession in conjunction with the explosive external debt situation in several large countries in the region.

By necessity this study focuses only on two aspects of the differences in policy behavior in the two regions, namely, the control of inflation and trade policy reforms. Time permitting, I would have examined other aspects of the differences, including the role of government, savings behavior, and the influence of differing resource endowments and population pressure.

In preparing the present study, I am indebted to many people. In particular, I would like to thank Charles Adams, Carl P. Blackwell, James Blalock, Patricia Brenner, Ke-Young Chu, Michael Deppler, E. C. Hwa, Mohsin S. Khan, Malcolm D. Knight, Jose Saul Lizondo, Hernan Puentes, Gustav Ranis, Rudolf Rhomberg, Brian Stuart, and John Williamson for their comments on earlier versions of some of the chapters; Sarra Chernick for editorial comments; Kaija-Leena Rikkonen and Youkyong Kwon for statistical assistance; and Doreen Bradford for secretarial assistance.

I would also like to express my sorrow at the sudden death of Professor Carlos F. Diaz Alejandro. I met him only briefly at Yale, but my interest in Latin American problems was originally stimulated by his work on Argentina. His death represents a great loss to our profession, and to me also the loss of learning his points of view on ideas in this book.

Part of chapters 2 and 4 formed "East Asia and Latin America as Contrasting Models," which was presented to the conference "Why Does Overcrowded, Resource-Poor East Asia Succeed—Lessons for the LDCs?" held at Vanderbilt University on October 17 to 19, 1986. I am grateful to Anthony M. Tang and James S. Worley for inviting me to the conference; to the section chairperson, Kathryn H. Anderson, for introducing me; and to the two discussants, Arnold C. Harberger and Samuel A. Morley, as well as Bela Balassa, Anne Romanis Braun, Andrew Crockett, Michael Deppler, D. Gale Johnson, Anthony Lanyi, and Elizabeth Milne for many useful comments. These comments helped improve the final draft which is included in this volume.

Neither the persons mentioned above nor the International Monetary Fund are responsible for opinions expressed in this book.

* * *

The Chinese province of Taiwan and the Republic of Korea are here referred to respectively as Taiwan and South Korea.

LATIN AMERICA
vs EAST ASIA

Chapter 1

INTRODUCTION

During the early 1980s, a number of Latin American countries experienced severe debt-service problems, rapid inflation, and stagnant economic growth. The list included not only Chile and Argentina, countries whose economic performance was below average during the 1960s, but also Brazil and Mexico, countries that were considered successful prior to the oil shocks. By contrast, most East Asian countries, which had attained rapid economic growth and stable domestic prices during the 1960s, managed to control the resurgent inflation and external deficits rapidly, thereby resuming noninflationary economic growth along with the recovery of the world economy in 1983.

What caused this divergence in economic performance between many countries in the two regions? Why were the East Asian countries able to take advantage of the favorable global environment in the 1960s to establish a sustainable pattern of economic growth while many Latin American countries were not? In the aftermath of oil shocks and the severe worsening in the global environment in the 1970s and the early 1980s, why were most East Asian countries able to control the resurgent inflation and external deficits rapidly while many Latin American countries were not? This study attempts to answer these questions by examining the major Latin American countries' economic problems and development experiences in light of the more successful stabilization and development experiences of the East Asian countries, particularly Taiwan and South Korea. In addition to the Introduction, the volume contains the following four chapters.

Chapter 2 is titled "Policy Reforms, International Competitiveness, and Export Performance: Chile and Argentina versus Taiwan and South Korea." It first investigates why Chile and Argentina continued to suffer from a vicious circle of recurrent balance of payments crises, persistent inflation, and sluggish economic growth during the 1960s when the global environment was favorable, while Taiwan and South Korea were able to take advantage of the favorable external environment to establish a sustainable pattern of economic growth with rapid export expansion, accelerated economic growth, and stable domestic prices. The chapter then reviews the more extensive stabilization and liberalization efforts of Chile and Argentina in the 1970s and discusses their problems in light of the more successful policy reform experiences of Taiwan and South Korea in the 1960s.

Chapter 3, "Policy Response to External Shocks: Brazil versus Taiwan and South Korea," investigates why, in the aftermath of two oil shocks, Brazil experienced hyperinflation and severe debt-service problems while Taiwan and South Korea controlled the resurgent inflation and external deficits without experiencing a prolonged recession. The chapter examines Brazil's macroeconomic policy behavior and its consequences in comparison to the developments in Taiwan and South Korea. In this study, South Korea is treated as an intermediate case between Brazil and Taiwan in terms of stabilization efforts and external adjustment.

Chapter 4 is titled "Controlling Rapid Inflation: East Asia versus Latin America." It discusses the divergent experiences of price stabilization in a number of countries in East Asia and Latin America, the underlying causes, and the interactions with the economic growth process. In tracing the differing policy attitudes toward the control of inflation between the East Asian and the Latin American countries, the chapter goes back to the early postwar period when the East Asian countries (not only Taiwan and South Korea, but also Japan and mainland China) experienced hyperinflation because of the chaotic wartime and postwar economic and political conditions, while the Latin American countries experienced only moderate inflation largely caused by the pursuit of inward-oriented development policies. The chapter then reviews the policy and institutional reforms in the East Asian countries that enabled a sustainable pattern of economic growth, and the relative lack of such reforms in the Latin American countries that led to the perpetuation of recurrent balance of payments crises, persistent inflation, and sluggish economic growth. The chapter then discusses the differing policy responses to the worsening external environment that occurred in the 1970s and the resulting further divergence of economic conditions in East Asia and Latin America.

The concluding chapter summarizes the divergent experiences of the East Asian and the Latin American countries with respect to export expansion, economic growth, and price stabilization, and discusses the policy implications for the Latin American countries from the perspective of the East Asian countries.

Some explanations are in order concerning the choice of countries for comparison. For the study of export performance and its bearing on the pattern of economic growth, Chile and Argentina are chosen for comparison to Taiwan and South Korea. The former two countries have had a long history of import-substituting industrialization and their labor forces are more susceptible to industrial discipline compared to many other Latin American countries, considering their predominantly European origins and their relatively advanced educational standards. This leaves population density and policy management as the two major factors explaining the differences in export performance between them and the two East Asian countries. Moreover, since population density is presumed to affect the composition of exports more than its rate of growth, we are left with policy management as the main factor explaining the divergence in export performance between the countries concerned.

For the study of policy response to external shocks and its after-effects, Brazil is chosen for comparison to Taiwan and South Korea because Brazil was one of the most successful countries in Latin America in attaining rapid economic growth in the decade or so before the first oil shock. The question is: why would a Latin American country which was successful during the 1960s get into difficulties during the 1970s and the 1980s, while Taiwan and South Korea in East Asia would not? For this study, Mexico is not chosen because of its subsequent oil bonanza, whereas Chile and Argentina are not chosen because of the presumption that if they did not do well during the favorable global environment of the 1960s, they would not do better in the turbulent external environment of the 1970s.

Lastly, for the study of the control of rapid inflation, the country coverage is widened to include Japan and China in East Asia and Mexico and Peru in Latin America. The first two countries are added because they, like Taiwan and South Korea, started postwar economic development with the control of hyperinflation that originated in the chaotic conditions of World War II and the immediate postwar years. The latter countries are added because their inflation and economic performance, like Brazil's, worsened during the 1970s and the early 1980s despite (or rather, because of the expectation of) the oil bonanza. The addition of these countries thus serves to accentuate the differences in economic policy management between the countries in East Asia and Latin America.

Chapter 2

POLICY REFORMS, INTERNATIONAL COMPETITIVENESS, AND EXPORT PERFORMANCE: CHILE AND ARGENTINA VERSUS TAIWAN AND SOUTH KOREA

Introduction and Summary

The export and macroeconomic performances of Chile and Argentina in the period before the first oil shock are compared here to the performances of Taiwan and South Korea, with discussion of the key factors underlying the divergence in performance including the differences in trade policies and in the control of inflation. In addition, this chapter reviews the extensive policy reforms of Chile and Argentina in the 1970s and discusses the associated difficulties in light of the more successful reform experiences of Taiwan and South Korea in the early 1960s.

Throughout the postwar decades, several Latin American countries experienced a vicious circle of balance of payments crises, persistent inflation, and sluggish economic growth. In countries such as Argentina, Chile, Peru, and Uruguay, recurrent balance of payments crises and persistent inflation compelled the national authorities to pursue intermittent stabilization policies which resulted in a stop-go growth pattern. Because of the sluggish growth of real income, the distribution of income became an important political issue, further constraining the authorities' policy options in breaking the inflationary spirals and improving the balance of payments.

How can these countries break out of this predicament? This analysis suggests that a key prerequisite is a rapid and sustained growth of export earnings, amply demonstrated by the experience of several countries in East Asia, particularly Taiwan and South Korea. In both of these countries, a strong export performance in the 1960s and the attendant improvement in credit standing enabled the authorities to remove the import and saving constraints they faced in the 1950s. The resulting expansion of investment, imports, and productive capacity, combined with the enlargement of domestic markets through the growth of export incomes, improved the operating efficiency and export competitiveness of domestic industry. The higher productivity growth restrained the rise of unit labor costs, and this, combined with the stable import prices then prevailing, facilitated the maintenance of domestic price stability. The rapid growth of income also enabled a rising savings ratio, and this ratio, in conjunction with the stabilizing price trends, facilitated the growth of domestic finances in order to support the expansion of economic activity. A virtuous circle of high export growth, rapid economic expansion, and stable domestic prices was thus generated.

By contrast, sluggish volume growth or sharp fluctuations in export prices continued to characterize the export patterns of Chile and Argentina because both countries failed to significantly diversify the commodity composition of their exports. Why did countries like Chile and Argentina, with long histories of industrialization, fail to develop significant exports of manufactures during the 1960s comparable to Taiwan and South Korea? Two major reasons are suggested.

First, behind the successful development of manufactured exports in Taiwan and South Korea was a thorough reform of the incentive systems in favor of export activity. These policy reforms received full government support, and the direction of policy reforms remained unchanged over time. By contrast, policy reforms in Chile and Argentina tended to fluctuate in intensity, partly because of frequent shifts in government policies and partly because of the persistent inflation. As a consequence, the relative profitability of export activity fluctuated widely and the focus of the entrepreneurial activity in the industrial sector remained directed mainly to the domestic markets.

Second, the rapid growth of manufactured exports in Taiwan and South Korea was supported by their very competitive factor cost position. Throughout the postwar decades, unit labor costs increased at a much slower pace in Taiwan and South Korea than in Chile and Argentina because of slower growth in money wages combined with faster growth in labor productivity. The slower growth of money wages both in Taiwan and in South Korea resulted from, and enabled the maintenance of, lower rates of inflation. In turn, these lower inflation rates enabled them to attain a higher rate of growth of exports, per capita income, and real wages than in Chile and Argentina. In Chile and Argentina, real wages increased only modestly during the 1960s despite a tremendous expansion in money wages caused by persistent inflation.

While the unfavorable domestic cost position can be ameliorated by the use of a flexible exchange rate, frequent exchange depreciations perpetuate chronic inflation through the built-in wage and cost adjustment mechanisms. Moreover, the persistence of inflationary psychology is inimical to the development of manufactured exports, which require constant product improvement and cost control in order to compete successfully in the international markets. This suggests that in order to establish a viable pattern of economic growth Chile and Argentina and other countries similarly situated must not only undertake policy reforms in order to shift incentives in favor of export activity, but must also pursue intensive stabilization efforts to create a domestic environment conducive to the attainment of economic efficiency and productivity growth.[1]

The chapter is organized as follows. The next section reviews the divergence in export growth between Chile and Argentina on the one hand, and Taiwan and South Korea on the other, during the decades before the first oil shock and the associated disparity in macroeconomic performance between them. The third section discusses both the initial similarity in the four countries' growth patterns and incentive systems in the early 1950s and the differences in the subsequent policy reforms instituted by the two East Asian countries and the two Latin American countries, respectively. The fourth section examines the divergence in the control of inflation and manufacturing unit labor costs in Chile and Argentina compared to Taiwan and South Korea, and discusses the major factors underlying the disparate movements of wages and productivity. Then a section reviews the more extensive policy reforms undertaken in Chile and Argentina in the 1970s and considers these countries' continuing economic difficulties in light of the more successful reform experience of Taiwan and South Korea in the 1960s. The last section provides concluding remarks.

Comparative Export and Macroeconomic Performances

The contrast in export and macroeconomic performance between Taiwan and South Korea, on the one hand, and Chile and Argentina, on the other, in the decade before the first oil shock is most striking. From 1960 to 1973, the export earnings (in U.S. dollars) of Taiwan and South Korea increased by 29 percent and 42 percent per year, respectively, compared to 7.4 percent for Chile and 8.9 percent for Argentina. As a consequence, the shares of Taiwan and South Korea in world exports (excluding the centrally planned economies other than the International Monetary Fund [IMF] members) increased rapidly while those of Chile and Argentina declined (Tables 2.1 and 2.2).

The sharp expansion of export earnings, under relatively stable world prices, enabled Taiwan and South Korea to boost their import capacity sharply. It also greatly improved their credit worthiness and their reputation as competitive producers of labor-intensive products, thereby inducing an increased inflow of bank credit and foreign capital. As a consequence, both capital investment and imports expanded sharply. In turn, these expansions led to a marked acceleration in the growth of real output and real income as well as a significant expansion of domestic markets. From 1960 to 1973, manufacturing production increased by 18 percent per year in Taiwan and by 17 percent in Korea, compared to 13 percent and 12 percent in the preceding decade. Real GDP increased by 10.4 percent and 8.9 percent per year, compared to 7.6 percent and 3.8 percent. An even greater acceleration occurred in the growth of import volume (Table 2.1).

Compared with the rapid acceleration in economic growth attained by Taiwan and South Korea, the rate of economic growth changed little in Chile and Argentina. From 1960 to 1973, the real export earnings of Chile and Argentina did increase somewhat, due to the steady expansion of the world economy. However, at 5 to 6 percent per year, this growth was not adequate to support a significant expansion in domestic demand and imports. Moreover, this growth fluctuated sharply over time because of cyclical demand changes or random supply factors. The resulting balance of payments difficulties and the persistent double-digit inflation compelled the authorities to

Table 2.1

Growth of Export Earnings, Import Purchasing Power of Exports, Import Volume, Manufacturing Production, and Real GDP, 1949–60, 1960–73, and 1973–85 (In percentage changes)

	1949–60[1]	1960–73	1973–85
1. *Export earnings* (US$)			
Chile	4.7	7.4	9.9
Argentina	0.3	8.9	8.0
Taiwan	4.3	28.7	17.3
South Korea	2.1	42.3	20.5
2. *Real export earnings*[2]			
Chile	4.3	5.9	3.2
Argentina	0.1	5.0	2.3
Taiwan	6.1	23.9	7.5
South Korea	3.9	38.8	12.6
3. *Import volume*			
Chile	4.7	4.4	1.3
Argentina	0.6	0.8	− 0.9
Taiwan	7.8	17.0	5.0
South Korea	6.2	21.3	10.4
4. *Manufacturing production*			
Chile	3.2	4.2	− 0.3
Argentina	3.8	6.8	− 0.5
Taiwan	13.0	18.1	10.1
South Korea	13.4[3]	17.9	15.4
5. *Real GDP*			
Chile	2.0[5]	3.4	1.8
Argentina	3.6[5]	3.1	0.3
Taiwan	7.6[5]	10.4	7.3
South Korea	3.8[5]	8.9	7.3
Reference items			
a. *Import unit value* (US$)			
Chile[4]	0.4	1.4	6.5
Argentina[4]	0.4	3.7	5.6
Taiwan	− 1.7	3.9	9.1
South Korea		2.5	7.0
b. *World import volume*	6.6	8.4	3.6

Sources: International Monetary Fund, *International Financial Statistics Yearbook* (various issues); United Nations, *Monthly Bulletin of Statistics* (various issues); and Council for Economic Planning and Development, *Taiwan Statistical Data Book, 1985* (Taipei, 1985).

[1]1952–60 for Taiwan and Korea, except where otherwise noted.
[2]Export earnings deflated by import unit values.
[3]For Korea, 1954–60.
[4]For Chile, based on import unit value index reported for Colombia; for Argentina, based on export unit value index reported for industrial countries.
[5]For Argentina, 1950–60; for Taiwan, 1952–60; and for Chile and Korea, 1953–60.

Table 2.2

Share of World Exports, Ratio of Exports to GDP, and Share of Manufactures in Total Exports, 1952, 1960, 1973, and 1984 (In percent)

	1952	1960	1973	1984[1]	Changes 1952–73	Changes 1973–84
Share of world exports[2]						
Chile	0.61	0.41	0.23	0.21	−0.38	−0.02
Argentina	0.92	0.91	0.61	0.46	−0.47	−0.15
Taiwan	0.16	0.14	0.84	1.71	0.68	0.87
South Korea	0.04	0.03	0.60	1.66	0.54	1.06
Ratio of exports to GDP[3]						
Chile	15.3	13.8	13.1	24.3	−2.2	11.2
Argentina	7.0*	9.5	10.1	14.6**	3.1	4.5
Taiwan	8.1	11.3	46.8	57.6	38.7	10.8
South Korea	2.1	3.3	29.9	37.5	27.8	7.6
Share of manufactures in total exports						
Chile[4]		4	4	8	(—)	4
Argentina[4]		4	19	24	(15)	5
Taiwan	8	32	85	92	77	7
South Korea		14	78	92	(73)	14
Share of manufacturing in GDP						
Chile		21	26	20	5[5]	−6
Argentina	11	29	29	28	−[5]	−1
Taiwan		7	36	33	19[5]	−3
South Korea		14	25	28	11[5]	3

Sources: International Monetary Fund, *International Financial Statistics Yearbook* (various issues); United Nations, *Handbook of International Trade and Development Statistics* (various issues); Council of Economic Planning and Development, *Taiwan Statistical Data Book, 1985* (Taipei, 1985); and World Bank, *World Development Report* (various issues).

[1] 1982 for the lower two panels; [2] World total excludes exports of U.S.S.R. and Eastern Europe, except Hungary, Romania, and Yugoslavia; [3] Exports include nonfactor services; [4] Manufactured exports exclude metals; [5] Changes in 1973 over 1960; *For 1950-52 average and **For 1983.

restrain periodically the growth of domestic demand. These developments resulted in sluggish economic performance in both Chile and Argentina.

From 1960 to 1973, real GDP increased by only 3 to 3.5 percent per year in the two countries (or less than 1.5 percent on a per capita basis), a pace not much different from that of the preceding decade. The growth of manufacturing output picked up somewhat, but the growth of import volume, reflecting a continued inward bias in the trade policies, remained as low as in the 1950s (Table 2.1).

The export expansion of Taiwan and South Korea was spearheaded by labor- and skill-intensive manufactured goods. As a result, along with the expansion of export activity, significant changes occurred in the commodity composition of exports and in the structure of domestic production. In the early 1950s, manufactured goods accounted for less than 10 percent of the exports of both Taiwan and South Korea; by 1973, the ratio had risen to 85 percent and 78 percent, respectively. During the same period, the share of manufacturing in domestic output increased from around 10 percent in both countries to 36 percent and 25 percent, respectively.

In comparison, in Chile and Argentina, there were relatively small changes in both the commodity composition of exports and in the structure of domestic production. In Chile, the share of manufactures (excluding nonferrous metals) remained at less than 5 percent of total exports throughout the 1950s and the 1960s. In Argentina, this share increased significantly during the 1960s, but, at 19 percent in 1973, the amount remained far below that of the East Asian countries. The ratio of exports to domestic output, which was higher than or comparable to those of Taiwan and South Korea in the early 1950s, did not increase at all in contrast with the sharp expansion in the two East Asian countries during the 1960s. Similarly, the share of manufacturing in domestic production, which was much higher than that of Taiwan or South Korea in the early 1950s, was by the early 1970s similar to or even lower than that of the East Asian countries (Table 2.2).

Through the expansion of exports, the economies of Taiwan and South Korea succeeded not only in removing the balance of payments constraints on the growth of imports and investment, but also in realizing economies of scale by circumventing the limitations of the originally smaller domestic markets. As a result, Taiwan and South Korea were able to gradually upgrade their industrial structures in terms of capital, technology, and scale of operation, and to increasingly shift the composition of their exports from labor-intensive products to more skill-intensive and higher quality products. These developments, combined with various factors that helped restrain the rapid growth of labor costs, enabled Taiwan and South Korea to establish a trade pattern based on a dynamic comparative advantage—exporting relatively labor- and skill-intensive products to the more advanced countries and relatively capital- and technology-intensive products to the less advanced countries.[2]

By contrast, in Chile and Argentina, the failure to develop new exports and to attain a faster and steadier expansion of export earnings led to continuing foreign exchange shortages, inadequate domestic savings, and small domestic markets. As a consequence, the growth of labor productivity and the improvement in operating efficiency were limited. This situation, combined with the rapid growth of unit labor costs and inadequate export incentives, inhibited the improvement of export competitiveness, thereby perpetuating the vicious circle between low export growth and low economic growth. Despite the steady expansion of the world economy in the 1960s, both Chile and Argentina were unable to take full advantage of the favorable external environment to strengthen their economies and to establish a viable pattern of economic growth.

Clearly, the expansion of exports has helped Taiwan and South Korea embark on sustained economic growth with comparative price stability, whereas low export growth has constricted Chile and Argentina to a difficult situation of recurrent balance of payments crises, persistent inflation, and sluggish economic growth. The question, therefore, is why Taiwan and South Korea were able to expand their exports while Chile and Argentina were not.

To some extent, the divergence in export performance between these Latin American and East Asian countries can be explained by the difference in their resource endowments and export composition, because world export demand for manufactures grew much faster than demand for agricultural and nonfuel primary products (14 percent versus 7 to 11 percent per year in terms of U.S. dollars) during the period 1960–1973 (Table 2.3). However, this difference can provide only part of the explanation, since the export growth of Chile and Argentina also fell short of the growth of world trade in agricultural and mineral products whereas the growth of Taiwan and South Korea

Table 2.3

The Growth of World Trade by Major Commodity Classes, 1955–60, 1960–73, and 1973–82 (Annual compound rate of change of U.S. dollar value)

	1955–60	1960–73	1973–82
All commodities[1]	6.5	12.2	13.8
Food	4.0	10.1	10.1
Agricultural raw materials	2.8	7.3	8.3
Ores and metals	7.9	10.5	7.7
Fuels	4.1	13.3	23.6
Manufactures	9.1	13.9	13.4

Source: United Nations, *Monthly Bulletin of Statistics* (various issues).
[1]The grouping of commodities, according to Standard International Trade Classification is as follows: food, Sections 0, 1, and 4, plus Division 22; agricultural raw materials, Section 2, except Divisions 22, 27, and 28; ores and metals, Divisions 27, 28, 67, and 68; fuels, Section 3; and manufactures, Sections 5, 6, 7, 8, except Divisions 67 and 68.

far surpassed the growth of world trade in manufactures (Tables 2.1 and 2.3). Moreover, other countries similar to Chile and Argentina in resource endowments and population density, such as Canada and Australia, achieved much better export and overall economic performances than Chile and Argentina.[3] This suggests the importance of other factors, such as differences in trade policy and export competitiveness, in explaining the divergence in export performance between the Latin American and East Asian countries.

Differences in Trade Policy Reform during the 1960s

The four economies considered here began their postwar economic development with an inward-oriented industrialization policy.[4] In fact, both Chile and Argentina embarked on such industrialization much earlier than Taiwan and South Korea. In both Chile and Argentina, manufacturing production to replace imports was started in the 1930s in response to the severe shortfalls of export earnings during the Great Depression.[5] These activities were continued during World War II because of shortages of imported supplies. After the war, the momentum for import-substitution initially slackened because of increased imported supplies, but then, after the Korean War boom, momentum picked up with greater intensity because of the stagnation in export earnings and because of the rising aspirations for economic development among the developing countries.

In comparison, both Taiwan and Korea were under Japan's colonial rule until the end of World War II and economic activity in the prewar period was largely geared to satisfying Japan's economic needs. Because of the availability of hydropower in Taiwan and its strategic location between Southeast Asia and Japan, Taiwan's industrialization during the colonial period started with the processing of minerals imported from Southeast Asia. In Korea, the hydropower supply was located in the present North Korea and so was the budding industrial activity. In Taiwan, some rudimentary import-substituting activity was started during the years of wartime shortages, but in both Taiwan and South Korea, intensive import-substituting industrialization did not start until after World War II when these countries became independent economies. This effort was given strong impetus by the severe shortages of foreign exchange and imported industrial goods. These shortages were caused by the loss of the Japanese markets for their primary exports and by the rapid expansion of domestic demand caused by the massive influx of refugees from mainland China and North Korea.[6]

While there were some variations, the policy instruments employed by the four economies to promote import-substituting industrialization were largely similar. These instruments included import controls, tariffs, and selective allocation of foreign exchange and bank credit. In addition, Chile and Argentina relied on export taxes on traditional exports while agricultural land reforms were an important factor in Taiwan and South Korea.[7] Under these systems, the production of import substitutes was encouraged by enhancing the expected profitability of domestic production through exclusion of foreign competition; by the allocation of foreign exchange, bank credit, and essential inputs at preferential rates; and by exemptions from, or remissions of, certain taxes and duties. At the same time, the production of traditional exports was discouraged by unfavorable exchange rate and pricing policies.[8] These systems, which were often the result of circumstance rather than design, nevertheless served the purpose of expediting the reallocation of resources from the traditional export sector to the new urban-centered industrial sector at a time when there were severe shortages of domestic savings, foreign exchange, trained labor, and industrial entrepreneurs.[9]

However, because of its inimical effects on exports and industrial efficiency, this system is basically transitional in nature. Ultimately, this system needs to be replaced by one which is more conducive to export expansion and industrial efficiency. The failure to execute such a change may impede the further growth of the economy by inducing recurrent foreign exchange shortages and prolonged industrial stagnation.[10] What set the experiences of Taiwan and South Korea apart from those of Chile and Argentina, therefore, did not lie in the initial conditions and the incentive systems, which were largely similar, but in the subsequent policy reforms which were successful in Taiwan and South Korea and unsuccessful in Chile and Argentina.

In both Taiwan and South Korea, the initial stage of import substituting industrialization and the subsequent saturation of domestic markets by "easy" manufactures were followed by a thorough reform of the incentive systems in order to encourage the export of manufactures and to encourage industrial efficiency. Partly because of these changes, import substitution and the export of manufactures ceased to be a dichotomy and became a continuing sequence of development.[11] By contrast, in Chile and Argentina, the substitution of "easy" manufactures was followed by that of the more difficult intermediate products—durable consumer goods and transport equipment. Moreover, the commitment to policy reforms tended to fluctuate, partly because of frequent changes in governments and government policies and partly because of the persistence of inflation.[12] As a consequence, the relative profitability of export activity fluctuated widely and the attention of industrial entrepreneurs remained mainly focused on domestic markets.

In Taiwan, the basic policy reforms occurred toward the end of the 1950s. Along with substantial devaluations and the elimination of multiple exchange rates, the system of policy incentives underwent profound changes, resulting in a substantial increase in incentives to exports compared with incentives to domestic sales.[13] These changes included the following: the proportion of foreign exchange retention awarded to exporters of manufactures was raised to a level far in excess of their actual need for importing raw materials; the harbor charge on export products was eliminated and its rate on imports raised; low-cost loans were initiated to meet the working capital needs of exporters; the scope of tax remission applicable to export activity was expanded substantially; the establishment of sectoral industrial-cum-trade associations which promoted exports through a system of mutual subsidies was encouraged; and the inflow of foreign capital related to export

Table 2.4

Taiwan: Evolution of Export Incentives and Nominal and Real Effective Export Exchange Rates, 1956–70
(In local currency per unit of U.S. dollar)

	Nominal export rate	Export incentives[1]	Effective Export Rate			Percentage excess of incentives over nominal rate	Relative wholesale prices[4]
			Nominal[2]	Real[3]	Percentage change		
1956	24.71	0.22	24.93	33.6		0.9	74.1
1957	25.53	0.29	25.82	33.6	—	1.1	76.9
1958	34.13	0.67	34.81	42.9	27.7	2.0	81.2
1959	39.38	1.60	40.98	46.1	7.5	4.1	88.8
1960	39.73	2.40	42.13	42.1	−8.7	6.0	100.0
1961	39.83	2.88	42.71	41.8	−0.7	7.2	102.1
1962	39.83	3.12	43.15	40.9	−2.2	8.3	105.5
1963	39.87	3.34	43.21	39.6	−3.2	8.4	109.1
1964	40.00	3.67	43.67	38.9	−1.8	9.2	112.3
1965	40.00	4.11	44.11	41.8	7.5	10.3	105.5
1966	40.00	4.39	44.39	43.2	3.3	11.0	102.8
1967	40.00	4.78	44.78	43.7	1.2	11.8	102.4
1968	40.00	4.70	44.70	43.7	—	11.9	105.1
1969	40.00	4.85	44.85	44.3	1.4	12.1	101.2
1970	40.00	5.51	45.51	45.6	2.9	13.8	99.8

Source: Based on Kuo-shu Liang and Ching-ing Hou Liang, "Trade and Incentive Policies in Taiwan," in Kwoh-ting Li and Tzong-shian Yu (eds.), *Experiences and Lessons of Economic Development in Taiwan* (Taipei: Academia Sinica, 1982), pp. 224–227.

[1]Includes export credit interest subsidy and tariff and indirect tax rebates, but excludes foreign exchange entitlement premium and industry-specific export bonus managed by industrial associations.

[2]Nominal export rate plus export incentives.

[3]Deflated by the index of relative wholesale prices.

[4]Taiwan's wholesale price index deflated by major trading partners' weighted average wholesale price indexes, each expressed in terms of respective national currencies.

activity was encouraged through the establishment of duty-free export processing zones and other measures. In the meantime, the permissible excess of domestic prices of import substitutes over the estimated import cost of products under import control was made more stringent, and import duties on a number of import substitutes were reduced substantially.[14]

As a consequence of these policy changes, both the permissible and actual levels of effective protection over domestic manufacturing were reduced substantially over time, and the effective exchange rates governing export sales were made substantially more favorable compared to those governing domestic sales[15],[16] (Table 2.4, column 6). These changes in the incentive systems exerted a strong impact on the direction of entrepreneurial activity. In the first half of the 1950s, the main concern of the traders-cum-manufacturers was directed to the acquisition of foreign exchange allocations at the official rate and to the related import quotas. By the middle of the 1960s, this concern had shifted to a scramble for profitable export items or outlets.

Similarly, in South Korea from the late 1950s to the mid-1960s, major reforms were undertaken to correct the gross overvaluation of the exchange rate and to increase the incentives for exports relative to domestic sales. While the more decisive Korean measures did not come until 1964, several years after the Taiwan reform, the Korean export promotion efforts, once started, were more aggressive than those of Taiwan.[17] In addition to a massive devaluation in May 1964, an extensive system of export incentives was implemented in early 1965. The latter included preferential treatment on taxes and interest rates; the exemption of customs duties on imported raw materials and capital equipment; the sale on the domestic markets of surplus raw materials imported duty-free for export processing (so-called wastage allowance); and imports for domestic sales of otherwise restricted consumer goods. The scope of these incentives was extended over the years so that the amount of national currency receivable per unit of U.S. dollar export earning, inclusive of various export incentives, exceeded the basic rate by about 28 percent in 1968 compared to 2 to 3 percent in the late 1950s. Moreover, the effective export exchange rate thus defined, which used to be much lower than the effective import exchange rate inclusive of tariffs and tariff equivalents, now exceeded the rate by a wide margin (Table 2.5, columns 9 and 10).

In addition to pecuniary incentives, the Korean authorities, like their Taiwanese counterparts, also provided various kinds of administrative

Table 2.5

South Korea: Evolution of Nominal Exchange Rate, Tariff and Tariff Equivalents, Export Incentives, Effective Import and Export Exchange Rates, and Real Export Exchange Rate, 1958–70 (In local currency per U.S. dollar)

	Official exchange rate for both imports and exports	Tariff and tariff equivalents[1]	Effective import exchange rate[2]		Export incentives[3]
			Nominal	Percentage excess of tariff over official rate	
1958	50.0	11.6	61.6	23.2	1.2
1959	50.0	27.3	77.3	54.6	1.3
1960	62.5	29.7	92.2	47.5	1.2
1961	127.5	17.6	145.1	13.8	8.5
1962	130.0	23.3	153.3	17.9	21.5
1963	130.0	12.0	142.0	9.2	19.6
1964	214.3	21.0	235.3	9.8	27.4
1965	265.4	27.7	293.1	10.4	39.2
1966	271.3	25.1	296.4	9.3	51.6
1967	270.7	25.5	296.2	9.4	62.4
1968	276.7	25.9	302.5	9.3	77.7
1969	288.2	24.5	312.7	8.5	75.1
1970	310.7	25.7	336.4	8.1	86.5

Effective export exchange rate

	Nominal[4]	Real[5]	Percentage change	Percentage excess of export incentives over nominal export rate	Effective export rate relative to effective import rate	Relative wholesale prices[6]
1958	51.2	124.9		2.4	0.83	41.0
1959	51.3	122.7	−1.8	2.6	0.66	41.8
1960	63.7	137.9	12.4	1.9	0.69	46.2
1961	136.0	261.0	89.3	6.7	0.94	52.1
1962	151.5	263.9	1.1	16.5	0.99	57.4
1963	149.6	217.8	−17.5	15.1	1.05	68.7
1964	241.7	261.9	20.9	10.3	1.03	92.3
1965	304.6	304.6	16.3	14.8	1.04	100.0
1966	323.9	306.1	0.5	19.0	1.09	105.8
1967	332.7	298.9	−2.4	23.1	1.12	111.3
1968	354.4	299.1	0.1	28.1	1.17	118.5
1969	363.3	295.6	−1.2	26.1	1.16	122.9
1970	397.2	307.2	3.9	27.8	1.18	129.3

Source: Based on Charles R. Frank, Jr., Kwang Suk Kim, and Larry E. Westphal, *Foreign Trade Regimes and Economic Development: South Korea* (New York: National Bureau of Economic Research, 1975), pp. 70–73.

[1]Includes actual tariff and foreign exchange tax collected, but excludes foreign exchange resulting from export certificate, export-import link, and import restrictions.

[2]Official rate plus tariff and tariff equivalents.

[3]Includes cash and interest subsidies and tariff and internal tax exemption and rebates, but excludes export certificate or export-import link premium.

[4]Official rate plus export incentives.

[5]Deflated by the index of relative wholesale prices.

[6]South Korea's wholesale price index deflated by major trading partners' weighted average wholesale price indexes.

Table 2.6

Argentina, Taiwan, and South Korea: Nominal Protection, Effective Protection, Effective Tax and Credit Incentives on Exports, Total Effective Incentives, and Bias Against Exports, 1969[1] (In percent)

	Nominal protection[2]	Effective protection[3]	Effective tax and credit incentives on exports	Total effective incentives[4]		
				Exports	Domestic sales	Bias against exports[5]
1. *All industries*						
Argentina	36	47	3	-17	55	87
Taiwan	9	5	20	16	2	-12
South Korea	13	10	9	9	10	1
2. *Manufacturing*						
Argentina	51	97	9	-31	110	204
Taiwan	13	19	27	23	24	1
South Korea	11	-1	9	12	-9	-19
3. *Agriculture, forestry, and fishery*						
Argentina	-10	-13	2	-11	-11	0
Taiwan	2	-4	4	2	-8	-10
South Korea	17	18	6	-10	23	37
4. *Mining and energy*						
Argentina	30	32	1	-11	33	49
Taiwan	0	-7	5	2	-10	-12
South Korea	7	3	4	3	5	2
5. *Processed foods*						
Argentina	2	24	5	-25	41	88
Taiwan	8	1	37	30	1	-22
South Korea	3	-17	5	2	-25	-26
6. *Beverages and tobacco*						
Argentina	50	87	2	-446	94	-156
Taiwan	48	-6,471	1,126	747	-5,812	-774
South Korea	2	-19	17	15	-26	-36
7. *Construction materials*						
Argentina	29	31	12	16	30	12
Taiwan	0	-10	8	5	-15	-19

South Korea	4	−11	11	6	−17	−22
8. Intermediate products I						
Argentina	27	142	8	−18	144	198
Taiwan	11	10	36	29	36	6
South Korea	10	14	8	43	−30	−51
9. Intermediate products II						
Argentina	67	122	12	−106	127	3,683
Taiwan	12	16	35	30	26	−3
South Korea	19	24	17	17	20	3
10. Nondurable consumer goods						
Argentina	56	48	9	−1	49	51
Taiwan	10	8	12	10	9	−1
South Korea	9	−9	7	5	−21	−25
11. Durable consumer goods						
Argentina	88	144	13	−100	143	0
Taiwan	14	29	33	30	44	11
South Korea	31	51	7	2	38	35
12. Machinery						
Argentina	87	117	21	19	119	84
Taiwan	9	1	12	11	−3	−13
South Korea	28	43	18	5	31	25
13. Transport equipment						
Argentina	109	207	14	10	206	51
Taiwan	27	55	30	−23	66	236
South Korea	54	164			159	

Sources: Estimates for Argentina, Taiwan, and South Korea are adopted from articles by Julio Berlinski and Daniel M. Schydlowsky; T. H. Lee and Kuo-shu Liang; and Larry E. Westphal and Kwang Suk Kim, respectively, published in Bela Balassa and associates, *Development Strategies in Semi-Industrial Economies* (Baltimore: Johns Hopkins University Press, 1982).

[1] For Korea, based on the 1968 tariff table.

[2] The rate of nominal protection expresses the effects of protective measures on the price received for a product by its domestic producers. Such protective measures include, in addition to import duties, indirect taxes, quantitative restrictions, export taxes and subsidies, and advanced deposits for import payments.

[3] The rate of effective protection relates the joint effects of protective measures on the price of the product and the prices of its inputs to value added in the production process. The estimates shown used the so-called Balassa method, although alternative estimates using the so-called Corden method are also available.

[4] Total incentives relate the combined effects of protective measures and credit and tax preferences to value added.

[5] This bias is defined as the percentage excess of domestic value added obtainable as a result of protection in producing for domestic markets over that obtainable in exporting, here estimated as the ratio 1 + rate of total effective incentives on domestic sales/1 + rate of total effective incentives on exports, minus one.

and technical assistance to exporters. A good illustration in the Korean case was the initiation in 1966 of the monthly export promotion committee meeting with the president, attended by cabinet members and business leaders. In the meetings, business leaders were asked to report their problems, difficulties, and opportunities, and the government officials were required to respond before the president to criticisms of past government performance and to make recommendations for improvement. These meetings served to emphasize the importance of the export drives and to expedite government decision making.[18]

In Chile and Argentina during the 1960s various incentives were also provided to promote nontraditional exports. In Chile, starting from 1958, a special regime was established for specific exports including (1) exemptions from indirect taxes and customs duties on material inputs, (2) tax rebates if an exporter could demonstrate that the taxes affected the cost of his exports, and (3) automatic tax refunds at specific percentages for copper sheets and plates and for bulk wine shipments. In 1963, new lines of preshipment credit were established for agricultural and nonagricultural exports. These tax and credit incentives were expanded in 1966 to cover more products, with the number of products receiving special treatment ultimately reaching 331 before being reduced in 1969.[19]

In Argentina, starting in 1962–1963, exporters of industrial products received reimbursement of tariffs which they and their suppliers had paid; and from 1967, the exporters also received the reimbursement of internal taxes. A preferential credit facility for nontraditional exports was created in 1963 and revised in 1965. In addition, from 1967, exporters were allowed to deduct 10 percent of the value of their exports from taxable income.[20]

However, compared with the all-out export drives of Taiwan and South Korea, the promotion of exports by Chile and Argentina appears inadequate. Their incentive systems remained heavily biased against exports despite the introduction of various export incentives. This is evidenced by the rates of effective protection and export incentives estimated for these countries. Based on estimates by the Balassa group, which, however, do not cover Chile, the rate of effective protection (on value added) on all industries remained at the end of the 1960s as high as 47 percent in Argentina compared to 5 percent in Taiwan and 10 percent in South Korea.[21] For manufacturing, the corresponding figures were 97, 19, and –1 percent, respectively.[22] In the same year, tax and credit incentives for all merchandise exports amounted to only 3

Table 2.7

Chile: Implicit Tariff Rates and Effective Protection Rates, 1961 and 1967 (In percent)

	Implicit tariff rates[1]		Effective protection rates[2]	
	1961	1967	1961	1967
All industries	83	48	254	168
Agriculture	43	1	50	−7
Fishing	21		25	
Mining				
Copper	37		31	
Nitrate	2		−7	
Food products	82	32	2,884	365
Beverages	122	7	609	−23
Tobacco	106	0	141	−13
Textiles	182	99	672	492
Footwear and clothing	255	23	386	16
Wood and cork	35	0	21	−4
Furniture	129	0	209	−5
Paper and its products	55	44	41	95
Printing and publishing	72	0	82	−15
Leather and its products	161	25	714	18
Rubber products	102	125	109	304
Chemical products	94	38	89	64
Petroleum and coal products	50	55	45	1,140
Nonmetallic mineral products	139	27	227	1
Basic metals	66	25	198	35
Metallic products	59	80	43	92
Nonelectrical machinery	84	56	85	76
Electrical machinery	105	162	112	449
Transport equipment	84	150	101	271

Source: Jere R. Behrman, *Foreign Trade Regimes and Economic Development: Chile* (New York: National Bureau of Economic Research, 1976), p. 138.
[1]The ratio to the c.i.f. price of the difference between the Chilean domestic price (net of normal distribution costs) and the c.i.f. price.
[2]The ratio to the domestic value added of the difference between domestic value added and international value added.

percent of these industries' value added in Argentina, compared to 20 percent in Taiwan and 9 percent in South Korea. For manufacturing, the corresponding figures were 9, 27, and 9 percent.

For all industries combined, because of the combination of low effective protection and high effective tax and credit incentives for exports at the end of the 1960s, exports actually received more incentives than domestic sales in Taiwan while these incentives were about the same between exports and domestic sales in South Korea. In Argentina, however, because of the combination of high effective protection and low tax and credit incentives for exports, the bias against export activity remained as high as 87 percent of value added. In manufacturing, the incentives for exports and domestic sales were about the same in Taiwan, whereas in South Korea they were much greater for exports than for domestic sales. By contrast, in Argentina the bias against exports amounted to as much as 204 percent[23] (Table 2.6).

Comparable estimates of effective incentives for exports and domestic sales are not available for Chile, but available estimates indicate that effective protection on manufacturing in Chile was even higher than in Argentina during the 1960s. Based on Teresa Jenneret's estimates, Chile's effective protection in 1961 amounted to 96 percent on all goods production and 208 percent on manufacturing.[24] Jere R. Behrman's estimates, shown in Table 2.7, indicate an effective protection of 254 percent in 1961 and of 168 percent in 1967, on all goods production.[25] From these estimates, it is clear that there was a strong bias against exports in Chile during the 1960s.

The relatively high overall protection rates of Argentina and Chile reflected the extremely high effective protection of intermediate products and transport equipment. In 1969, Argentina had an effective protection of 142 percent for the less sophisticated intermediate products and a 122 percent rate for the more sophisticated intermediate products. Chile's protection of intermediate products appeared more selective, with the effective rates ranging from 1 percent for nonmetallic mineral products to 1,140 percent for petroleum and coal products in 1967.

In comparison, the effective protection rates for intermediate products were only 10 to 24 percent in Taiwan and South Korea in 1968–1969. For transport equipment, the rate of effective protection was 207 percent in Argentina[26] and 271 percent in Chile, compared to 55 percent in Taiwan and 164 percent in South Korea. For durable consumer goods, the rate of effective protection was much higher in

Argentina (144 percent) than in Taiwan (29 percent) and South Korea (51 percent). A similar pattern is found in the protection of nondurable consumer goods. For textiles, for instance, Chile's effective protection amounted to nearly 500 percent in 1967. In both Chile and Argentina, the production of machinery was heavily protected, but less so in South Korea and virtually unprotected in Taiwan (Tables 2.6 and 2.7).

The high protection rates of Chile and Argentina for intermediate products, machinery, and transport equipment indicate the continued emphasis on import-substituting industrialization during the 1960s, while the relatively low protection rates of Taiwan for these products reflect the authorities' shift to export-led industrialization during the same period. The intermediate protection rates of South Korea for these products reflect the authorities' continued pursuit of import substitution while emphasizing export expansion at the same time.

Divergence in the Control of Inflation and Unit Labor Costs

Taiwan and South Korea were not only more consistent in the reform of trade policies, but they were also more successful in controlling inflation and the rise of manufacturing unit labor costs. This success enabled them to avoid relying excessively on exchange rate devaluations in order to maintain their international competitiveness.

In contrast, Chile and Argentina were not only less consistent in the reform of trade policies, but also less successful in controlling inflation and the rise of manufacturing unit labor costs. The latter, in turn, compelled them to rely more on exchange rate devaluations in order to maintain their international competitiveness. Such devaluations, although useful and necessary, tended to perpetuate the inflationary pressure through upward adjustments in import costs and, frequently, a worsening in the government's fiscal position.

The control of inflation

Inflation and stabilization efforts

In both Taiwan and South Korea, the transition to an outward oriented development in the 1960s was preceded in the early to the mid-1950s by the control of hyperinflation, an inflation caused by the chaotic conditions that prevailed in these countries in the immediate postwar period.

CHART 2.1

TAIWAN AND SOUTH KOREA
CONSUMER PRICE INFLATION AND GROWTH OF REAL OUTPUT, 1951-83

(In percent)

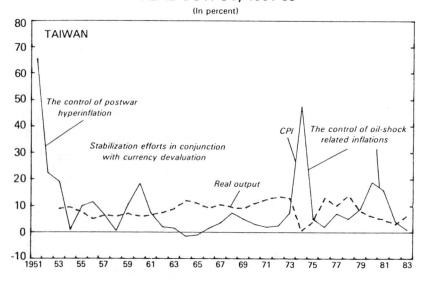

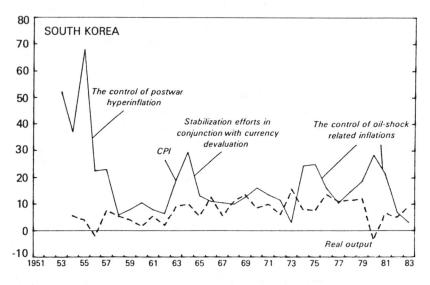

In the subsequent years until the onslaught of worldwide inflation in the 1970s, the authorities displayed determination in controlling any resurgence of inflation, such as that occurring in Taiwan during 1959 and 1960

CHART 2.2

CHILE

CONSUMER PRICE INFLATION AND
GROWTH OF REAL OUTPUT, 1952-83

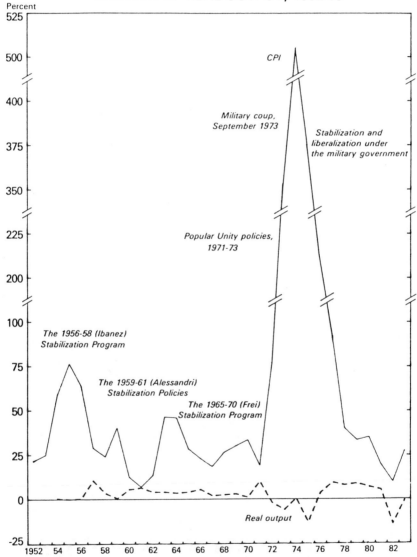

and in South Korea during 1963 and 1964 when exchange devaluations and special factors combined to threaten price stability[27] (Chart 2.1).

By contrast, in Chile and Argentina the failure to control inflation

CHART 2.3

ARGENTINA

CONSUMER PRICE INFLATION AND
GROWTH OF REAL OUTPUT, 1952-83

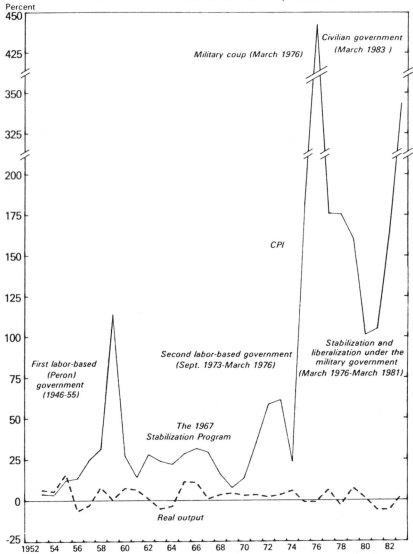

constricted the authorities' reform of trade policies. During the 1950s and the 1960s, the rate of inflation in these two countries remained more than 20 percent per year, with periodical upsurges to more than 50 percent and even several hundred percent per year, as happened in

Chile in 1954 to 1956, 1963 to 1964, and 1972 to 1978, and in Argentina in 1958 to 1959, 1971 to 1973, and 1975 to the present (Charts 2.2 and 2.3). These inflations were largely internally originated, as they occurred at a time when the global environment was rather favorable, with world export demand expanding by 7 to 8 percent per year while import prices were rising by only 3 to 4 percent per year in dollar terms. (See reference items in Table 2.1.)

These differing policies with respect to the control of inflation between Taiwan and South Korea on the one hand, and Chile and Argentina on the other, can be explained by their divergent experiences with respect to inflation and economic development during the war-time and early postwar years. In Taiwan and South Korea the majority of the population had suffered from severe inflation and economic disruptions, and this made them more willing to accept the short-run deflationary effects of the stabilization policies, while reducing the national authorities' political cost in pursuing these policies.[28] By contrast, Chile and Argentina did not suffer from the ravages of hyperinflation during the wartime and the early postwar years, and this made them less inclined to accept the short-run stabilization costs. Moreover, much of the inflation experienced by Chile and Argentina in the early postwar years stemmed from the inward-oriented development policies pursued by the authorities in order to sustain economic growth.

These policies tended to generate inflationary pressures through various channels, including the deficit financing of increased government expenditures for development; the proliferation of industrial inefficiencies resulting from prolonged heavy protection; and the shortage of foreign exchange caused by the policy bias against export activity. These inflationary pressures were also present in Taiwan and South Korea in the 1950s and the early 1960s, but the authorities took decisive measures to control inflation and to shift policy emphasis in favor of export activity. By contrast, the aversion to the initial deflationary impact of stabilization policies combined with the periodic relaxation of the foreign exchange constraint occasioned by the cyclical expansion of primary exports made the Chilean and Argentinean authorities reluctant to pursue effective stabilization policies.

The differing attitudes with respect to controlling inflation coalesced with the differing emphases with respect to trade policy to enhance performance in Taiwan and South Korea and weaken it further in Chile and Argentina. In Taiwan and South Korea the success of export promotion policies enabled them to remove the dual constraints of foreign exchange shortage and low savings ratio. This led to expanded imports, higher investment, and improved domestic supply conditions. The resulting growth in per capita income and domestic savings in conjunction with the stabilizing price trends led to increased holding of financial assets (particularly bank deposits) and increased intermediation of savings and investment by the financial institutions. These developments contributed to both productivity growth and financial stability.

By contrast, the continued pursuit of inward-oriented development policies and the cyclical behavior of primary exports led Chile and Argentina to experience balance of payments difficulties. This led to frequent exchange rate devaluations, associated wage and cost adjustments, and the pursuit of stop-go monetary policies. As a consequence the growth of imports, investment, and productivity remained modest over time; domestic savings increased only slowly; domestic finances did not improve; and inflationary pressures remained strong.

These forces were exacerbated by the increasing tendency for inflation in both Chile and Argentina to become self-perpetuating once begun. A major reason for this development was the rapid spread of indexation mechanisms for wages, exchange rates, and financial liabilities.[29] Such indexing, while useful in maintaining the real value of wages, exchange rates, financial liabilities, and the associated expenditure flows, distracts the authorities' attention from the necessity of taking the politically difficult measures to control inflation. Such control is necessary in order to cultivate a mentality compatible with the development of manufactured exports. To be competitive, manufactured exports require constant product improvement and cost control. Such activity tends to be neglected in an environment of rapid inflation where marginal gains derived from product improvements and cost control are often dwarfed by large changes in both absolute and relative prices.

Nominal and real exchange rate movements

During the period from 1960 to 1973, Taiwan's unit labor costs in manufacturing increased by less than 2 percent per year while South Korea's rose by 12.6 percent per year. However, even the higher Korean rate was dwarfed by the corresponding developments in Chile and Argentina. In Chile, following an increase of more than 24 percent in the 1950s, these costs increased by about 40 percent per year in the period from 1960 to 1973. In Argentina, they increased by 23 percent per year in both the 1950s and the 1960s (Table 2.8).

Because of its stable unit labor costs, Taiwan did not have to devalue again during the 1960s, following major devaluations in the late 1950s Table 2.8). In fact, under the par value system, its strong competitive position led to continued improvement in its trade balance, thus necessitating a revaluation against the U.S. dollar in March 1973 in the wake of the latter's floating. In comparison, South Korea undertook two major devaluations in the first half of the 1960s in order to strengthen its competitive position because of its diminished but still high rate of inflation. Even more frequent or greater was the rate of devaluation in Chile and Argentina because of their higher, fluctuating inflation. Chile adopted a dual exchange rate system from 1962 through 1973, and its banker rate for merchandise trade was adjusted bimonthly from 1965 onward until termination by the Popular Unity government in 1971. Argentina also briefly experimented with a flexible exchange rate system (1963 to 1966), but otherwise made periodical devaluations following periods of fixed rate with increasing overvaluation.

In real terms, Taiwan's exchange rate was also most stable[30] (Chart 2.4 and Table 2.9). South Korea's real exchange rate fluctuated sharply during the late 1950s and the early 1960s, but then the authorities succeeded in maintaining its real depreciation during the second half of the decade, as the inflation rate stabilized at the 10 percent level and as more frequent rate adjustments were made following the 1964 devaluation. In comparison, because of mini-devaluations, the Chilean real exchange rate was relatively stable during the 1960s despite the much higher rate of inflation. However, the Chilean real rate became highly unstable during the early 1970s following the termination of the flexible exchange rate system. Even worse was the situation in Argentina, whose real exchange rate not only experienced a large swing in the 1960s but also a severe overvaluation in the early 1970s.

Wage and productivity growth

Contrasting movements of nominal wages, labor productivity, and real wages

The divergence in the inflation of unit labor costs between the East Asian and the Latin American countries resulted from differences in the behavior of both nominal wages and labor productivity. In Taiwan

Table 2.8

Increases in Nominal and Real Wages, Production, Employment, Labor Productivity, and Unit Labor Costs in Both National Currency and U.S. Dollars, in Manufacturing, 1949–60, 1960–73, and 1973–85 (In annual compound rate of change)

	1949–60[1]	1960–73	1973–85[6]
1. *Nominal wage*			
Chile	27.9[2]	45.5	101.0
Argentina	27.6	29.0	199.5
Taiwan	11.9	11.4	15.6
South Korea		19.1	23.1
2. *Production*			
Chile	3.2	4.2	−1.4
Argentina	4.1	6.8	−1.1
Taiwan	13.0	18.1	8.9
South Korea	13.4	17.9	15.0
3. *Employment*			
Chile	0.5	0.9	−0.3
Argentina	0.6	1.8	−1.6
Taiwan	4.5	8.1	4.8
South Korea		11.4	5.8
4. *Labor productivity*			
Chile	2.7	3.3	−1.1
Argentina	3.5	4.9	0.5
Taiwan	8.1	9.3	3.9
South Korea		5.8	8.7
5. *Unit labor costs*[3]			
Chile	24.5[2]	40.9	103.2
Argentina	23.6	23.0	198.0
Taiwan	3.5	1.9	11.3
South Korea		12.6	13.2

6. *Exchange rate*[4]			
Chile		43.6	85.4
Argentina		20.5	178.9
Taiwan		−0.4	0.4
South Korea		15.1	6.7
7. *Unit laobr costs in U.S. dollars*[5]			
Chile		−1.9	9.6
Argentina		2.1	6.8
Taiwan		2.3	10.9
South Korea		−2.3	6.1
8. *Consumer prices*			
Chile	33.7	42.9	85.4
Argentina	28.1	27.5	192.1
Taiwan	10.8	3.7	9.1
South Korea	49.8	12.7	13.8
9. *Real wages*			
Chile	4.3[2]	1.8	8.4
Argentina	−0.4	1.2	2.5
Taiwan	1.0	7.4	6.0
South Korea		5.7	8.2

Sources: International Labour Office, *Yearbook of Labour Statistics* (various issues); International Monetary Fund, *International Financial Statistics* (various issues); United Nations, *Monthly Bulletin of Statistics* (various issues); supplemented by James W. Wilkie and Stephen Haber (eds.), *Statistical Abstract of Latin America*, vol. 22 (Los Angeles: University of California, 1983), and national publications. Data on Taiwan are based on Council for Economic Planning and Development, *Taiwan Statistical Data Book* (Taipei, 1983).
[1]For Taiwan, 1952–60; for South Korea, 1950–60.
[2]The accuracy of these estimates may be questioned owing to several changes in the base of the wage index. However, a shorter wage index for 1949–57 on a consistent basis shows an even greater erosion of real wages for the period.
[3]The index of nominal wages deflated by the index of labor productivity.
[4]Index of national currency per U.S. dollar, based on *IFS* annual average implicit or market rates.
[5]The index of unit labor costs deflated by the index of exchange rate.
[6]1973–84 for Chile and Argentina.

CHART 2.4

REAL EXCHANGE RATE, FIRST QUARTER 1957
THROUGH FOURTH QUARTER 1973

(Index of national currency per unit of U.S. dollar,
deflated by the index of relative wholesale prices; 1960 = 100)

the control of unit labor costs was achieved through both moderate growth in nominal wages and rapid growth in labor productivity. From 1950 to 1973, nominal wages in manufacturing increased by 11 to 12 percent per year, while labor productivity increased by 8 percent per year in the 1950s and 9.3 percent per year in the 1960s. In Korea unit labor costs increased more rapidly than in Taiwan during the 1960s because of greater nominal wage increases while labor productivity increased at a slower pace.

In comparison with Taiwan and South Korea, the growth of nominal wages was much faster in Chile and Argentina, and the growth of labor productivity much slower. In Chile, nominal wages in manufacturing increased by 28 percent per year in the 1950s and by more than 45 percent per year in the 13 years ending in 1973. Chilean labor productivity in manufacturing increased by 2.7 and 3.3 percent yearly during the corresponding periods, only about one third of the Taiwan rates. Argentina's manufacturing nominal wages increased by 27.6 percent yearly from 1949 to 1960 and by an even higher rate from 1960 to 1973, while its manufacturing labor productivity increased by 3.5 and 4.9 percent per year in the corresponding periods.

Contrary to the movements of nominal wages, real wages increased much faster in Taiwan and South Korea, at 7.4 and 5.7 percent per year from 1960 to 1973, compared to a mere 0.9 and 1.2 percent in Chile and Argentina (Table 2.8). This reversal in nominal and real wage movements was important, demonstrating that (1) by controlling inflation and restricting the growth of nominal wages and unit labor costs, combined with the successful promotion of exports, Taiwan and South Korea were able to attain a faster growth of real output and real wages; and that (2) by failing to control inflation and restrict the growth of nominal wages and unit labor costs and by unsuccessfully promoting exports, Chile and Argentina were condemned to a much lower growth of real output and real wages.

Specific factors relating to the labor supply

In addition to the successful control of inflation, the moderation of wage demand in Taiwan and South Korea was helped by the following factors: (1) improvements in agricultural labor productivity and (2) increased participation of female workers in manufacturing. These factors made possible an ample supply of industrial workers for the labor-intensive export industries and helped make the labor market competitive.

Improvements in agricultural labor productivity. Whereas all four countries under review were major exporters of agricultural products before the war, Taiwan and South Korea differed widely from Chile and Argentina in the mode of operation of their agricultural sectors. Be-

Table 2.9

Wholesale Price Index, Nominal and Real Exchange Rates: Estimated Trend and Coefficient of Variation, Based on Quarterly Data for 1957–73, 1957–65, and 1966–73

	Chile			Argentina[1]		
	1957–73	1957–65	1966–73	1957–73	1957–65	1966–73
1. *Wholesale price index*						
Trend[2]	0.066**	0.049**	0.097**	0.057**	0.069**	0.061**
Coefficient of variation[3]	363.7	59.5	257.8	116.9	62.2	71.9
2. *Nominal exchange rate*[4]						
Trend[2]	0.063**	0.045**	0.087**	0.038**	0.034**	0.027**
Coefficient of variation[3]	332.4	55.5	237.1	59.3	30.0	24.8
3. *Real exchange rate*[5]						
Trend[2]	0.001**	−0.003**	−0.000	−0.009**	−0.017**	−0.024**
Coefficient of variation[3]	9.4	6.3	10.1	22.1	15.6	26.0

Source: Computed from International Monetary Fund Data Fund.
[1]1959–73 and 1959–65 for exchange rate.
[2]Estimated by fitting a semi-log trend.
[3]Standard deviation divided by the arithmetic mean.
[4]Index of national currency per unit of U.S. dollar.

cause of their high population density, agricultural production in the two East Asian countries had been characterized by a heavy application of both human and intermediate inputs (the latter including R and D, irrigation, and chemical fertilizers) and an intensive use of the land since the 1930s.[31] This resulted in the generation of high agricultural value added per unit of agricultural land in Taiwan and South Korea, in sharp contrast with the situation in Chile and Argentina, where low population density and ample agricultural lands resulted in a light use of human and intermediate inputs and an extensive use of the land (Table 2.10).

Following the chaotic wartime and early postwar periods during which agricultural output declined, this pattern of agricultural development was resumed and intensified in Taiwan and South Korea partly because their separation from Japan and the massive influx

Table 2.9 (continued)

	Taiwan			South Korea	
1957–73	1957–65	1966–73	1957–73	1957–65	1966–73
0.008**	0.013**	0.009**	0.027**	0.030**	0.021**
16.6	13.7	11.4	50.1	36.4	20.1
0.002**	0.006**	−0.001**	0.0354**	0.056**	0.016**
6.6	8.7	1.5	56.1	63.8	16.2
−0.002**	−0.006**	0.000	0.013**	0.027**	0.005**
7.9	9.6	4.5	26.5	32.6	7.2

[5]Index of national currency per unit of U.S. dollar, deflated by the index of relative wholesale prices.
 * = The estimated coefficient is significant at the 10 percent level.
** = The estimated coefficient is significant at the 5 percent level.

of refugees necessitated the reorientation of agricultural production from exporting to satisfying the sharply increased domestic demand. In both economies, the postwar agricultural development was facilitated by the institution of land reforms early in the late 1940s through the early 1950s. Land reform, consisting of rent reduction and redistribution of government lands and private lands exceeding a certain maximum, raised incentives for tenants and owner-cultivators and accelerated the diffusion of new agricultural practices and product varieties.

Nevertheless, the recovery of agricultural output was faster in Taiwan than in South Korea, partly because Taiwan attained political and economic stability much earlier than South Korea and also because Taiwan strengthened its organizational base for agricultural R and D and extension inherited from the colonial regime.[32] Thus, during the

Table 2.10

Agricultural Value Added per Unit of Agricultural Land and Labor Force, 1970–72 Average

	Taiwan	South Korea	Chile	Argentina
1. *Agricultural value added* (U.S.$ equivalent)				
a. Per hectare of:				
Arable and permanent crop land	904	1,098	153	104
Crop land plus pasture	904	1,098	49	19
b. Per economically active agricultural population	479	451	1,139	2,299
2. *Cereals output per hectare* (metric ton)	4.7[1]	3.8	1.7	2.0
3. *Fertilizer consumption per hectare* (in kilograms of nutrient)	229[2]	247	32	2
Memorandum				
a. Agricultural value added (US$mn equivalent)	814	2,525	797	3,448
b. Agricultural land (million hectares):				
Arable and permanent crop lands	0.9	2.3	5.2	33.2
Permanent pasture	—	—	11.0	144.5
c. Economically active population in agriculture (million)	1.7	5.6	0.7	1.5
d. Population density:				
Per sq. kilometer of total area	300	254	10	7
Per sq. kilometer of agricultural land	1,242	1,169	54	12

Sources: Food and Agriculture Organization, *FAO Production Yearbook* (various issues), and Council for Economic Planning and Development, *Taiwan Statistical Data Book* (Taipei: Council for Economic Planning and Development, 1985).
[1]For 1969–71 average.
[2]Estimated on the basis of the ratio of plant nutrients to the aggregate weight of chemical fertilizers applied to the rice fields.

more than two decades prior to the first oil shock, Taiwan's agricultural production increased by 4.3 percent per year through the growth of labor productivity by 4.4 percent per year (Table 2.11). These developments not only helped stabilize the prices of wage goods in the domestic markets, but also relieved the wage pressure in the urban sectors by providing a large, albeit diminishing, pool of surplus labor.[33] Thus, during the 1960s, the agricultural sector's share of Taiwan's rapidly growing labor force declined from 50 to 37 percent, while the industrial sector's share increased from 21 to 28 percent (Table 2.12).

Table 2.11

Comparative Agricultural Performance, 1952–60, 1960–73, and 1973–84 (In percentage changes)

	1952–60	1960–73	1973–84
1. Chile			
Production[1]	2.9	−0.1	4.5
Employment	0.2	−2.1	1.2
Labor productivity	2.7	2.0	3.3
2. *Argentina*			
Production[1]	−0.1	1.9	1.7
Employment	−1.5	−0.8	−1.3*
Labor productivity	1.4	2.7	3.0*
3. *Taiwan*			
Production[1]	4.5	4.2	1.8
Employment	0.7	−0.5	−1.9
Labor productivity	3.8	4.7	3.9
4. *South Korea*			
Production[1]	1.9**	4.3	2.9
Employment		1.4†	−3.2
Labor productivity		2.9	6.3

Sources: Food and Agriculture Organization, *Production Yearbook* (various issues); United Nations, *Yearbook of National Account Statistics* (various issues) Markos J. Mamalakis, *Historical Statistics of Chile: Demography and Labor Force, Vol. 2* (Westport Conn.: Greenwood Press, 1980); Central Bank of Chile, *Economic and Social Indicators, 1960–82*; Carlos F. Diaz Alejandro, *Essays on the Economic History of the Argentine Republic* (New Haven: Yale University Press, 1970); Council for Economic Planning and Development, *Taiwan Statistical Data Book* (Taipei, 1983); Economic Planning Board, *Major Statistics of Korean Economy* (Seoul, various issues); and *Korea Statistical Yearbook* (various issues).
[1]Based on the FAO index of total agricultural production for the period 1952–60, and on the national account data for the other periods.
*For 1973–82.
**For 1955–60.
†For 1963–73.

Compared to Taiwan, South Korea's agricultural growth was much slower during the 1950s, thus requiring heavy imports of foodstuffs to supplement the domestic needs. Nevertheless, Korean agricultural productivity improved during the 1960s and accelerated sharply during the 1970s, thus enabling a significant release of rural labor for urban industrial activity (Tables 2.11 and 2.12).

Compared to Taiwan, agricultural performance in Chile and Argentina in the 1950s and the 1960s was not impressive. In Chile agricultural output increased by 2.9 percent per year during 1952 to 1960 and

Table 2.12

**Sectoral Allocation of Labor Force, 1960, 1970, and 1980
(In percent of total)**

	Agriculture[1] 1960			Industry[2] 1970			Services[3] 1980		
Taiwan	50	37	20	21	28	42	29	35	38
South Korea	66	51	36	9	14	27	25	35	37
Chile	31	23	19	20	21	19	49	56	62
Argentina	20	18	13	36	32	34	44	50	53

Sources: World Bank, *World Tables: The Third Edition. Vol. II. Social Data from the File of the World Bank* (Baltimore: Johns Hopkins University Press, 1983); *World Development Report, 1986* (New York: Oxford University Press, 1986); and Council for Economic Planning and Development, *Taiwan Statistical Databook* (Taipei: Council for Economic Planning and Development, 1985).
[1]Including agriculture, fishery, and forestry.
[2]Including mining, manufacturing, construction, and utilities.
[3]Including all other sectors.

changed little during 1960 to 1973. In Argentina it changed little during 1952 to 1960 and increased by 2.2 percent per year during 1960 to 1973 (Table 2.10). In both countries, as in Taiwan and South Korea during the early 1950s, economic activity in the rural sector was penalized by the unfavorable exchange rates and the often adverse domestic terms of trade, which resulted from the authorities' pursuit of inward-oriented industrialization policies.

In Taiwan and South Korea these price disincentives were offset to a varying degree through the government's provision of irrigation, agricultural research, and many other supporting services. Also, in Taiwan the exchange rates and domestic terms of trade unfavorable to the rural sector were largely corrected during the 1960s (Chart 2.5). In comparison, both the Chilean and Argentine governments did relatively little to improve agricultural productivity. Not until the late 1950s did the Argentine government begin to expand activity in agricultural education, research, and in the extension of agricultural credit.[34] The continuing lag in the intensity of agricultural development and land use in Chile and Argentina was reflected in their extremely low fertilizer inputs and agricultural value added as late as the early 1970s, in contrast to Taiwan and South Korea (Table 2.10).[35]

Participation of female labor force in manufacturing. In both

CHART 2.5

TAIWAN AND ARGENTINA

PRICES OF AGRICULTURAL GOODS IN RELATION TO THOSE OF NON-AGRICULTURAL GOODS, 1949-82

(1935-37 = 1 in Taiwan; 1939 = 1 in Argentina)

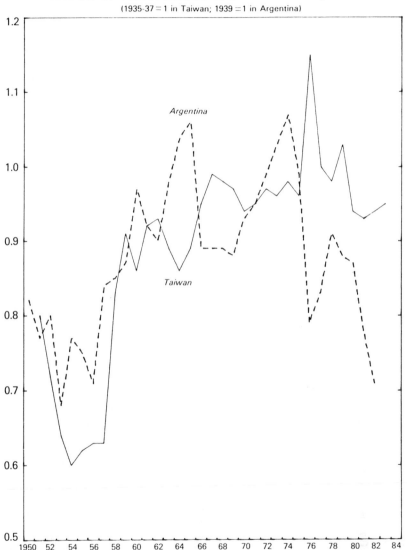

Taiwan and South Korea the rapid growth of labor intensive manufactured exports during the 1960s was supported by the elastic supply of young female workers whose wages were much lower than those of the

Table 2.13

Comparative Trends in Female Labor Force Participation
(In percent)

	Rate of change			Percentage share			
	1950–60[1]	1960–73[2]	1973–84[3]	1950[4]	1960	1973[5]	1984[6]
1. Chile							
Employment							
Male	1.7	1.2	1.3	75.0	77.6	76.9	69.7
Female	−0.1	1.4	4.3	25.0	22.4	23.1	30.3
Manufacturing employment							
Male	2.1	0.3	2.0	67.7	76.2	73.8	72.6
Female	−3.2	0.8	2.0	32.3	23.8	26.2	27.4
Labor force participation rate[7]							
Male				77.2	72.7	77.0	68.0
Female				20.1	19.6	21.2	28.3
2. Argentina							
Employment							
Male	3.9	0.6		78.4	77.4	74.6	
Female	4.6	2.9		21.6	22.6	25.4	
Manufacturing employment							
Male	5.0	−1.0		75.3	78.1	76.6	
Female	3.8	−0.5		24.7	21.9	23.4	
Labor force participation rate[7]							
Male				79.2	77.7	72.6	76.4
Female				21.7	21.8	24.0	27.4

3. *Taiwan*							
Employment							
Male	2.3	3.7	2.7	73.2	78.4	69.5	63.8
Female	-0.6	7.6	3.4	26.8	21.6	30.5	36.2
Manufacturing employment							
Male	5.7	9.7	7.9	89.8	88.4	61.3	50.4
Female	7.0	21.0	9.0	10.2	11.6	38.7	49.0
Labor force participation rate[7,8]							
Male				92.5	87.3	77.1	76.1
Female				35.2	25.0	41.5	43.3
4. *South Korea*							
Employment							
Male		3.0	2.3		64.7	62.1	61.5
Female		4.2	2.5		35.3	37.9	38.5
Manufacturing employment							
Male		9.5	6.0		69.9	61.4	62.1
Female		13.7	5.8		30.1	38.6	37.9
Labor force participation rate[7]							
Male					76.4	73.9	67.3
Female					36.3	40.8	40.6

Sources: International Labour Office, *Yearbook of Labour Statistics* (Geneva: various issues); Markos J. Mamalakis, *Historical Statistics of Chile: Demography and Labor Force, Vol. 2* (Westport, Conn.: Greenwood Press, 1980); James W. Wilkie and Adam Perkal (eds.), *Statistical Abstract of Latin America*, vol. 23 (Los Angeles: University of California, 1984); Director-General of Budget, Accounting and Statistics, *Yearbook of Labor Force Statistics, Republic of China* (Taipei, various issues); and National Bureau of Statistics, *Korea Statistical Yearbook* (Seoul, various issues).

[1] 1952–60 for Chile and 1947–60 for Argentina.
[2] 1960–70 for Chile and Argentina, and 1963–73 for Korea.
[3] 1970–83 for Chile.
[4] 1952 for Chile and 1947 for Argentina.
[5] 1970 for Chile and Argentina.
[6] 1983 for Chile and 1980 for Argentina.
[7] Economically active population as a percent of working age population.
[8] Data for 1950 and 1960 are based on household registration, whereas those for 1973 and 1984 are based on labor force survey.

CHART 2.6

TAIWAN
FEMALE PARTICIPATION IN LABOR FORCE, 1951-80

(In percent)

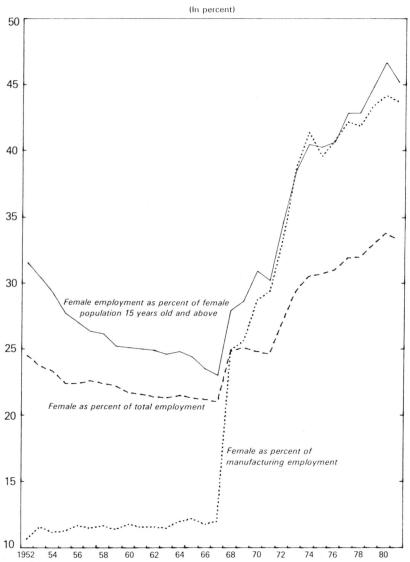

average male workers.[36] As a consequence, in Taiwan female employment in manufacturing jumped by 21 percent per year in the period
1961 to 1973, compared to 7.0 percent per year in the preceding

decade. Meanwhile, the female labor force participation rate (represented here by the ratio of female employment to female population 15 years and older) increased rapidly from 23 percent in 1966 to more than 41 percent in 1973 (Table 2.13 and Chart 2.6). By the end of the 1970s, female workers accounted for 43 percent of the manufacturing work force, with the ratio exceeding 70 percent in a number of export oriented, labor intensive industries.

Similarly, in South Korea, where export expansion was also built on cost-competitive labor intensive products, female workers accounted for an increasing share of both manufacturing and total employment from the mid-1960s. Over the decade ending in 1973, female employment in manufacturing increased by 13.7 percent per year, compared to 9.5 percent per year for male workers. As a result, the share of female workers in manufacturing employment increased from 30.1 percent to 38.6 percent, and the female labor force participation rate increased to 40.8 percent in 1973, about the same as in Taiwan (Table 2.13).

In contrast with the rising female participation in manufacturing and total employment in Taiwan and South Korea, such participation declined in Chile in both the 1950s and the 1960s. In 1952, female workers accounted for 32.3 percent of manufacturing employment and 25.0 percent of total employment in Chile. By 1960, this had declined to 23.8 and 22.4 percent, respectively, with only a slight increase during the ensuing decade. As a consequence, the female labor force participation rate declined from 20.1 percent in 1950 to 19.8 percent in 1980. This decline was at least partly attributable to the shortage of employment opportunities caused by the sluggish economic growth because the growth of male and female employment at 1.4 and 0.7 percent per year during the two decades fell far short of the growth of the respective population groups 12 years and older (Table 2.13). For Argentina, comparable data on female employment in manufacturing are not readily available. Its female labor force participation rate increased modestly over time, but, like Chile's, remained far below those of Taiwan and South Korea.[37]

Labor productivity and capital efficiency

The rapid growth of labor productivity in Taiwan and South Korea in the 1960s occurred in conjunction with the rapid growth of capital investments and a sharp improvement in the operating efficiency of

Table 2.14

Growth of Manufacturing Labor Productivity, Capital Stock per Employee, and Output/Capital Ratio, 1960–73 and 1973–82 (Percentage changes)

	Labor productivity Y/L	Capital stock in constant prices K	Capital stock per employee K/L	Output/ capital ratio[1] Y/K
Taiwan				
1960–73	8.3	8.6[2]	0.5	7.8
1973–82	4.4	11.0[2]	6.0	−1.5
South Korea				
1960–73	5.8	11.8[3]	0.4	5.4

Sources: Author's estimates based on sources noted below and those shown in Table 8.

[1]Obtained by using the relationship $Y/K = Y/L \div K/L$.

[2]This estimate is obtained by using the census value of capital stock in 1971 as a base year value. The latter is then adjusted by the annual value of gross fixed capital formation in constant prices to create a time series of capital stock. The census data are reported in the Committee on Industrial and Commercial Censuses, *Commercial Censuses of Taiwan and Fukien Area, Vol. III, Manufacturing* (Taipei, June 1973). The capital formation data are estimated from Council for Economic Planning and Development, Executive Yuan, *Taiwan Statistical Data Book, 1983* (Taipei, 1983).

[3]Estimates of capital stock for Korea are based on Wontack Hong, "Export Promotion and Employment Growth in South Korea," in Anne O. Krueger, et al. (eds.), *Trade and Employment in Developing Countries*, vol. I (Chicago: University of Chicago Press for National Bureau of Economic Research, 1981).

capital stock.[38],[39] Based on estimates shown in Table 2.14, real manufacturing capital stock increased by 8.6 percent per year in Taiwan and by nearly 12 percent per year in Korea in the period 1961 to 1973. However, the growth of employment was almost as rapid, so that the growth of capital stock per employee was modest, around .5 percent per year in both countries. By contrast, real output per unit of real capital stock increased by nearly 8 percent per year in Taiwan and by 5.4 percent per year in South Korea. This rapid increase in the operating efficiency of the capital stock occurred in conjunction with the rapid growth of manufactured exports, the resulting change in the output mix of the manufacturing industry, and the improved utilization of capacity. In addition, it is possible that the quality of both the capital stock and the labor force improved over time as new equipment replaced old and the workforce (both labor and management) gained more experience (Tables 2.8 and 2.14, and Chart 2.7).

While the lack of the manufacturing capital stock data for Chile and

CHART 2.7

TAIWAN
CHANGES IN LABOR PRODUCTIVITY, CAPITAL-LABOR RATIO, AND
OUTPUT-CAPITAL RATIO IN MANUFACTURING, 1953-82
(In percent)

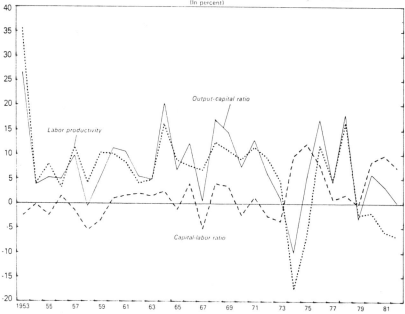

Argentina precludes analysis on the above basis, the behavior of the incremental capital-output ratio for the economy as a whole indicates that the gain in capital efficiency in both countries during the 1960s, if any, was much less impressive than in Taiwan and South Korea. These ratios, measured on three-year moving averages, fluctuated sharply and frequently in Chile and Argentina throughout the post-war decades, except for a brief period of stability in Chile during the second half of the 1950s and the early 1960s. In comparison, the ratios of both Taiwan and South Korea were much more stable, moving in a narrow range between 2.5 and 3.5 except for a sharp rise at the end of the 1970s and the early 1980s. In both Taiwan and South Korea there was a decline in the incremental capital-output ratio for the whole economy during the first half of the 1960s, in line with the rise of the output-capital ratio for manufacturing mentioned earlier (Charts 2.8, 2.9, and 2.10).

The sharp and frequent fluctuation of the incremental capital output ratios of Chile and Argentina largely reflected similar movements in their real output caused by the frequent stop-go stabilization-cum-

CHART 2.8

TAIWAN AND SOUTH KOREA

INCREMENTAL CAPITAL-OUTPUT RATIO, 1952-81

(In three-year moving averages, with changes in real output lagged by one year)

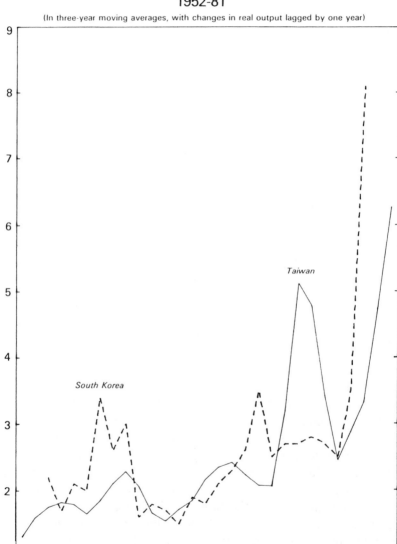

adjustment efforts, while the relative stability of the Taiwanese and Korean ratios reflected their success in attaining a steady expansion of output and price stabilization without causing a prolonged adverse

CHART 2.9

CHILE

INCREMENTAL CAPITAL-OUTPUT RATIO, 1951-80

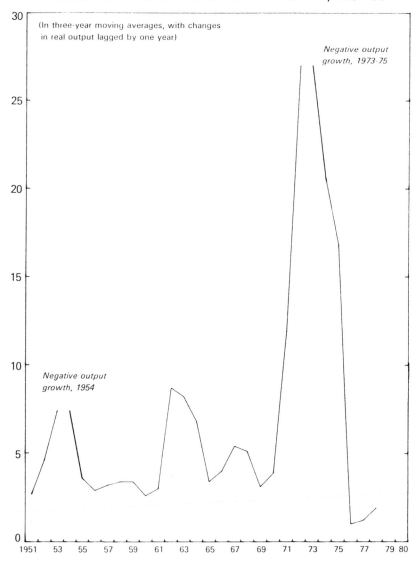

impact on economic growth.[40] The higher ratios of Chile and Argentina even during the 1960s when the external environment was more favorable may also reflect the relatively capital-intensive nature of their investment patterns and the continued inward-orientation of their man-

CHART 2.10

ARGENTINA

INCREMENTAL CAPITAL-OUTPUT RATIO, 1951-80

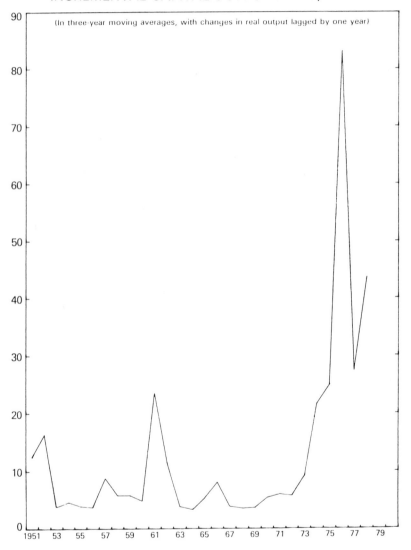

(In three-year moving averages, with changes in real output lagged by one year)

ufacturing production that precluded the realization of the economy of scale.[41] In contrast, the decline of these ratios in Taiwan and South Korea during the first half of the 1960s apparently reflected the overwhelming impact of the rapid expansion of labor-intensive exports, the resulting expansion in imports and production, and the realization of both internal and external economies. Under these favorable circumstances, export expansion and productivity growth apparently tended to bolster each other, leading to much improved economic performance. While the incremental capital-output ratio rose in both Taiwan and South Korea during the 1970s, reflecting the effects of increased investment in intermediate goods and the impact of the much worsened external environment, the ratio, at around 3.5, remained much lower than in Chile and Argentina during the same period.

Policy Reforms in Chile and Argentina in the 1970s

The failure to control inflation and to establish a sustainable pattern of economic growth over a long period of time and the frustrations thus generated ultimately led to more fundamental reforms of economic policies and the incentive systems in both Chile and Argentina during the 1970s. These reform efforts were indeed commendable, but unfortunately they did not succeed in establishing a sustainable pattern of economic growth. In order to understand why, and to help Chile and Argentina (and countries in similar situations) search for a workable model of economic development, it is useful to examine these countries' policy reform experiences in the 1970s in light of the more successful reform experiences of Taiwan and South Korea in the 1960s.

An overview of the Chilean and Argentine reform programs

Chile[42]

The Chilean policy reforms occurred only after the country had experimented with the "Chilean Road to Socialism" under President Allende in 1970–1973, including nationalization of financial and industrial enterprises, redistribution of farmlands, and worker participation in factory management. However, the lack of a political consensus within the country to support such an experiment and the neglect of fiscal and monetary discipline soon caused a sharp deterioration in the Chilean economy's internal and external balances, thereby prompting a military takeover of the government in September 1973.[43] The new government not only totally reversed Allende's socialist programs, but undertook extensive policy reforms to control inflation and to liberalize the economy. Under the military regime, both labor union and political activities were severely curtailed, and the economic policy makers were given a virtual free hand to pursue stabilization and liberalization goals.

The program implemented by the Chilean authorities can be divided into three phases: a first phase, from September 1973 to mid-1976, when fiscal and monetary restraints were applied to stabilize the economy and various measures were taken to restore market mechanisms; a second phase, from June 1976 to June 1979, when the exchange rate was used as a tool to accelerate price stabilization; and a third phase, from June 1979 to June 1982, when many of the programs were reversed or revised and a passive monetary policy was followed in conjunction with the adoption of a fixed exchange rate against the U.S. dollar.

During the first phase, the exchange rate in Chile was devalued sharply at the outset and followed by frequent minidevaluations designed to maintain the real value of the peso. The large public sector deficit, which had reached 24 percent of GDP in 1973, was reduced sharply by restraining government expenditures and increasing taxes, the latter through the introduction of a 20 percent value-added tax (Chart 2.11). At the same time, several direct taxes affecting capital were reduced or eliminated; prices were decontrolled; properties taken over by the previous government were returned; collective bargaining was suppressed; and labor union activity was severely curtailed. In addition, an extensive tariff reduction program was announced at the beginning of 1974. The program, as amended subsequently, reduced the average tariff rate from over 90 percent in 1973 to a uniform 10 percent in 1979. Finally, the financial market was gradually liberalized by denationalizing large segments of the banking sector and establishing private financial companies that operated with little restriction.

As a result of these programs, the fiscal deficit declined from 25 percent of GDP in 1973 to 2.6 percent in 1975. However, the decline in the rate of inflation was painfully slow (with the CPI still rising by more than 340 percent in 1975), partly because of the interaction between inflation and exchange rate devaluations. Moreover, both industrial production and real GDP declined sharply in 1975 and unemployment increased from less than 5 percent in 1973 to 14.5 percent in 1975 (excluding those participating in the Minimum Employment Program) (Charts 2.2, 2.12, and 2.13).

CHART 2.11

CHILE AND ARGENTINA

EVOLUTION OF GOVERNMENT REVENUES AND EXPENDITURES, 1971-83

(As percent of GDP)

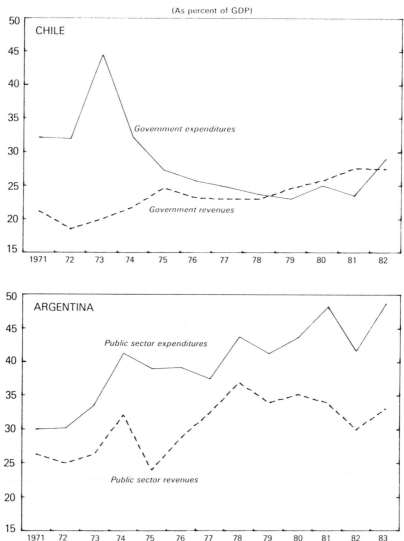

These developments prompted phase two in Chile, characterized by a shift in the emphasis of the anti-inflation strategy from restraining domestic demand to curbing cost pressures and price expectations. In

CHART 2.12

CHILE

PUBLIC SECTOR DEFICIT IN RELATION TO GDP, REAL DOMESTIC CREDIT, AND GOVERNMENT'S SHARE IN THE INCREMENTAL DOMESTIC CREDIT, 1971-82

(In percentage change or ratio)

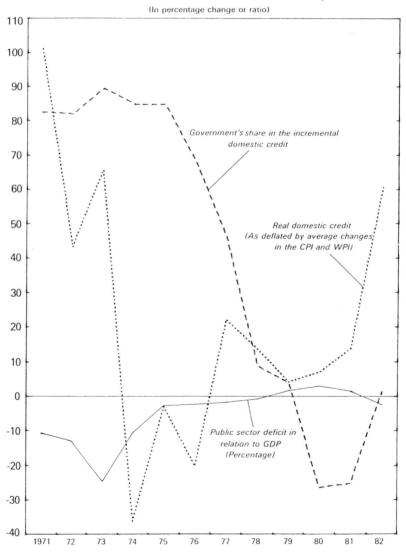

June 1976, at the beginning of the second phase, the peso was revalued by 10 percent and a 30-day preannounced value for future exchange rates was established as a way of influencing inflationary expectations.

CHART 2.13

CHILE AND ARGENTINA

INDEX OF MANUFACTURING OUTPUT AND REAL GDP, 1967-83

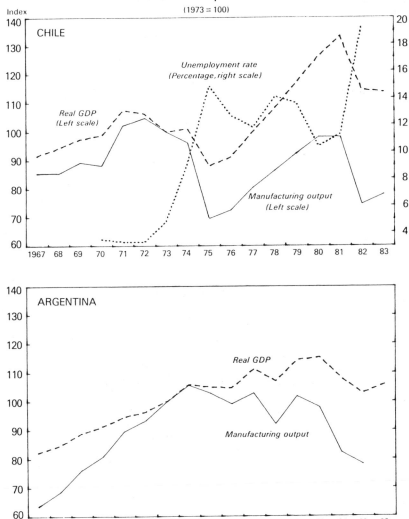

This new approach was complemented by additional large tariff reductions to further dampen domestic price pressures,[44] and, from 1977, by a gradual deregulation of external capital flows. The new policies, helped by a more favorable external environment, reduced the rate of

CHART 2.14

CHILE AND ARGENTINA

BALANCE OF PAYMENTS DEVELOPMENTS, 1972-83

(In billions of U.S. dollars)

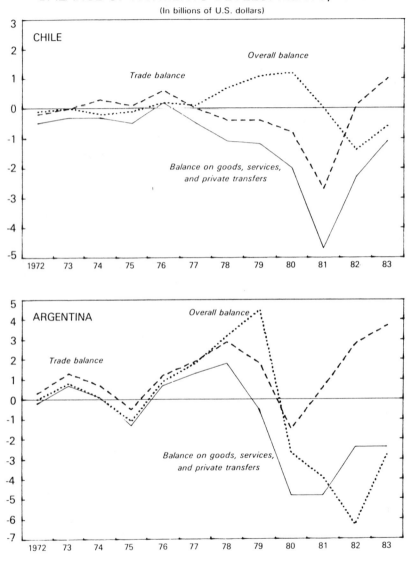

consumer price inflation to 37 percent by 1978 while a vigorous economic recovery, led by housing construction, nontraditional exports
and production, trade, and financial activities, sustained the growth of
real GDP at between 8 and 10 percent per year for three consecutive

years (1977 to 1979) (Chart 2.13). At the same time, the lessening of exchange risks under the preannounced (crawling peg) devaluations and the very high differentials between domestic and overseas interest rates stimulated large inflows of foreign capital from 1977 onward (Chart 2.14). These inflows largely took the form of short- and medium-term credits to the private sector for financing the growing imports of consumer goods and the boom in construction and service activities, and for taking over many denationalized enterprises at greatly depressed prices. In comparison, direct foreign investment in production activity was relatively small, and the unemployment rate remained high despite growth of real output. During this period, the marked widening of the current account deficit was more than covered by large net capital inflows, which in fact also led to a large accumulation of foreign reserves.

In 1979 the Chilean economy appeared to enter a new era. The once large fiscal defecit was all but eliminated and the high barriers to foreign trade and capital transactions were largely removed. Both government regulations and labor union activity were severely curtailed. Foreign capital inflows and foreign reserves continued to expand, and the recovery of economic activity, although skewed, was sustained. The remaining problems in Chile were the continuing high level of unemployment and inflation, which remained at nearly 40 percent per year. (Charts 2.2, 2.12, 2.13, and 2.14)

At this point, in June 1979, the Chilean experiment moved into its third phase, with the authorities hastening the price deceleration by fixing the value of the peso against the U.S. dollar. With the authorities' passive stance toward the creation of money, it was hoped that such a monetary policy would reduce the domestic inflation rate to that of the world inflation rate. At the same time, however, the authorities introduced a Labor Plan to restore collective bargaining while allowing wage adjustment based on past inflation.

While the strategy was successful in reducing higher inflation to less than 10 percent by 1981, the originally much higher domestic inflation rate combined with the appreciation of the U.S. dollar led to increasing overvaluation of the domestic currency (Chart 2.15). In continuation with the deepening world recession, this real appreciation caused a sharp expansion in the current account deficit, which reached 15 percent of GDP in 1981.

At the same time, the sharp rise in international interest rates, the increased risk of currency devaluation, and the slowdown in the growth of the monetary base resulting from the attainment of fiscal surplus led to a sharp rise in real domestic interest rates, which averaged 35 percent in 1981.[45] This rise, combined with the rising "product" wages, generated strong cost pressure on Chilean industry which was already suffering from a severe loss in effective demand[46] (Chart 2.15). As a consequence, business failures mounted and unemployment increased rapidly, reaching 21 percent in 1982, excluding those workers participating in the Minimum Employment Program. By June 1982, the deepening economic crisis compelled the government to reverse or modify several of the stabilization and liberalization programs instituted since 1973. In addition to repeated exchange rate devaluations, the authorities reintroduced exchange controls and preferential exchange rates, temporarily raised import tariffs to a uniform 20 percent level, terminated formal wage indexation, and intervened to rescue faltering banks and some important industrial and commercial firms.

Thus, eight years after the initiation of the stabilization and liberalization efforts, the Chilean economy faced great uncertainty. While the once rampant inflation was finally reduced to 10 percent, this accomplishment took nearly a decade and was accompanied by huge losses in real output, particularly in manufacturing; a sharp increase in unemployment; and a significant worsening in the distribution of income. In 1982, when several of the new programs were abandoned, manufacturing output was 25 percent lower than in 1973, the unemployment rate had reached 21 percent, domestic savings and productive investment were depressed, and the burden of servicing external debt was increasing rapidly (Chart 2.13).

Argentina[47]

Although not the same as in Chile, developments in Argentina were equally dramatic. As in Chile, the deterioration of economic conditions under the labor-based government of Isabel Peron led to a military takeover in March 1976. At that time, the Argentine economy was in a hyperinflationary recession, with a huge public sector deficit, negative output growth, and three-digit inflation (Charts 2.3 and 2.16). Also as in Chile, the new economic policy team was given a broad mandate to transform the economy by means of various liberalization programs while trying to control the virulent inflation. The policies pursued by the Argentine authorities can be divided into two phases: a first phase, from March 1976 to December 1978, when various liberalization pro-

CHART 2.15

CHILE

DEVELOPMENTS OF REAL EXCHANGE RATE
(Per U.S. dollar) AND
MANUFACTURING PRODUCT WAGE, 1967-83

(1973 = 100)

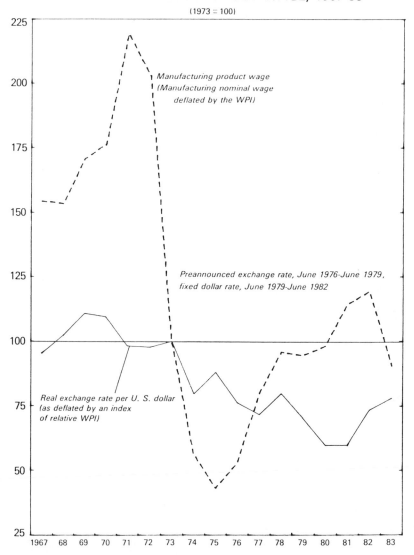

grams were introduced; and a second phase, from January 1979 to
March 1981, during which exchange rate policy was primarily geared
to the control of inflation, as in Chile.

CHART 2.16

ARGENTINA

PUBLIC SECTOR DEFICIT IN RELATION TO GDP, REAL DOMESTIC CREDIT, AND GOVERNMENT'S SHARE IN THE INCREMENTAL DOMESTIC CREDIT, 1972-82

(In percentage changes or ratio)

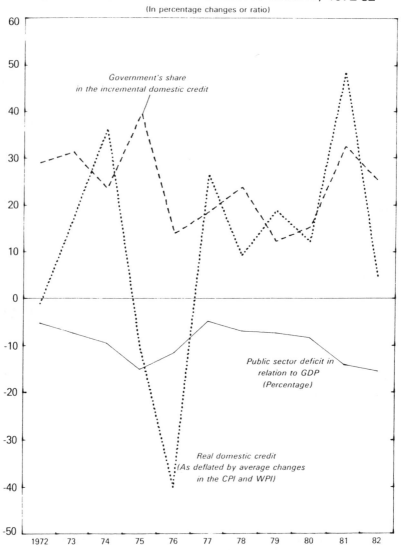

During the first phase, the Argentine authorities placed more emphasis on opening up the economy than on controlling inflation. The following measures were taken. The policy of crawling peg devaluations was made more effective through the imposition of indexation arrangements; many quantitative restrictions and the heavy taxes on meat, wheat, and other traditional exports were removed; various incentives to nontraditional exports were also phased out; and the extraordinarily high tariffs were reduced in several steps, although a preannounced tariff reduction program in the Chilean style was not put into effect until January 1979. In addition, the authorities moved to decontrol the banking system by allowing market determined interest rates on time deposits; by removing restrictions on the composition of banks loan portfolios; and by removing many of the restrictions on international capital flows. Moreover, the Argentine government imposed severe controls on wage adjustments while removing price controls and taking steps to compel public enterprises to reduce operating deficits.[48] Unlike Chile, however, no comprehensive measure was taken to reform the tax system, which remained a potpourri of individual taxes.

These reforms initially led to sharp improvements in both fiscal and external balances. The consolidated public sector deficit, which had amounted to 15 percent of GDP in 1975, was reduced to 7 percent by 1978 through a sharp increase in government revenues and a moderation in expenditures. Meanwhile, the sizable deficit in the current account of the balance of payments turned into a large surplus as both agricultural and nonagricultural exports responded to the real devaluation, while imports were restrained by the tightening in fiscal and monetary policies (Charts 2.14 and 2.16). However, consumer price inflation, which decelerated from 440 percent in 1976 to 180 percent in 1977, remained unchanged in 1978; and real output remained stagnant at its 1975 level except for a brief recovery in 1977 (Charts 2.3 and 2.13).

Confronted with the difficulty of short circuiting the inflationary spiral, the authorities decided to resort to a policy of preannounced exchange rate adjustments as a means of influencing inflationary expectations. In December 1978, at the beginning of phase two, the authorities issued an exchange rate table setting forth a diminishing rate of planned devaluations in the official rate for the peso for the period through August 1979. A subsequent table extended the schedule to March 1981. At the same time, restrictions on capital were relaxed further, and a schedule of tariff reductions for the years 1979 through 1984 was published. The schedule, in five annual steps, intended to reduce the tariff rates from a rate ranging from 21 to 85

CHART 2.17

ARGENTINA

REAL EXCHANGE RATE (Per U.S. dollar) AND MANUFACTURING PRODUCT WAGE, 1972-83

(1973 = 100)

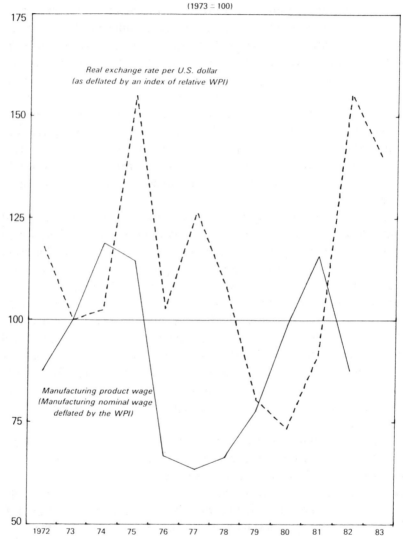

percent ad valorem to one ranging from 10 to 40 percent.[49]

As a consequence of these policies, the inflation rate did fall further to around 100 percent in 1980, but real interest rates rose sharply since nominal interest rates remained high because of continuing inflationary expectations.[50] The higher real interest rate combined with the reduced exchange risks under the preannounced exchange rates induced a sharp expansion of speculative capital inflows in 1979, while the holders of peso-denominated assets who remained skeptical about the viability of these exchange rates scrambled to shift their assets into foreign currency (Chart 2.14).

In the course of these developments, the business sector's external indebtedness grew rapidly. Under the combined squeeze of increased market competition and rising financial and wage costs, business failures mounted in 1979 and early 1980[51] (Chart 2.17). The resulting financial difficulties of several major banks prompted the central bank to intervene, thus reversing its restrictive monetary stance. Despite these difficulties, the authorities decided in July 1980 to continue the policy of preannounced exchange rate adjustments. Moreover, regulations governing external borrowing were liberalized further, and the pace of tariff reduction was intensified with the issuance of a new schedule designed to establish a uniform 20 percent tariff rate by 1984.

These measures failed to bolster confidence in the currency. The economy and the fiscal balance continued to deteriorate and, partly because of the financing needs of the public sector, external indebtedness increased rapidly. The fiscal deficit rose sharply during 1980 to 1982—both before and during the Falkland (Malvinas) conflict of mid-1982—as government spending on defense, wages, and interest on the public debt increased sharply while revenues sagged (Chart 2.11). By the first quarter of 1981 these developments led to large speculative capital outflows which caused a sharp drop in international reserves and, later, sharp devaluations of the peso. (The devaluations occurred in March, May, and again in June with the adoption of a floating exchange rate.) At the same time, inflation accelerated once again and the real economy continued to deteriorate. In 1982, six years after the initiation of the liberalization and stabilization effort, the Argentine public sector deficit (at 15 percent of GDP) and the inflation rate (at 165 percent) were back at levels comparable to those prevailing before the liberalization effort began. Real GDP was 1.2 percent lower than in 1975 and manufacturing output was down by as much as 39 percent. Many industrial and financial enterprises were in deep financial difficulties, and the nation was saddled with a huge external debt.

The Chilean and Argentine difficulties in light of the Taiwanese and Korean reform experiences

The unfavorable outcomes of Chilean and Argentine reform efforts are regrettable, especially considering the leeway given to policy makers in their policy experiments and the economic and social costs.[52] What went wrong? Were the disappointing outcomes attributable to the unfavorable circumstances under which the authorities operated, or were there serious flaws in the design and execution of the liberalization and stabilization programs?

Compared to the global environment in which Taiwan and South Korea carried out their policy reforms in the late 1960s, the state of the world economy in the mid- to late 1970s was much more unfavorable. Instead of a steady growth in world export demand, stable exchange rates, and moderate inflation of world trade prices, the Argentine and Chilean authorities had to cope with the ramifications of two major oil shocks, wide swings in external demand and in key exchange rates, and, in the later stages, an upsurge in international interest rates. These changes in external environment undoubtedly contributed greatly to the difficulties encountered by the Chilean and Argentine authorities in their liberalization and stabilization efforts.[53]

Nevertheless, several features of the Chilean and Argentine experiences stand out compared with the stabilization and liberalization experiences of Taiwan and South Korea in the 1960s.

The sequencing of inflation control and trade policy reform

In both Chile and Argentina, the opening up of the economies to external competition through reducing tariff rates and removing exchange and import controls in the 1970s occurred largely at the same time as the authorities were trying to control hyperinflation through fiscal and monetary restraints. This greatly exacerbated the difficulties confronting domestic industry, which therefore needed to cope simultaneously with the deflationary impact of fiscal and monetary restraints and the initially revenue-restraining effect of increased foreign competition. In comparison, the control of hyperinflation in Taiwan and South Korea occurred in the early to mid-1950s, i.e., well ahead of their trade and industrial restructuring efforts in the 1960s (Charts 2.1, 2.2, and

2.3). This interval allowed the domestic industries time to adjust first to the impacts of stabilization policies and then to the re-orientation of trade policy, and to minimize the losses in real output and employment.

The sequence of export promotion and import liberalization

Neither Taiwan nor South Korea opened up their economies to strong foreign competition until their export promotion policies had taken effect and their trade balances had improved. In both economies, while tariff rates were originally much lower than in Chile and Argentina, they were not systematically reduced until the 1970s, i.e., well after the onset of the reform efforts. The same is true of import and exchange controls, the primary tool used by these countries to protect their infant industries. Their trade liberalization measures initially consisted primarily of allowing the duty-free importation of intermediate products for use in export processing. Instead of wholesale reductions in tariffs, Taiwan required domestic producers of import substitutes to reduce their domestic sale prices relative to potential imports in order for their products to remain under import control. Systematic decontrol of imports in Taiwan did not occur until the early 1970s, and in South Korea the share of restricted import items remained as high as 40 to 45 percent in the 1970s.[54] (For evidence on Taiwan, see Table 2.15.)

Compared with the two East Asian countries' cautious policy regarding the liberalization of imports, both Chile and Argentina opened up their economies to strong foreign competition without first strengthening their export sectors. This caused great hardships for their domestic industries and led to an undue number of bankruptcies, and to excessive unemployment. The policy approach of the two Latin American countries may have been based on the theoretical argument about the equivalency of removing import restrictions and granting export subsidies. In reality, however, the adverse effect on domestic industry of removing import restrictions is often immediate, while the development of an export industry takes time.

Exchange rate as a tool for price stabilization
versus export promotion

The difficulty of quickly contracting hyperinflation in an economy accustomed to widespread indexations led the Chilean and Argentine

Table 2.15

Taiwan: Evolution of Import Control, Tariff Rate, and Tariff Burden, Selected Years, 1956–81 (In percent)

	The share of items under import control[1]	The share of items with a tariff rate of[2]			The ratio of tariff revenue to total imports
		0–30%	31–60%	61–165%	
1956	46.0	46.6*	34.7*	18.7*	27.8
1960	40.5	39.5**	45.0**	15.5**	16.8
1966	41.9	58.7***	28.0***	13.3***	18.5
1970	41.0				16.1
1972	17.9	39.8†	34.1†	26.2†	12.7
1974	2.3				11.5
1976	2.7	46.0††	31.1††	22.9††	11.7
1980	2.5	58.1 (65.1)	25.8 (25.3)	16.1 (9.6)	9.6
1981	3.1				9.1

Sources: Based on Tables 2–4 attached to S. C. Tsiang and Wen Lang Chen, ''Developments Toward Trade Liberalization in Taiwan'' (mimeo, December 24, 1984).
*Effective January 1955.
**Effective August 1959.
***Effective September 1965.
†Effective August 1971.
††Effective August 1977.
[1]The share of controlled items in the 1970s exclude those whose imports are limited by sources of origin or importing agencies.
[2]The parenthetical figures for 1982 apply to most favored nations.

authorities to use preannounced exchange rate devaluations as a tool to control inflation. To be successful such a policy requires the support of compatible wage, fiscal, and monetary policies. This support, combined with the relatively stable import prices during 1976 to 1978, contributed to the success of the Chilean experiment. Such support was lacking in Argentina, both because of its failure to contain the fiscal deficit and because of the resurgence of import prices following the second round of oil price increases leading to increased overvaluation of the exchange rate as well as a substantial rise in the domestic real interest rate. At the same time, the Chilean and Argentine authorities also condoned (and even encouraged) short-term capital inflows unrelated to productive investment, thereby exacerbating the currency appreciation and the risk of a sudden reversal of capital flows.[55] Moreover, decision makers persisted in these policies despite the evidently serious damage that such measures were inflicting on the domestic industry and the financial system.

Such a doctrinaire attitude toward exchange rate policy contrasted sharply with the pragmatic attitudes of Taiwan and South Korea in the 1960s. In both economies not only was the exchange rate not used as a tool for price stabilization, but the effective exchange rate (inclusive of various policy-related incentives) was also heavily and consistently set in favor of export activity in order to influence entrepreneurial activity. With respect to capital inflows, the authorities of both economies have actively solicited foreign capital investment and technology transfer in generous terms (with respect to the percentage of foreign ownership, income tax payment, depreciation allowance, and imports of necessary raw materials and intermediate inputs, and so forth), but they have also emphasized the necessity of exporting a relatively large proportion of the planned output.

On short-term flows, in particular, Taiwan has been cautious.[56] South Korea has been more liberal with respect to the use of short-term foreign credits, which were partly attracted by maintaining a relatively high nominal interest rate during the late 1960s. Partly because of this interest rate, however, Korea experienced more difficulties than Taiwan in controlling inflation during the 1960s and the 1970s. Moreover, because of the resulting relatively high debt service ratios, the Korean balance of payments has also been less stable. Nevertheless, unlike Chile and Argentina, South Korean authorities have always acted to prevent the balance of payments from degenerating into a crisis through their steadfast export orientation and resolute price stabilization efforts.[57]

The role of government

The policy reforms of Chile and Argentina in the 1970s involved a redefinition of the role of government in the process of economic development. In an over-reaction to the inefficiencies and persistent inflation under prolonged industrial protection, the authorities in these countries (particularly Chile) turned to laissez-faire liberalism as a model of economic development. This model was manifested in the denationalization of public enterprises, the liberalization of merchandise trade and capital flows, the sharp reduction of import tariffs, the severe curtailment of labor union activity, and in the case of Chile, the pursuit of a neutral fiscal policy and a passive monetary policy. Many of these measures were indeed necessary in order to invigorate the economy. Yet the hasty pace of their implementation facilitated speculative capital flows and, in Chile, rapid concentration of private wealth and massive unemployment.[58]

In contrast to Chile and Argentina, the authorities in Taiwan and South Korea have succeeded in improving the overall efficiency of the economy while maintaining an active role in the process of economic development.[59] In both Taiwan and South Korea, partly because of tradition the state has dominated society not only in politics, but also in the operation of the economy. In both countries, the governments have owned and operated many key services including railways, electric power, piped water, telephones and other telecommunications, commercial banks, and the cigarette and tobacco monopoly. In Taiwan the state has also dominated a number of manufacturing industries (petroleum refining, chemical fertilizers, integrated steel mills, and shipbuilding). Both governments pursued policies to create an institutional framework conducive to economic development and the growth of private enterprise.

Both have also acted strongly in provision of public welfare programs, in addition to being highly restrictive on labor union activity. The latter deficiency has been compensated by the authorities' pragmatic approach to economic policymaking. Through a successful control of inflation and timely, active promotion of exports and industrial efficiency both governments have helped create a viable pattern of economic growth based on their dynamic comparative advantages. This has enabled Taiwan and South Korea to rapidly increase employment and improve the living standards of the majority of the population while permitting an increasing liberalization of their economies.[60] Such liberalization in turn has contributed to the improvement of resource allocation and the attainment of overall economic efficiency. Thus the experiences of Taiwan and South Korea indicate that the role of government in the development process need not be passive. In fact, it should be active and growth promoting, not growth retarding.

Conclusions

This comparative review indicates that the superior economic performance of Taiwan and South Korea in the 1960s owed much to the successful reform of trade incentives by the respective governments, while the poor economic performance of Chile and Argentina was attributable at least partly to the half-hearted efforts of the national authorities in this regard. Moreover, the East Asian countries' policy reforms were preceded by the successful control of hyperinflation, a success which greatly facilitated the task of restructuring trade and industry. By contrast, the two Latin American countries were unable to control inflation on a sustained basis even under the favorable world economic environment of the 1960s, greatly complicating their trade and industrial restructuring efforts.

As a consequence of the policy reforms, the focus of the entrepreneurs in Taiwan and South Korea shifted from domestic to export activity. This focus, combined with the formation of a competitive labor supply, enabled Taiwan and South Korea to develop a growth pattern based on their dynamic comparative advantages. In both economies productivity growth accelerated, and a virtuous circle of rapid export expansion, high economic growth, and stable domestic prices developed. By contrast, in Chile and Argentina the bias against exports remained significant during the 1960s and the effective protection of domestic industry remained high. Largely because of these policies their exports failed to grow rapidly enough to support a satisfactory expansion of domestic demand and imports.

The failure to establish a viable pattern of economic growth and the pressures thus generated ultimately led the Chilean and the Argentine authorities to undertake extensive liberalization and stabilization efforts in the 1970s. While these efforts were commendable and indeed overdue, they ultimately failed partly because of the lack of pragmatism in the management of economic policies. The hasty opening up of the economy through drastic tariff reductions and the liberalization of short-term capital inflows as well as the prolonged experiment of using preannounced exchange rate devaluation as a tool for price stabilization caused unnecessarily severe hardships for the domestic industry and the workers.

Such a doctrinaire attitude to economic policy management contrasted sharply with the highly pragmatic attitude displayed by the authorities in Taiwan and South Korea in their economic policy conduct. These authorities were resolute in their pursuit of price stabilization and export promotion goals, but they were more cautious and eclectic about the liberalization of imports and capital inflows unrelated to productive investment. In this regard, the success of the East Asian countries in attaining price stabilization without causing prolonged recession and in achieving rapid economic growth without worsening the income distribution should be of interest to many developing countries (particularly Chile and Argentina) which have so far failed to do so, and which are therefore searching for an alternative development model.

Chapter 3

POLICY RESPONSE TO EXTERNAL SHOCKS: BRAZIL VERSUS TAIWAN AND SOUTH KOREA

Introduction and Summary

Brazil and Mexico in Latin America, like Taiwan and South Korea in East Asia, were considered model developing countries in the decade prior to the first oil shock. During that decade, all four countries experienced rapid economic growth, relatively stable domestic prices or a stabilizing price situation, and no serious balance of payments problems. Since then, however, both Brazil and Mexico have diverged widely from Taiwan and South Korea in important aspects of their macroeconomic performance. The two Latin American countries experienced hyperinflation and severe debt service problems, while the two East Asian countries controlled inflation and balance of payments deficits without causing a prolonged recession in their economies. What caused this divergence in economic performances? Was there a difference primarily because Brazil and Mexico were too anxious to maintain economic growth while they neglected to control inflation until it was too late? Was it also because of some defects in the two Latin American countries' development strategies, such as their renewed inward-orientation while neglecting to maintain export growth, or their excessive reliance on external borrowing while neglecting to strengthen domestic finances? Why could Taiwan restore domestic price stability and external balance while sustaining a relatively high rate of economic growth despite the severe disturbances in the world economy? How did South Korea manage to escape the entrapment of runaway inflation and severe debt service problems despite its heavy reliance on external credits to sustain economic growth? Are the experiences of Taiwan and South Korea relevant to countries like Brazil and Mexico?

This paper attempts to answer these questions by contrasting the policy responses and development experiences of Brazil in the 1970s and the early 1980s with those of Taiwan and South Korea. The experience of Mexico—similar to Brazil's in important aspects but nevertheless different in certain areas particularly because of Mexico's subsequent emergence as a major oil exporter—is not discussed in the rest of the paper, both in order to reduce the complexity of the comparative analysis and to emphasize the significance of South Korea as an intermediate case between Brazil and Taiwan in policy management and development experience. Briefly, this chapter attributes the ultimate divergence in macroeconomic performance between Brazil and Taiwan to the authorities' contrasting policy stances with respect to price stabilization and external adjustment when they were confronted with the vast changes in external environment that occurred in the 1970s and the early 1980s.

During this period, the authorities in these countries, like many other governments, were confronted with two major oil price shocks, sharp swings in external demand and commodity prices, wild fluctuations in the key currency exchange rates, and during the early 1980s, sharp rises in the real interest rates in the international financial markets. Taken together, these developments represented a sharp break in the external environment from the stable and predictable world of the 1960s, with steady expansion of external demand, mild inflation in world trade prices, and stable relationships between major currencies.

Faced with this new situation, in particular the large losses in terms of trade and surging import cost pressures, how should the national authorities react to attain their long-term growth objectives without causing runaway inflation or severe external payments problems? Should they adjust their priority in favor of short-term price stabilization, or try to sustain domestic growth through enlarged external borrowing? What should these countries do in order to reduce external deficit—reduce domestic demand, increase exports, or reduce imports? These were the kind of policy issues confronting the national authorities in the 1970s.

Whereas the Taiwanese authorities, when confronted with the ramifications of the first oil shock, took drastic policy actions to curtail the excess demand emanating from the 1972 and 1973 export booms in order to control the surging inflation and the sharply widened external deficits, Brazil did not take effective action to stop the acceleration of inflation and relied heavily on external borrowing to sustain economic

growth through import-substitutions and massive domestic development projects. The successful control of inflation and the attendant
restoration of international competitiveness enabled Taiwan to take full
advantage of the subsequent recovery in export demand that occurred
during 1976 to 1978.[1] This control, combined with the authorities'
prudent attitude toward import substitutions and external borrowing,
enabled Taiwan to overcome the economic difficulties related to the
second oil shock that occurred in 1979 to 1980.

By contrast, the failure to control inflation after the first oil shock
and the continued heavy reliance on external credits at variable market
rates placed Brazil in an untenable position when the world economy
went into a prolonged recession following the second oil shock. Brazil's trade balance worsened sharply because of the unfavorable terms
of trade and export demand, while its debt service obligations expanded
drastically, partly because of the extraordinary rise in international
interest rates. Meanwhile, the authorities continued to use full wage
indexing and monetary corrections despite severe losses in trade and
consecutive crop failures. As a result, Brazil's resurgent inflation
deteriorated rapidly to exceed 100 percent a year despite the use of the
preannounced monetary target and exchange rate adjustment as a tool
to influence price expectations. By the second half of 1982, Brazil
experienced a severe liquidity shortage and mounting debt service
problems amid disruptions in the international financial markets. This
finally prompted the government to undertake intensive stabilization
and adjustment measures (with the assistance of the IMF) which it had
avoided for a decade.

While South Korea, like Brazil, also relied on heavy external borrowing to sustain domestic growth after the first oil shock, it was much
more successful than Brazil in maintaining export expansion (including
the sale of construction services to the oil-exporting countries) and in
containing inflation. Moreover, faced with deteriorating internal and
external balances in the wake of the second oil shock, the Korean
authorities quickly undertook intensive stabilization and adjustment
measures in 1980. These measures were successful in restoring price
stability, reducing external deficit, and resuming economic growth by
1982.

In this chapter the next section compares the macroeconomic performance of Brazil with Taiwan and South Korea in the period since the
first oil shock. The causes of divergence in inflation between the three
countries, focusing on differences in monetary policy and wage behav-

Table 3.1

Brazil, Taiwan, and South Korea: Selected Indicators of Macroeconomic Performance, Before and After the First Oil Shock (In annual percentage changes, except debt service ratio)

	1966-73	1971-73	1974-75	1976-78	1979-80	1981	1982	1983
Brazil								
Real output	8.5	12.2	7.6	6.8	6.8	-1.6	0.9	-3.2
CPI inflation	23.3	16.7	28.3	41.5	67.1	105.6	98.0	142.0
Foreign trade gap[1]	-29.4	-39.5	-74.9	-46.4	-57.7	-43.5	-69.4	-28.4
Taiwan								
Real output	11.0	13.0	2.7	12.4	7.3	5.0	3.9	7.1
CPI inflation	4.5	4.6	24.6	5.1	14.3	16.3	3.4	1.8
Foreign trade gap[1]	2.6	12.9	-13.1	15.1	-1.5	2.0	8.8	15.4
South Korea								
Real output	11.5	9.8	7.7	11.2	2.1	6.9	5.5	9.5
CPI inflation	11.3	9.3	24.8	13.3	23.4	21.3	7.3	3.4
Foreign trade gap[1]	-43.6	-27.7	-36.1	-3.9	-22.7	-17.2	-9.5	-5.6

Sources: International Financial Statistics, national sources, and IMF staff estimates.
[1] Current account deficit (balance on goods, services, and private transfers) as percent of exports of goods and services.

ior, are presented and followed by the patterns of external adjustment and financing from 1974 to 1978. The chapter then reviews the three countries' macroeconomic policy responses to the second oil shock and the divergent outcomes. The last section discusses further the policy requirements for Brazil to control inflation and reduce the debt burden in light of the two East Asian countries' development experiences.

Comparative Macroeconomic Performance, before and after the First Oil Shock

In the less than a decade that followed the stabilization efforts in 1964, Brazil experienced sharp improvements in its economic conditions, with a steady decline in the rate of inflation and a marked acceleration in the rate of investment and output growth that was supported by large inflows of foreign capital. By the early 1970s, the Brazilian economic performance had become comparable to that of Taiwan and South Korea, the star performers among the developing countries (Table 3.1 and Charts 3.1, 3.2, and 3.3).

In the subsequent decade following the first oil shock of 1973 to 1974, however, the Brazilian economic performance deteriorated and diverged widely from Taiwan and South Korea. Between 1973 and 1983 Brazil's real GDP increased yearly by only 4.4 percent, compared to 8.5 percent in the period 1966 to 1973. In comparison, Taiwan's real output increased by 7.3 percent per year compared to 11.0 percent, while South Korea's increased by 7.7 percent compared to 11.5 percent (Table 3.1).

The steep decline in Brazil's economic growth rate occurred only after 1980. Until then, despite the worsened external conditions, Brazil's economic growth rate was maintained at nearly 7 percent yearly (Chart 3.1 and Table 3.1). However, this growth was sustained by large external borrowing at variable market rates and was accompanied by worsening inflation and debt service obligations. From a low point of less than 13 percent per year in 1973, Brazil's CPI inflation accelerated year after year to reach more than 100 percent by 1980 (Chart 3.2). Meanwhile, its current account deficit, which expanded to over 80 percent of exports of goods and services in 1974, had remained at the 40 to 60 percent range, with the resulting annual debt services increased from 13 percent of export earnings (including services) in 1973 to 31 percent in 1978 and 34 percent in 1980. From 1980 to 1983,

CHART 3.1

BRAZIL, TAIWAN, AND SOUTH KOREA:

EVOLUTION OF REAL OUTPUT AND
REAL DOMESTIC DEMAND, 1971-83

(In percentage change)

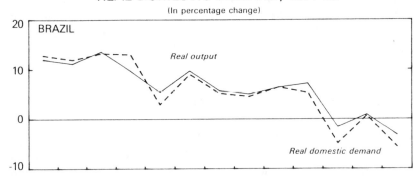

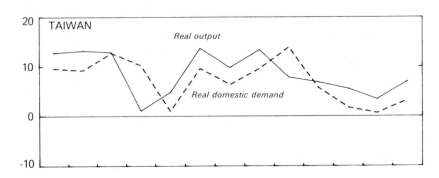

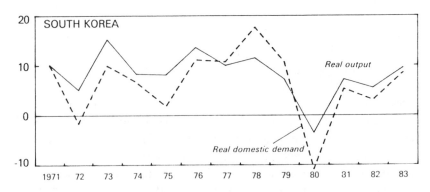

Brazil's real output declined by 3.9 percent (8.3 percent per capita) because of the world recession and the domestic stabilization policies, but its CPI inflation rose even higher, to exceed 150 percent in 1983. Its

CHART 3.2

BRAZIL, TAIWAN, AND SOUTH KOREA:

CONSUMER PRICE INFLATION, 1951-83

(In percentage change)

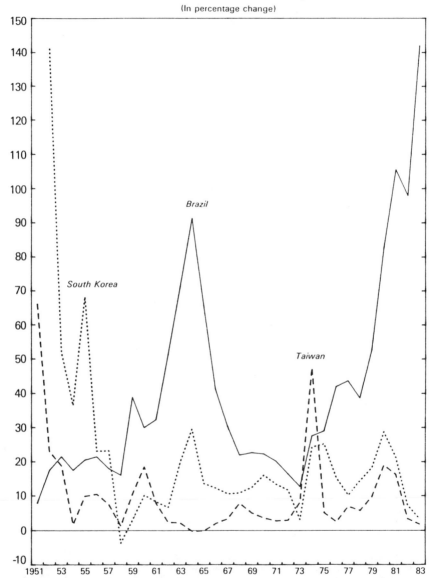

current account deficit was cut back to 30 percent of export earnings in 1983, at great cost to domestic growth, but its debt service ratio has remained very high (Charts 3.2, 3.3, and 3.4 and Table 3.1).

CHART 3.3

BRAZIL, TAIWAN, AND SOUTH KOREA:

CURRENT ACCOUNT DEFICIT IN RELATION TO EXPORTS OF GOODS AND SERVICES, 1967-83[1]

(In percentages)

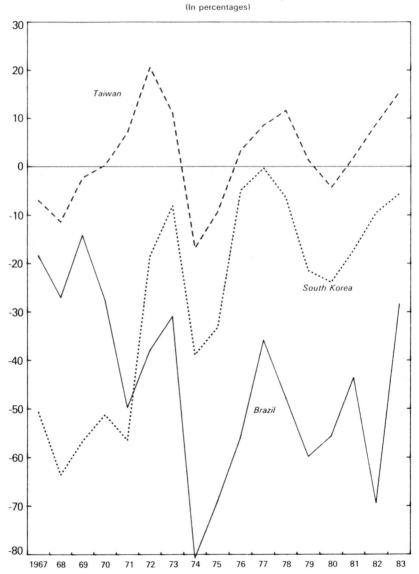

[1]Current account deficit is defined as the balance on goods, services, and private transfers.

CHART 3.4

BRAZIL VERSUS TAIWAN AND SOUTH KOREA:

DEBT-SERVICE RATIO, 1971-83

(Amortization and interest payments as percent of exports of goods and services)

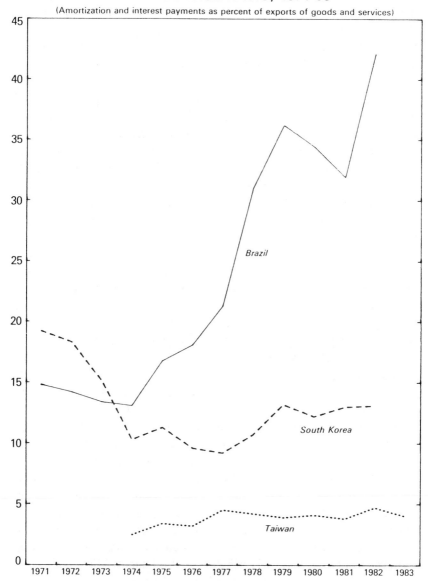

Compared to Brazil, Taiwan's inflation and current account deficit were controlled quickly after an initial severe worsening. Taiwan's CPI inflation, jumping from less than 10 percent in 1973 to nearly 50

percent in 1974, was brought down quickly to around 5 percent in 1975 and remained stable during the following three years. The price resurgence in 1980 in the wake of the second oil shock was contained at less than 20 percent per year even though it lasted two years instead of one. By 1982, however, Taiwan's CPI inflation was again brought down to less than 5 percent per year (Chart 3.2). Similarly, Taiwan's current account balance, which had shifted from a surplus amounting to over 10 percent of export earnings in 1973 to a deficit amounting to 17 percent in 1974, was quickly restored to a surplus position of 25 percent of export earnings in 1976. The renewed worsening in external deficit that occurred in 1979 and 1980 was much smaller, and its adjustment even swifter (Chart 3.3). As a consequence, Taiwan's debt service ratio increased very little during the last decade. In fact, Taiwan's gross foreign reserves, which declined to 10 to 20 percent of annual import payments (goods only) during the period 1974 to 1980, were restored to the 40 to 45 percent level by the early 1980s, comparable to the situation in the 1960s (Chart 3.5). However, reflecting the influences of the protracted world recession and the authorities' extremely cautious demand management, domestic investment declined markedly in the early 1980s and the growth of real output also slowed down (Table 3.1).

South Korea occupied the middle ground between Brazil and Taiwan with respect to price stabilization and external adjustment. The Korean inflation in the wake of the first oil shock was milder than in Taiwan, at only about 25 percent per year, but it lasted longer and also turned upward much faster than in Taiwan after being reduced to the 10 percent level in 1977. By 1979 and 1980, in the wake of the second oil shock following a strong expansion of domestic demand, the Korean inflation was back to 24 percent per year compared to around 14 percent in Taiwan. Only strong monetary and fiscal restraints in 1980 and 1981 brought the inflation down to 7 percent in 1982 (Chart 3.2). Similarly, South Korea's current account deficit widened much more sharply than Taiwan's following both the first and the second oil shocks. Compared to the Brazilian experience, however, South Korea's external adjustment was swifter on both occasions. During the first oil shock adjustment, help came from a strong export expansion at the time of the 1976/1978 world economic recovery; and during the second from the combination of an early initiation of adjustment measures and a successful price stabilization (Charts 3.2 and 3.3). Consequently, South

CHART 3.5

BRAZIL, TAIWAN, AND SOUTH KOREA:

GROSS RESERVES IN RELATION TO
ANNUAL MERCHANDISE IMPORTS, 1953-82

(In percent)

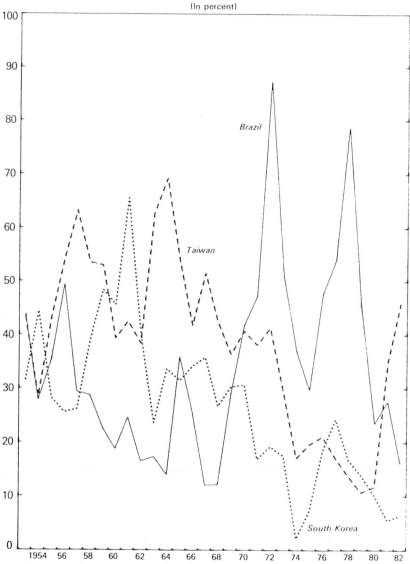

Korea's debt service ratio actually declined from 15 percent in 1973 to 9.2 percent in 1977, before rising to over 13 percent in 1979 (Table 3.1 and Chart 3.4).

Table 3.2

Brazil, Taiwan, and South Korea: Exports, Import Unit Value, Money Supply, and Domestic Credit in Both Nominal and Real Terms, and Real Domestic Demand, Selected Periods from 1966 to 1983 (In percentage changes)

	1966–71	1972–73	1974	1975	1976–78	1979–80	1981–83
Brazil							
Exports (US$)	10.5	46.1	28.3	9.0	13.5	26.1	2.8
Import price (US$)	1.8	15.5	46.2	8.7	4.5	23.8	0.5
Money supply (M2)	30.0	44.1	32.7	44.5	44.8	67.2	98.8
Domestic credit	19.4	47.9	50.8	54.2	50.7	78.8	120.2
Inflation[1]	25.4	19.2	28.3	28.0	41.2	72.9	117.4
Real money supply[2]	3.7	20.9	3.4	12.9	2.5	–3.3	–8.6
Real domestic credit[2]	–4.8	24.0	17.5	20.5	6.7	3.4	1.3
Real domestic demand[3]	9.9	12.5	13.0	2.9	6.2	5.8	–3.3
Taiwan							
Exports (US$)	28.9	47.5	25.8	–5.9	33.7	22.6	12.2
Import price (US$)	2.3	20.7	47.6	–4.2	7.7	22.8	2.5
Money supply (M2)	21.4	31.1	24.7	28.0	29.6	15.6	22.8
Domestic credit	19.7	31.9	42.2	30.3	21.8	22.8	17.0
Inflation[1]	2.9	9.6	44.1	—	4.1	16.0	4.5
Real money supply[2]	18.0	19.6	–13.5	28.0	24.5	–0.3	17.5
Real domestic credit[2]	16.3	20.3	–1.3	30.3	17.0	5.9	12.0
Real domestic demand[3]	10.2	10.9	10.2	1.0	8.5	9.7	1.8

South Korea

Exports (US$)	35.2	73.7	38.3	13.9	35.7	17.3	11.8
Import price (US$)	-0.1	16.3	55.5	2.9	1.9	21.2	-2.4
Money supply (M2)	49.3	35.1	24.1	28.2	36.0	25.7	22.3
Domestic credit	47.8	29.3	52.6	31.5	29.8	39.4	23.9
Inflation[1]	10.3	8.8	33.2	26.0	12.1	25.9	9.4
Real money supply[2]	35.4	24.2	-6.8	1.7	21.3	-0.2	11.8
Real domestic credit[2]	34.0	18.8	14.6	4.4	15.8	10.7	13.3
Real domestic demand[3]	10.7	4.0	6.6	1.8	13.1	-0.7	5.6

Sources: *International Financial Statistics*, national publications, and author's estimates.
[1] Average rate of change in the CPI and WPI.
[2] Deflated by an average rate of changes in the CPI and WPI.
[3] Estimated by using the relation Domestic demand equals GNP minus Exports plus Imports, in volume terms.

85

Price Stabilization and External Adjustment after the First Oil Shock

Divergence in the control of inflation

The better control of inflation in Taiwan and South Korea after the first oil shock can be ascribed to the following three factors: (1) The authorities in Taiwan, and to a lesser extent in South Korea, took the task of price stabilization more seriously than their counterparts in Brazil, and they undertook strong stabilization measures much sooner. (2) Unlike Brazil and several other Latin American countries, restrictive monetary policy proved effective in containing inflation in Taiwan and South Korea partly because of the lack of rigid wage indexing. (3) The continued pursuit of outward-looking policies helped domestic price stabilization in Taiwan and South Korea, while the intensified import restrictions and the renewed emphasis on import substitutions exacerbated import cost pressures in Brazil.

Similarity of initial conditions and the first oil shock

At the time of the first oil shock, all three countries experienced strong export expansion and rapid economic growth helped by strong booms in the world economy and substantial effective depreciation of their currencies that occurred in conjunction with the multilateral currency realignment in late 1971 and the generalized floating in early 1973. (See Chart 3.6 for the "real" effective depreciation of the three countries' currencies against the SDR in 1971 to 1973.) In fact, during 1972 and 1973, export earnings (in U.S. dollars) expanded yearly by 46.1 percent in Brazil, 47.5 percent in Taiwan, and 73.7 percent in South Korea compared to 10.5, 28.9, and 35.2 percent in the preceding six years. As a result, foreign reserves accumulated rapidly, and the monetary authorities' base money increased at extraordinary rates. The rapid growth of export earnings and money supply stimulated the growth of domestic demand and real output which was supported by a higher expansion of domestic credit by the banking system. During 1972 and 1973 real domestic demand increased by 12.7 percent per year in Brazil and 11.0 percent per year in Taiwan. In South Korea, which had just emerged from a recession, real domestic demand expanded by nearly 10 percent in 1973 compared to a negative 2 percent in 1972. During those two years, domestic credit expanded yearly by 47.9 percent in

CHART 3.6

BRAZIL, TAIWAN, AND SOUTH KOREA:

INDEX OF REAL SDR EXCHANGE RATE, 1970-83

(Index of national currency per unit of SDR, multiplied by the ratio of the index of industrial countries' wholesale prices to the domestic wholesale price index; 1973=100)

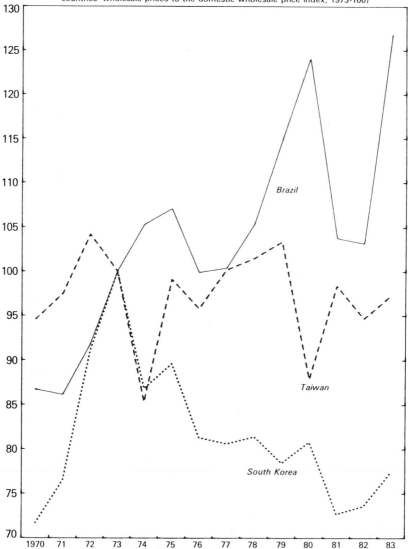

Brazil, 31.9 percent in Taiwan, and 29.3 percent in South Korea. (See Table 3.2 and Charts 3.7, 3.8, and 3.9 for the evolution of money supply and domestic credit in real terms.)

CHART 3.7

BRAZIL:

IMPORT UNIT VALUE, REAL DOMESTIC CREDIT, REAL MONEY SUPPLY, AND INFLATION, 1966-83

(In annual percentage changes)

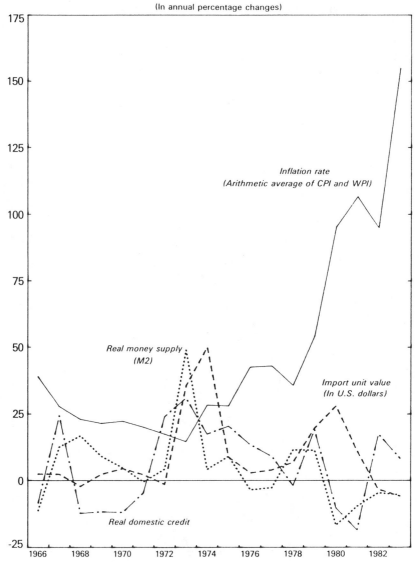

Under the circumstances, the quadrupling of oil prices in late 1973 gave a strong push to the accelerating inflation in Taiwan, while reversing the slowing price trend in Brazil and South Korea. However, be-

CHART 3.8

TAIWAN:

IMPORT UNIT VALUE, REAL DOMESTIC CREDIT, REAL MONEY SUPPLY, AND INFLATION, 1966-83

(In percentage changes)

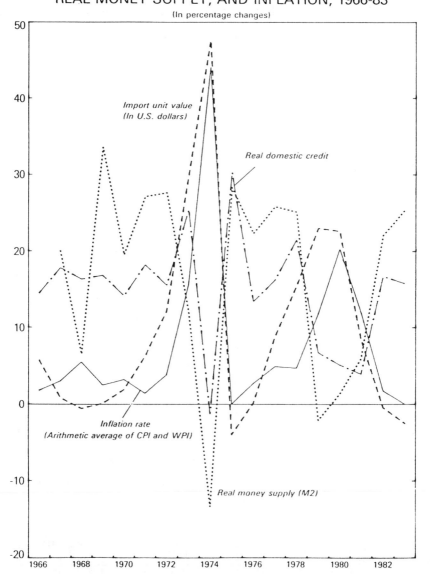

cause of the greater openness of the two East Asian countries,[2] the cost-push effect of the oil price jumps was felt more strongly in Taiwan and South Korea than in Brazil. Thus, while the import unit value (in U.S.

CHART 3.9

SOUTH KOREA:

IMPORT UNIT VALUE, REAL DOMESTIC CREDIT, REAL MONEY SUPPLY, AND INFLATION, 1966-83

(In annual percentage changes)

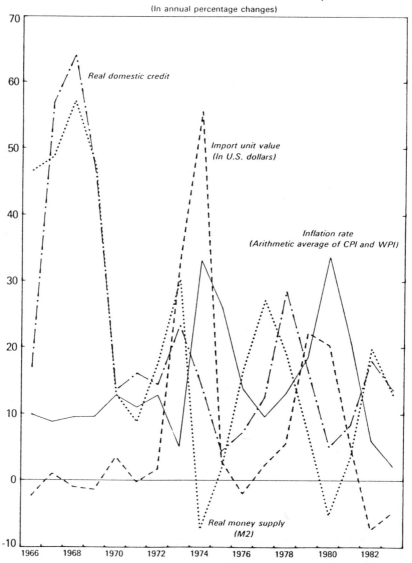

dollars) jumped by roughly the same magnitude in 1973 and 1974—by 100 percent in Brazil, 92 percent in Taiwan, and 106 percent in South Korea—domestic inflation accelerated faster in Taiwan and South Ko-

Table 3.3

Brazil, Taiwan, and South Korea: Terms of Trade Developments, 1971–83 (In percentages)

	Changes in merchandise terms of trade			GDP equivalent of changes in terms of trade[1]		
	Brazil	Taiwan	South Korea	Brazil	Taiwan	South Korea
1971	−7.0	−3.1	−1.0	−0.5	−0.9	−0.1
1972	14.7	−3.0	−0.4	0.7	−0.7	−0.2
1973	1.5	−3.6	−5.1	−0.3	−0.3	−2.2
1974	−13.8	−10.9	−18.6	−1.5	−3.7	−7.4
1975	−8.0	−1.8	−9.8	−0.8	−0.4	−2.4
1976	12.3	2.3	14.1	0.5	0.8	3.0
1977	17.5	−1.5	7.0	0.8	−0.5	1.8
1978	−13.9	−5.4	4.7	−0.8	−2.0	1.3
1979	−8.3	−3.2	−2.1	−0.5	−0.6	−1.2
1980	−17.3	−9.3	−13.2	−1.0	−4.8	−5.0
1981	−15.3	−4.0	−2.1	−0.9	−2.1	−0.9
1982	−2.9	1.1	4.3	−0.1	0.4	1.7
1983	−0.2	0.5	0.9	0.1	0.1	0.3
Average 1974–78	−2.8	−3.6	−1.3	−0.3	−1.2	−0.8
Average 1979–83	−9.0	−3.3	−2.6	−0.5	−1.4	−1.0

Sources: International Financial Statistics, and author's estimate.
[1]Difference between incremental exports and incremental imports at constant volume as a percent of current year GDP. The incremental imports and exports are estimated as a product of preceding year exports (imports) times the percentage change in export (import) unit value.

rea than in Brazil. In Taiwan, the average rate of inflation in the CPI and WPI jumped from a mere 3.8 percent in 1972 to 15.6 percent in 1973 and 44.1 percent in 1974. In South Korea, this rate rose to 33.2 percent in 1974, after decelerating from 12.8 percent in 1972 to 5.1 percent in 1973; and in Brazil, it rose to 28.3 percent, after decelerating from 17.5 percent to 14.7 percent (Charts 3.7, 3.8, and 3.9).

Similarly, due to the smaller size of their economies, the decline in terms of trade caused a greater deflationary effect on the domestic demand of Taiwan and South Korea than on Brazil's demand. In 1974 to 1975 the merchandise terms of trade declined yearly by 10.9 percent in Brazil, 6.4 percent in Taiwan, and 14.2 percent in South Korea. In relation to GDP, however, the yearly loss amounted to 2.1 percent in Taiwan, and 4.9 percent in South Korea, compared to only 1.1 percent in Brazil (Table 3.3).

Divergence in policy response between Brazil and Taiwan

Faced with strong cost pressures and sharply higher import payment requirements, the authorities in the three countries reacted quite differently. While both Brazil and South Korea sought to sustain economic growth through enlarged external borrowing, Taiwan placed more emphasis on stopping the surging inflation. As early as 1973 the Taiwanese authorities began to take various measures to alleviate the mounting inflationary pressures. In February the NT dollar was revalued by 5 percent against the U.S. dollar in the wake of the latter's downward floating. In April the inflow of short-term foreign credit was temporarily suspended and its use was replaced by domestic funds. In July the reserve requirements of the banking institutions for fixed deposits were raised from 5 percent to the maximum 10 percent; and in July and again in October interest rates for loans and deposits were raised. However, these measures proved inadequate to stem the surging inflation, and following the quantum jumps in oil prices in late 1973, the authorities strengthened the stabilization measures in January 1974 by raising the interest rates by 2.5 to 4.3 percentage points and sharply curtailing nonessential bank credits. As a consequence, real domestic credit, which had expanded by 25 percent in 1973, actually declined by 1 percent in 1974, and real money supply (M2), which had expanded by 12 percent in 1973, declined by as much as 13 percent partly because of the large loss in foreign reserves. The severe monetary restraint, combined with the weakened domestic demand caused by the falling real income and the reversal in inventory investment,[3] stopped the upward movements of domestic prices by the second half of 1974. During 1975, the wholesale price index declined by 5 percent while consumer prices increased by only 5 percent compared to 48 percent in the preceding year (See Chart 3.8 and Table 3.2).

Compared with Taiwan's highly restrictive monetary policy, the

Brazilian monetary stance in 1973 and 1974 was much more relaxed. Despite the tripling of foreign reserves in 1972 and 1973, the authorities allowed a sharp expansion of domestic credit through various public agencies. This resulted in an extraordinary 49 percent expansion of the real money supply in 1973. Following the oil price jumps, the expansion of consumer credit slowed down markedly because of the decline in real income and the much increased cost of operating motor vehicles.[4] However, credit expansion to the import-substituting industries and the agricultural sector continued, resulting in a relatively minor slackening in domestic credit expansion. In nominal terms, domestic credit expanded by 51 percent in 1974, about the same rate as in 1973. In real terms, it expanded by 17.5 percent compared to 31 percent. While the growth of the real money supply was much smaller in 1974 because of the sharp loss in foreign reserves, it remained positive compared to the sharp absolute decline suffered by Taiwan (Table 3.2 and Charts 3.7 and 3.8).

In addition to the more relaxed monetary stance, the Brazilian authorities allowed real gains in urban wages in 1974 and 1975 despite the severe losses in terms of trade and real income. This resulted in contrasting wage and price behavior between Brazil and Taiwan in those two years. In Taiwan the wage earners suffered a substantial loss in their purchasing power during 1974, but the resulting stabilization in costs and prices allowed the authorities to relax their monetary stance beginning from the second half of 1974. The recovery of economic activity, export expansion and productivity growth under stable domestic prices then enabled the wage earners to again obtain real wage gains in the following years (Charts 3.8, 3.10, and 3.11 and Table 3.4). By contrast, in Brazil the wage earners continued to obtain real wage gains in both 1974 and 1975 despite the declines in trade and labor productivity, but these gains inevitably resulted in higher unit labor costs and product prices, leading to the acceleration of inflation (Charts 3.10 and 3.12).

Another factor that contributed to the divergence of inflation between Brazil and Taiwan concerns the policies on external trade. After the first oil shock, the authorities in Taiwan continued to pursue the outward-looking policies that had brought rapid export expansion and high economic growth in the previous decade. During 1973 and 1974 the government took further measures to liberalize imports and reduce tariff rates. These measures, with the temporary freezing of the tax base for several essential commodities (such as sugar and cement)

Table 3.4

Brazil, Taiwan, and South Korea: Manufacturing Output, Employment, Labor Productivity, Wages in Both Nominal and Real Terms, Unit Labor Costs, and Wholesale Prices: Selected Periods from 1966 to 1982 (In annual percentage changes)

	1966–73	1974–75	1976–78	1979–80	1981–82
1. *Brazil*					
a. Real output	11.5	5.8	7.5	7.1	−5.1
b. Employment	7.9	6.2	3.6	1.5	−3.0
c. Labor productivity	3.3	−0.4	3.8	5.5	−2.2
d. Nominal wages	27.2	35.9	49.2	74.2	108.2
e. Unit labor costs	23.1	36.4	43.7	65.1	112.9
f. Consumer prices	23.3	28.3	41.5	67.1	101.8
g. Real wages	3.2	5.9	5.4	4.2	5.5
h. Terms of trade	1.1	−10.8	4.2	−12.7	−9.3
i. Wholesale prices	22.8	28.2	41.1	79.4	99.9
j. Excess of real wage gains over pro-ductivity growth	−0.1	6.3	1.6	−1.3	7.7
k. Excess of unit labor costs over WPI	0.3	8.2	2.6	−14.3	13.0
2. *Taiwan*					
a. Real output	21.0	0.7	21.6	7.7	2.5
b. Employment	11.1	3.4	7.5	6.3	0.5
c. Labor productivity	8.9	−2.6	13.1	1.3	2.0
d. Nominal wages	13.6	26.3	16.6	20.0	14.0
e. Unit labor costs	4.3	29.7	3.1	18.5	11.8
f. Consumer prices	4.5	24.6	5.1	14.3	9.7
g. Real wages	8.7	1.4	10.9	5.0	3.9
h. Terms of trade	−0.9	−6.6	−1.6	−6.3	2.0
i. Wholesale prices	4.4	15.5	3.0	17.6	3.3
j. Excess of real wage gains over pro-ductivity growth	−0.2	4.0	−2.2	3.7	1.9
k. Excess of unit labor costs over WPI	−0.1	14.2	0.1	0.9	8.5
3. *South Korea*					
a. Real output	23.6	24.2	25.2	4.9	9.2
b. Employment	10.5	11.1	11.3	−1.0	1.5
c. Labor productivity	11.9	11.8	12.5	6.0	7.6
d. Nominal wages	21.8	31.8	33.8	25.6	17.3
e. Unit labor costs	8.8	17.9	18.9	18.5	9.0
f. Consumer prices	11.3	24.8	13.3	23.4	14.1
g. Real wages	9.4	5.6	18.1	1.8	2.8
h. Terms of trade	0.9	−13.9	8.4	−11.2	1.7
i. Wholesale prices	8.6	34.1	10.9	28.5	12.2
j. Excess of real wage gains over pro-ductivity growth	−2.5	−6.2	5.6	−4.2	−4.8
k. Excess of unit labor costs over WPI	0.2	−16.2	8.0	−10.0	−3.2

Sources: International Monetary Fund, *International Financial Statistics*, International Labour Office, *International Labour Statistics*, and national publications.

CHART 3.10

BRAZIL, TAIWAN, AND SOUTH KOREA:

TERMS OF TRADE, AND LABOR PRODUCTIVITY
AND REAL WAGES IN MANUFACTURING, 1972-83

(In annual percentage changes)

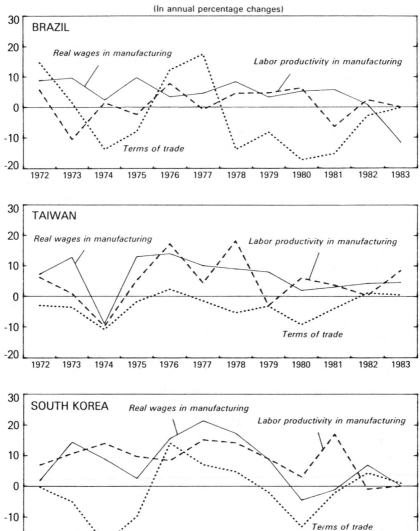

helped stabilize the domestic prices.[5] By contrast, Brazil raised tariffs on a large number of commodities, introduced various measures to restrict imports, and placed a renewed emphasis on import-substituting activity. These measures intensified the strong import cost pressures.[6]

South Korea as an intermediate case

Compared to Brazil and Taiwan, the Korean monetary stance in 1973 was mixed. Because of the aftereffects of a recession in 1971 and 1972, domestic prices were relatively stable in South Korea during the early part of 1973. In fact, during the early months of 1973 the Korean government lowered the nominal interest rates, thus continuing the policy action started in the previous year. In the course of 1973, however, the economy had increasingly become overheated, prompting the government to tighten monetary policy. In May, the minimum reserve ratios of the banking institutions were raised by 3 to 4 percentage points, and in December interest rates on short-term deposits were temporarily raised and a foreign currency time deposit was introduced for exporters in order to absorb excess liquidity. Following the oil price jumps, these stabilization measures were substantially strengthened in January 1974.

The strengthening of the stabilization measures in South Korea in early 1974 paralleled similar policy actions in Taiwan. However, in comparison with Taiwan, the Korean policies in 1974 were much more expansionary. For example, the Korean authorities took action to encourage the inflow of foreign credits, in contrast with the discouragement of short-term capital inflows by the Taiwanese authorities. To facilitate the inflow of these credits, in January 1974 the Korean authorities introduced a floating interest rate system. Interest rates on all loans in foreign currencies would fluctuate in relation to the average Eurocurrency rates of six-month maturity in the preceding month.[7] Moreover, in July 1974 the Korean authorities lowered the minimum reserve ratios of the banking institutions for deposits by 3 percentage points to relieve their worsened reserve position. As a consequence, domestic credit expanded by 53 percent in 1974, well above the 29 percent rate in the previous year. In real terms, the growth was nearly 15 percent compared to 23 percent. This compares with an absolute decline of 1.3 percent in Taiwan following a 25 percent growth in 1973. Lastly, in December 1974 the Korean authorities depreciated the won by 21 percent against the U.S. dollar, which helped to restore the international competitiveness of the Korean industry, but the price stabilization process was inevitably retarded by the interaction of currency depreciation

CHART 3.11

TAIWAN:

IMPORT UNIT VALUE, MANUFACTURING UNIT LABOR COSTS, AND WHOLESALE PRICES, 1966-83

(In annual percentage changes)

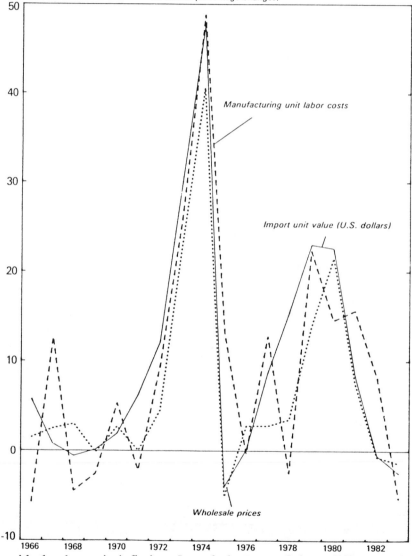

with the domestic inflation. Largely because of these differences in policy actions the deceleration of inflation was much slower in South Korea than in Taiwan (Table 3.2 and Charts 3.9 and 3.13).

CHART 3.12

BRAZIL:

IMPORT UNIT VALUE, MANUFACTURING UNIT LABOR COSTS AND WHOLESALE PRICES, 1966-83

(In percentage changes)

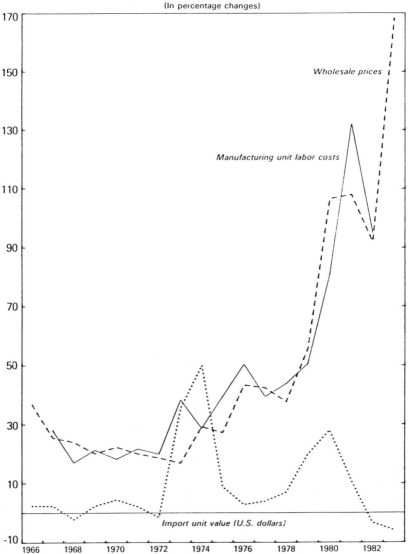

Nevertheless, as distinct from Brazil where the authorities started to relax monetary policy in early 1975, the Korean government continued to restrict credit expansion to the private sector through 1975 except for

CHART 3.13
SOUTH KOREA:
INDEXES OF NOMINAL AND REAL DOLLAR EXCHANGE
RATE AND REAL SDR EXCHANGE RATE, 1967-83
(1973=100)

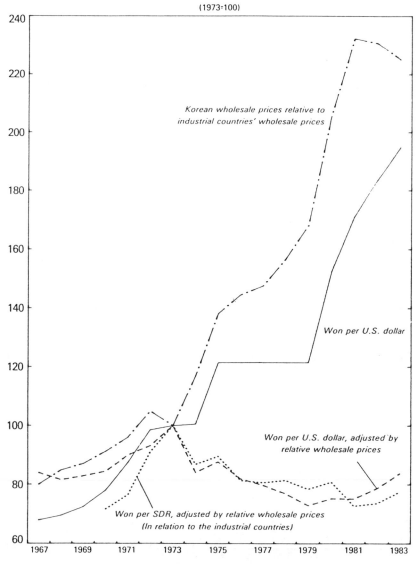

export industries. These differences in monetary policy resulted in a lower expansion of real domestic credit in South Korea than in Brazil during 1975 and 1976 (Chart 3.14 and Table 3.2). This reduced credit

CHART 3.14

BRAZIL, TAIWAN, AND SOUTH KOREA:

TERMS OF TRADE, REAL DOMESTIC CREDIT, AND REAL DOMESTIC DEMAND, 1972-83

(In percentage changes)

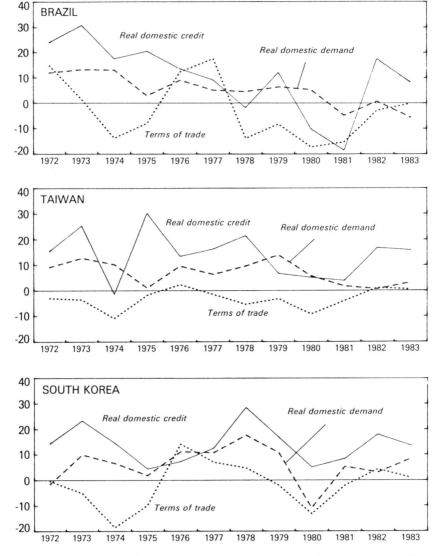

expansion, plus the better performance of Korean labor productivity, contributed to the divergence of price trends in these two countries during 1976 and 1977, with the rise of Korean manufacturing unit labor

CHART 3.15

SOUTH KOREA:

IMPORT UNIT VALUE, MANUFACTURING UNIT LABOR COSTS, AND WHOLESALE PRICES, 1966-83

(In percentage changes)

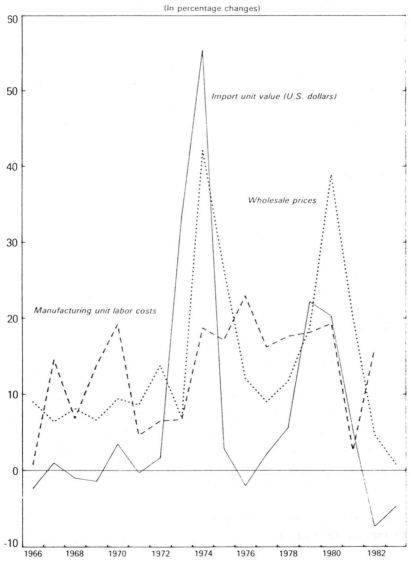

costs remaining at 16 to 20 percent per year, approximately one half of the Brazilian rate. The lower rate of unit labor cost inflation, combined with the marked stabilization of import prices in 1975 to 1977, made possible a downward movement on the Korean inflation while the Brazilian inflation remained at a much higher rate (Charts 3.10, 3.11, and 3.15 and Table 3.4).

Divergence in economic developments—1976 to 1978

During the three years from 1976 to 1978 economic conditions in the three countries diverged widely. In Brazil the persistence of inflation at over 40 percent per year encumbered the conduct of monetary policy and the development of domestic demand. Consequently, the expansion of real domestic credit decelerated steadily from 1975 to 1978, accompanied by a slowdown in the growth of real domestic demand from nearly 9 percent in 1976 to less than 4 percent in 1977 and 1978. By contrast, the early restoration of domestic price stability in Taiwan combined with sharp improvements in the current account balance allowed the authorities to relax their monetary stance, enabling a strong expansion of the domestic economy. During 1976 to 1978, the expansion of real domestic credit was maintained at 13 to 22 percent per year in Taiwan, facilitating the growth of real domestic demand at between 6 and 10 percent yearly (Chart 3.14 and Table 3.2).

In South Korea the stabilizing trend of inflation in 1976 and 1977 was accompanied by a moderate but steady expansion in both domestic credit and domestic demand in real terms. This, combined with a sharp improvement in the current account balance and the launching of an ambitious development plan covering the five years from 1977 to 1981 stimulated a sharp expansion in domestic investment. In 1978 real domestic credit expanded by nearly 30 percent and real domestic demand by 17 percent. Both of these rates of expansion were the highest since the early 1970s (Charts 3.9 and 3.14). As a consequence, employment increased rapidly in 1978—by 7.8 percent in manufacturing and 4.3 percent in aggregate—and inflation began to rise again from 10 percent in 1977 to 14 percent in 1978.

The pattern of external adjustment and financing, 1974 to 1978

In addition to a lag in the control of inflation, Brazil was also behind both Taiwan and South Korea in the adjustment of the external deficit that had expanded sharply after the first oil shock. In Taiwan the large current account deficit amounting to 17 percent of exports of goods and services in 1974 was restored to a surplus position of around 11 percent in 1978. In South Korea also the current account deficit, which had widened to nearly 40 percent of exports of goods and services in 1974, was cut back to a nearly balanced position in 1977 before expanding to 6 percent in 1978. By contrast, the Brazilian current account deficit of some 80 percent of exports of goods and services in 1974 was reduced gradually to 35 percent in 1977 before expanding again to 48 percent in 1978 (Chart 3.3).

Divergence in savings-investment behavior and external financing

Why did Brazil lag behind Taiwan and South Korea in effecting external adjustment after the first oil shock? This can be explained by the differences in both savings/investment behavior and external sector performance. Because of the authorities' intent to sustain economic growth through increased external borrowing. Brazil's investment ratio was sustained at a relatively high level despite a marked decline in the savings ratio caused by the large loss in terms of trade, the slower economic growth, and the sustained growth of real domestic consumption. In fact, Brazil's investment ratio rose initially from 30.5 percent of GNP in 1974 to 32.5 percent in 1975 before falling to around 26 percent in 1977 to 1978, while its gross savings ratio fell from 26 percent of GNP in 1975 to 22 percent in 1978. During the five years in the period from 1974 to 1978, per capita real consumption increased by 7.7 percent per year compared to around 6 percent in the preceding eight years, despite the loss in terms of trade by 2.8 percent yearly, and the slowdown in per capita real GDP from 5.6 percent yearly to 4.5 percent (Chart 3.16 and Table 3.5).

In contrast, Taiwan's investment ratio fell sharply from almost 40 percent of GNP in 1974 to 31 percent in 1975 to 1976, and 28.5 percent in 1977 to 1978. Its gross savings ratio, after a sharp fall to 25 percent of GNP in 1975, recovered strongly from 1976 onward along with the resurgence of export incomes.[8] The slowdown in investment demand was particularly evident in the private sector where radical changes in production costs and market prospects led to the postponement of various projects, although the decline was offset substantially by the initiation of a number of public sector projects. As distinct from the situation in Brazil, the growth of per capita real private consumption in Taiwan slowed down to 5.3 percent per year in the five years after the

Table 3.5

Brazil, Taiwan, and South Korea: Terms of Trade, Real Domestic Demand, Real Consumption, Per Capita Real Private Consumption, Import and Export Volume, and Import and Export Elasticities, 1966–73, 1974–78, and 1979–83

	1966–73	1974–78	1979–83
1. *Changes in terms of trade*			
Brazil	1.1	−2.8	−9.0
Taiwan	−0.9	−3.6	−3.3
South Korea	0.9	−1.3	−2.6
2. *Growth of real domestic demand*			
Brazil	9.9	6.8	0.3
Taiwan	10.2	7.2	4.9
South Korea	10.7	9.4	3.0
3. *Growth of real consumption*			
Brazil	8.8	10.4	5.6
Taiwan	8.7	6.9	6.0
South Korea	8.8	10.9	2.8
4. *Growth of per capita real private consumption*			
Brazil	6.0	9.3	3.0
Taiwan	6.3	5.3	4.1
South Korea	8.8	10.3	2.6
5. *Growth of import volume*			
Brazil	19.9	3.5	−6.5
Taiwan	19.2	10.5	2.9
South Korea	26.8	15.8	5.0
6. *Growth of export volume*			
Brazil	11.3	4.7	12.2
Taiwan	26.2	14.0	9.6
South Korea	37.2	19.9	9.9
7. *Import elasticity* (with respect to the growth of real output)			
Brazil	2.3	0.5	−3.6
Taiwan	1.7	1.3	0.5
South Korea	2.3	1.6	1.0
8. *Export elasticity* (with respect to the growth of world imports)			
Brazil	1.2	1.1	6.8
Taiwan	2.9	3.2	5.3
South Korea	4.1	4.5	5.5

Sources: Author's estimate based on *International Financial Statistics*. Data on Taiwan are based on Council for Economic Planning and Development, *Taiwan Statistical Data Book, 1983* (Taipei, 1983).

CHART 3.16

BRAZIL, TAIWAN, AND SOUTH KOREA:
GROSS DOMESTIC INVESTMENT AND GROSS SAVINGS IN RELATION TO GNP, 1966-83

(In percentages)

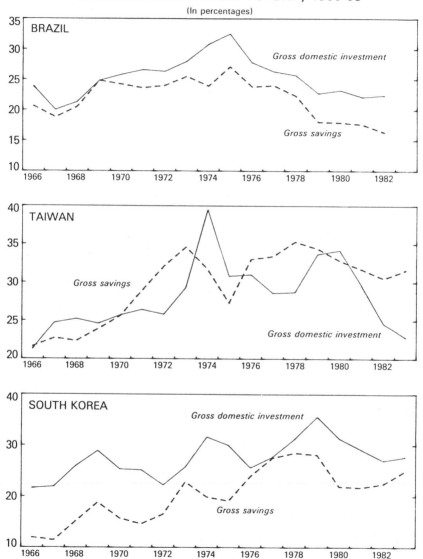

first oil shock, compared to 6.3 percent in the preceding eight years. While the growth of real consumption in Taiwan was held well below the growth rate of real output, the reverse was true in Brazil. As a

CHART 3.17

TAIWAN AND SOUTH KOREA:

BALANCE OF PAYMENTS DEVELOPMENTS, 1972-83

(In billions of U.S. dollars)

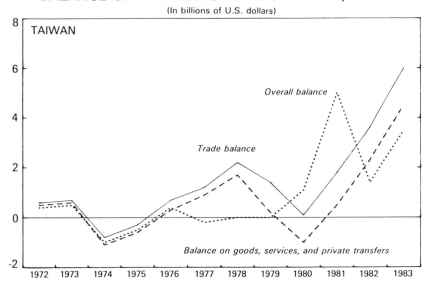

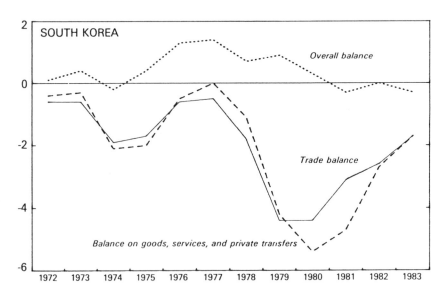

consequence, while Brazil's external debt continued to expand even during the period of strong world economic recovery in 1976 to 1978, Taiwan achieved a large export surplus or excess savings to offset the large current account deficit incurred in 1974 and 1975 (Chart 3.16 and Table 3.5).

As in Brazil, South Korea relied on large capital inflows to sustain a high rate of domestic investment. The latter declined moderately from 31 percent of GNP in 1974 to 25.5 percent in 1976, but increased steadily from 1977 to 1979 in conjunction with the launching of the fourth Five-Year Development Plan. As in Brazil, the growth of real consumption was sustained at a high level, far exceeding the growth of real output. However, as distinct from Brazil, South Korea's gross savings ratiò, after a two-year slide in 1974 and 1975, recovered strongly in 1976 and 1978 in conjunction with strong improvements in its trade and service balances (Chart 3.17). These differences in the trade performance and savings behavior between South Korea and Brazil, despite the similarity in their heavy reliance on external credit to sustain domestic investment, accounted for the divergence in their debt service burden. South Korea's debt service ratio initially declined from 15.1 percent in 1973 to 9.2 percent in 1977, before rising again to 10.7 percent in 1978, whereas the Brazilian ratio increased rapidly from 13.4 percent in 1973 to 31.0 percent in 1978[9] (Chart 3.4).

Disparity in trade balance and trade policy developments

In Taiwan and South Korea the recovery of domestic savings in 1976 through 1978 both reflected and supported the strong performance of their export sectors. In Taiwan the trade balance moved from a deficit of $0.7 billion in 1974 to a surplus of $1.7 billion in 1978. In South Korea the trade deficit of nearly $2 billion in 1974 and 1975 was reduced to zero in 1977 before increasing to over $1 billion in 1978. In both Taiwan and South Korea developments in the trade balance dominated the current account balance because their deficits on services and private transfers were relatively small and increased only modestly over time. In Taiwan this occurred because of its much smaller external debt, whereas in South Korea, which continued to maintain large capital inflows, the increase in service deficit was contained through a sharp expansion in the sales of construction services to the oil-exporting countries (Chart 3.17).

In Brazil, also, the trade balance improved strongly between 1974 and 1977. However, unlike Taiwan and South Korea, Brazil had a large deficit in the service account even before the first oil shock, and this deficit has since expanded sharply to dominate the current account

CHART 3.18

BRAZIL:

BALANCE OF PAYMENTS DEVELOPMENTS, 1972-83

(In billions of U.S. dollars)

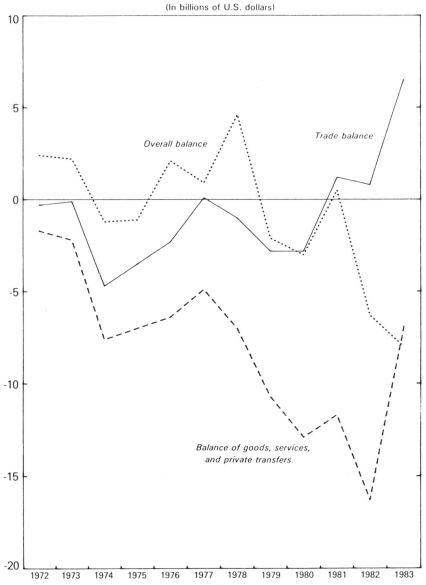

balance largely because of increased interest payments. In fact, net interest and other investment income payments increased from $0.3 billion in 1974 to $3.0 billion in 1977 and these payments continued to grow rapidly (Chart 3.18).

Moreover, the equally impressive improvements in the trade balance among the three countries actually resulted from quite diverse movements in terms of trade and the real trade balances. Taking the five years from 1974 through 1978 as a whole, the yearly loss in terms of trade was the largest in Taiwan, at 3.6 percent, followed by Brazil at 2.8 percent and South Korea at 1.3 percent. In turn, the improvement of the real trade balance was much greater in Taiwan and South Korea than in Brazil. During the five years between 1974 and 1978 export volume increased yearly by 14.0 percent in Taiwan, 19.9 percent in South Korea, but only 4.7 percent in Brazil. Although these rates represented a sharp slowdown compared with the records of the preceding eight years, the performance of export volume actually improved in both Taiwan and South Korea considering the decline in the growth of world demand that had occurred, while Brazil's relative export performance slipped somewhat.

In fact, the elasticity of the growth of Taiwan's export volume with respect to the growth of ''world'' import volume increased from 2.9 in 1966 to 1973 to 3.2 in the period 1974 to 1978. In Korea it increased from 4.1 to 4.5, while in Brazil there was a decline from 1.2 to 1.1 (Table 3.5). The recovery of strong export growth in the two East Asian countries was accompanied by a rapid growth of imports because of their heavy dependence on imported raw materials, intermediate inputs, and capital equipment, but both countries managed to appreciably reduce their import elasticity in relation to the growth of real output. In Taiwan this elasticity was reduced from 1.7 in the period from 1966 to 1973 to 1.3 during 1974 to 1978. In South Korea, this elasticity was reduced from 2.3 to 1.6. These declines, which mainly reflected the economizing on imported oil and raw materials, were significant but dwarfed by a much sharper cutback in Brazil. In Brazil, compared to a yearly growth of nearly 20 percent in 1966 to 1973, the volume of imports increased by only 3.5 percent per year during 1974 to 1978, indicating a reduction in the import elasticity from 2.3 to a mere 0.5 (Table 3.5).

The divergence in the trade volume developments among the three countries reflected their disparate trade and development strategies. Both the slight fall-off in Brazil's relative export performance and the sharp reduction in its import elasticity reflected the authorities' renewed inward orientation. While the policy of minidevaluations and the system of export incentives established in 1968 were left unchanged, various tariff and nontariff barriers were established after the first oil shock, thus increasing the relative incentives for domestic sales and new import-substituting projects. Beginning in 1974, widespread tariff increases were effected, resulting in an increase of the average nominal tariff rate for manufactured goods from around 57 percent in 1973 to 95 percent in 1978. In addition, a prior import deposit system was reestablished in 1975 (eliminated in 1979); increased direct controls were placed on imports of public corporations and agencies; and import licenses were suspended for a large number of products, in particular finished consumer goods.

Meanwhile, major government efforts were mounted under the framework of the Second National Development Plan (1975 to 1979) to encourage private investments in basic intermediate products and capital goods. General protection for these activities was provided along with substantial tax benefits and subsidized official credit. Also, measures were adopted to limit oil imports and to step up the production of alcohol to mix with gasoline. [10]

In contrast with Brazil's renewed inward-orientation, both Taiwan and South Korea continued to pursue outward-looking policies. In both countries the bias against exports in the incentive system was corrected in the course of the 1960s, and the level of protection on manufacturing was much lower than in Brazil. [11] During the early 1970s, both countries experienced sharp expansion of export earnings partly because their currencies underwent sizable effective depreciation in the process of multilateral currency realignment and generalized floating. The resulting inflationary pressure led the authorities to reduce export incentives somewhat and to accelerate import liberalization. In Taiwan, the number of items under import control was sharply reduced during 1973 and 1974, and the tariff rate was lowered for a large number of commodities. [12] In Korea quantitative import restrictions were also liberalized and tariffs were lowered in 1973 and again in 1977. [13] While import substitutions of selective intermediate products and capital goods (such as petrochemicals, steel products, and shipbuilding) also took place in both countries during the 1970s, these were promoted with protective measures less severe than in Brazil. In fact, export industries continued to enjoy duty-free imports of essential inputs in both countries.

However, because of their concern with inflation, both South Korea and Taiwan continued to maintain exchange parity with the U.S. dollar, with only sporadic adjustments (the large Korean devaluation in De-

CHART 3.19

TAIWAN:

INDEXES OF NOMINAL AND REAL DOLLAR EXCHANGE RATE AND REAL SDR EXCHANGE RATE, 1967-83

(1973=100)

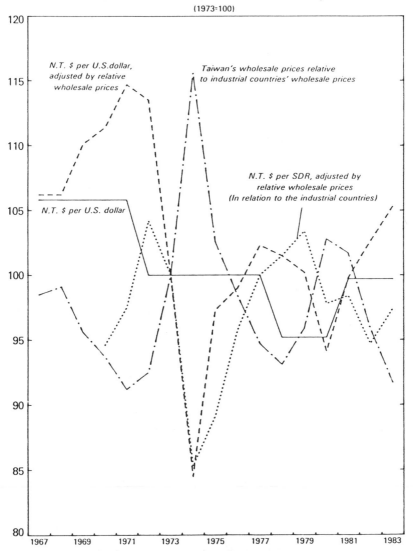

cember 1974 and the smaller Taiwan upvaluations in March 1973 and July 1978). These practices resulted in a sharp real appreciation of the currency in 1974, but an adverse impact on the external account was softened by the subsequent success of price stabilization in both countries.

In fact, during the period from 1975 to 1978, Taiwan's currency continued to depreciate in real terms because of its relative price stability compared with its major trading partners, particularly the United States (Chart 3.19). The resulting improvement in Taiwan's external position, particularly the achievement of a large trade surplus with the United States, finally induced the government to revalue its currency against the U.S. dollar by 5.6 percent in July 1978 while introducing a flexible management of the exchange rate. In comparison, South Korea's relative cost position did not improve during 1976 to 1978 because its inflation rate, lower than that of many developing countries, was still higher than the average of the industrial countries. This situation, combined with the overheating of the economy in 1978, caused a sharp expansion of imports and a renewed worsening of the external balance (Charts 3.13 and 3.17).

Policy Response to the Second Oil Shock

When the oil prices jumped again in 1979 and 1980 and both cost pressure and terms of trade worsened, the three countries were in widely different positions. The Brazilian economy differed with respect to the control of inflation and external adjustment. The Korean economy was overheating more than in 1973. The Taiwanese economy was ready to withstand another external shock. Unlike the results of the first oil shock, after the second shock the world recession became more protracted because of the earnest pursuit of disinflation by the United States and several other industrial countries. In particular, the U.S. monetary authorities changed the rule of monetary control in October 1979, which resulted in a sharp increase in interest rates in the international financial markets. These developments caused a protracted decline in the developing countries' export demand and a sharp rise in the real interest rates on their external debts. In the five years from 1979 to 1983, "world" import volume increased by only 1.8 percent yearly, compared with 4.4 percent in the preceding five years. Interest rates in the international financial markets, as represented by the three-month Eurodollar rate, averaged 13.2 percent per year from 1979 to 1983, compared with 7.7 percent from 1974 to 1978. By contrast, the non-oil developing countries' export unit value (in U.S. dollars) increased yearly by only an estimated 4.5 percent compared to 13.0 percent. As a

Table 3.6

Evolution of World Trade Volume, Eurodollar Interest Rate, Non-Oil Developing Countries' Import Unit Value, Export Unit Value, and the Real Interest Rate of Their External Bank Debt, 1973–83 (In percent)

	Changes in world trade volume	Eurodollar rate (60-days)[1]	Non-Oil Developing Countries			
			Changes in US$		Terms of trade	Real interest rate of Eurodollar credit[2]
			Import unit value	Export unit value		
1973	12.0	9.2	25.3	33.0	6.1	−17.9
1974	4.5	11.0	47.1	38.9	−5.6	−20.1
1975	−3.5	7.0	8.9	−1.0	−9.1	8.1
1976	11.0	5.6	0.9	7.1	6.1	−1.4
1977	5.0	6.0	7.5	14.5	6.5	−7.4
1978	5.5	8.9	9.6	5.4	−3.8	3.3
1979	6.5	12.1	18.6	19.5	0.3	−5.8
1980	2.0	14.2	20.5	16.0	−3.7	−1.6
1981	1.0	16.8	3.2	−1.8	−4.8	18.9
1982	−2.5	13.2	−3.2	−6.2	−3.1	20.9
1983	2.0	9.6	−4.3	−4.6	−0.3	14.9
Average: 1963–72	8.5	6.1	2.1	2.2	0.1	3.8
1974–78	4.4	7.7	14.8	13.0	−1.6	−3.5
1979–83	1.8	13.2	7.0	4.5	−2.3	9.4

Sources: International Monetary Fund, *World Economic Outlook* (1982, 1984, and April 1986); *International Financial Statistics* (1983 Yearbook).

[1]At an annual rate.
[2]Figures in column 2 deflated by column 4, as an approximation.

consequence, the proximate real interest rate of their short-term external bank debt jumped from a negative 3.5 percent per year to a positive 9.4 percent (Table 3.6).

Faced with this new, more difficult situation in the world economy, the authorities in the three countries again reacted quite differently, resulting in vastly different outcomes for their economies. The Brazilian authorities initially experimented in vain with some expansionary-cum-stabilization measures, but were compelled to undertake drastic adjustment measures after August 1982 when the country experienced a severe liquidity crisis in the wake of disturbances in the international financial markets. The Taiwanese authorities continued to emphasize price stabilization despite the protracted recession in the world economy, thus resulting in both a successful control of inflation and a severe underutilization of productive capacity. The South Korean government, in contrast with the situation following the first oil shock, undertook strong stabilization and adjustment measures relatively early in order to eliminate both internal and external imbalances.

Brazil's belated adjustment efforts

At the onset of the second oil shock Brazil was in a difficult situation considering its persistent, rapid inflation and the already heavy debt service burden. Yet, during 1979 and 1980, the Brazilian authorities chose to follow a set of economic policies that resulted in a continuing expansion of domestic demand and a sharper acceleration of inflation. During 1979 the government sought to combat the growing inflationary pressures through the expansion of output, particularly in the agricultural sector. As a consequence, both fiscal and monetary policies turned expansionary. The public sector deficit expanded from 5 percent of GDP in 1978 to over 8 percent in 1979, despite the steps taken to improve the central authorities' control over the public sector budget. Real domestic credit expanded by nearly 20 percent (Charts 3.7 and 3.14).

In November 1979 the Brazilian government introduced a new wage indexing formula which eliminated the adjustment factor for predicted future inflation but increased the frequency of wage adjustments from once to twice a year.[14] The new formula made the protection of real wages more automatic at a time of severe losses in trade when wage flexibility was needed to protect profit margins and employment. (See Charts 3.10 and 3.11 on the movements of real wages in manufacturing and unit labor costs.) Then, following a 30 percent devaluation of the cruzeiro in December 1979, the government announced for the following year the prefixing of the cumulative monetary correction at 45 percent and the exchange rate adjustment against the U.S. dollar at 40 percent. The purpose was to reverse inflationary expectations and promote external borrowing by Brazilian firms and financial institutions that were unsettled by the maxi-devaluation.

These policies resulted in a strong growth of real domestic demand and real output at 6 to 8 percent per year through 1979 and 1980, while inflation accelerated to 52 percent in 1979 and over 80 percent in 1980 (Charts 3.1 and 3.7). Meanwhile, current account deficit expanded to over $10 billion in 1979 and $12.5 billion in 1980 because of the combined effects of large losses in trade and the sharply higher international interest rates (Chart 3.18).

In the face of continuing rises in import costs and the current account deficit and expansionary public sector operations, the prefixation of the monetary target and exchange rate adjustment failed to attain the intended results of reversing inflationary expectations. Instead, by limiting the returns on financial assets through an inadequate monetary correction, this policy induced a shift in investment portfolios from financial to physical assets, thereby weakening the financial structure of the banking institutions and causing widespread credit rationing. Similarly, in the face of a sharper acceleration in inflation, the pre-announced exchange rate caused an appreciation in the purchasing power parity of the cruzeiro, particularly because much of the effect of the December 1979 devaluation was offset by the simultaneous removal of fiscal subsidies for manufactured exports and the import deposit requirement.[15]

In November 1980, faced with the continuing worsening of inflation and external balance, the government abandoned the pre-fixation of monetary correction and exchange rate adjustment. Instead, the authorities shifted to an increasingly restrictive monetary policy while encouraging the private sector to borrow abroad. Lending ceilings were made more effective and real domestic credit declined by nearly 20 percent in 1981 following a 10 percent decline in 1980 (Charts 3.7 and 3.14). Meanwhile, interest rates increased dramatically for most industrial capital and consumer credits, reaching 40 to 45 percent in real terms.[16] This increase led to a sharp cutback in the demand for consumer durables and widespread inventory liquidation. As a consequence, real GDP fell 1.6 percent in 1981, the first decline since 1947. The output decline was concentrated in the industrial sector, particularly in the capital goods and automobile industries.

During 1982 the world recession deepened and Brazil suffered a 10 percent decline in its export volume because of widespread declines in export demand. Meanwhile, in the face of Brazil's deteriorating balance of payments, international banks became increasingly reluctant to expand their loans to Brazil, even at high spreads above LIBOR. In August, with the balance of payments crises in Argentina and Mexico, lending by these banks virtually stopped for a few weeks, precipitating an external liquidity crisis for Brazil as manifested in a rapid depletion of liquidity reserves and an intensification of debt service problems. With its ready access to the international financial markets thus suspended, the Brazilian government was left with no choice but to undertake serious adjustment measures with the help of the IMF, which had been avoided for a decade. [17] The economic program supported by the IMF targeted a sharp cutback in both external and fiscal deficits, while aiming to lower inflation through wage moderation. In late February 1983 the cruzeiro was devalued by 30 percent against the U.S. dollar, followed by minidevaluations through the year to maintain the real exchange rate. (See Chart 3.6 on the movement of real exchange rate.) These devaluations, combined with a 5 percent decline in real domestic demand, were instrumental in reducing the current account deficit by about 4 percent of GDP in 1983, far exceeding the original target (Chart 3.18).

Meanwhile, in October 1983 a new wage formula was approved to permit a partial deindexation of wages. This formula allowed a cutback in the public sector wage bill in real terms which together with substantial reductions in investment outlays substantially reduced the operational portion of the deficit that amounted to 6.8 percent of GDP in 1982. However, this was more than offset by a jump in the deficit due to the indexation of the huge public sector debt. As a result, the overall deficit, instead of falling as planned, increased further by 4 percentage points of GDP in 1983 to reach 20.8 percent (Table 3.7). Largely because of this deficit increase, the monetary target was exceeded by a wide margin, and inflation, instead of falling, accelerated even further to 155 percent in 1983 as measured by the average of changes in the WPI and CPI[18] (Chart 3.7).

This pattern of external adjustment, with sharp cutbacks in domestic investment and imports and improvements in domestic savings and exports, continued into 1984. This enabled Brazil to attain a large trade surplus, thereby eliminating the current account deficit in that year.

Table 3.7

Brazil: Public Sector Borrowing Requirements, 1980–84
(As percent of GDP)

	1980	1981	1982	1983	Preliminary 1984
Total financing	7.1	12.6	16.6	20.8	23.3
Operational budget	3.6	5.6	6.8	3.6	2.0
General government[1]	0.9	2.6	2.6	0.3	0.1
State enterprises	2.7	3.0	4.2	3.3	1.9
Monetary correction	3.5	7.0	9.8	17.2	21.3
General government[1]	3.2	4.1	5.5	9.6	13.3
State enterprises	0.3	2.9	3.5	7.6	8.3

Sources: Brazilian authorities and IMF staff estimates.

[1]Includes central administration, state and local governments, and other institutions.

However, the rate of inflation continued to worsen (reaching 217 percent in 1984, based on average changes in the CPI and the WPI) because of the feedback effects of exchange rate depreciation on wages and material costs and the continued monetary expansion necessary to finance the fiscal deficit resulting from the indexed domestic debt.

Taiwan's continued focus on price stability

Compared with the dramatic experiences of Brazil and South Korea, Taiwan managed to survive the disturbances in the world economy with less difficulties. The current account, which had worsened during 1979 and 1980, returned to a surplus position in 1981 through sustained export growth and a decline in imports. The CPI inflation, accelerating to 18 percent in 1980 and 16 percent in 1981, was brought down to 4 percent in 1982 (Table 3.1 and Charts 3.8 and 3.17). These results were obtained with the help of a monetary policy that was cautious but not as tight as in 1974. In fact, real domestic credit in Taiwan increased by a moderate but steady yearly rate of 5 percent during the three years 1979 to 1981, compared with the sharp fluctuations in Brazil and South Korea during the same period (Chart 3.14). Moreover, as in 1974, Taiwan was ahead of Brazil and South Korea in tightening monetary policy during 1979, and thus helped contain the inflationary pressures generated by the combination of strong domestic demand and sharp jumps in import costs (Chart 3.7).

The moderation of inflation was also helped by a significant reduction in the tariff rates and in the taxable value of imports.[19] In addition, the government took several measures to improve the functioning of the financial markets. In February 1979 it initiated a managed floating of the exchange rate against the U.S. dollar;[20] in April 1980 an interbank loan market was established to facilitate reserve adjustments among the banking institutions; and in November 1980 the commercial banks were given greater authority to set interest rates.

During 1981 and 1982, however, the growth of exports continued to slow because of the prolonged recession in the world economy and the decline in the competitiveness of Taiwan's exports. Between 1978 and 1982 the unit labor costs of Taiwan's manufacturing industries increased by almost 15 percent per year because wage adjustments outstripped the growth in labor productivity (Table 3.4 and Chart 3.12). The worsening in Taiwan's relative cost position was exacerbated by the appreciation of its currency brought about by the continued rise in the U.S. dollar against other major currencies[21] (Chart 3.19). As a consequence, during 1981 and 1982, capacity utilization continued to decline, inventory liquidation became widespread, and private investment dropped sharply. During these two years, real domestic demand increased by only 1 percent per year (Chart 3.14 and Table 3.2). Faced with the deepening recession in the economy, the government took various measures during late 1981 and April 1982 to relax credit expansion and improve investment incentives. During 1983, supported by a resurgence in exports and expansionary fiscal and monetary policies at home, Taiwan's economic growth recovered to around 7 percent. Private investment, which had remained weak, showed signs of recovery toward the end of the year. This recovery continued into 1984, with a higher rate of growth of real output and continuing price stability.

The recovery in Taiwan's economic growth was primarily based, though, on the resurgence of export demand while domestic investment continued to decline in relation to GDP. This led to a sharp expansion of both excess savings and current account surplus, the latter particularly vis-à-vis the United States. This situation, in conjunction with the latter country's large external deficit (over $100 billion in 1984), subjected Taiwan to increasing protectionist pressures from its major trading partners. The root problem lay in the stagnation of private domestic investment caused by two major factors: the decline of private corporate profitability and the increased political uncertainty. The former stemmed from a combination of several factors—inadequate exchange flexibility during 1983 and 1984 amid the sharp dollar appreciation; increased export competition from lower-wage countries at a time when domestic labor costs were rising sharply (Table 3.4); and inadequate government actions to spur the acquisition and upgrading of technology and skills as well as to stimulate domestic demand.

The political uncertainty stemmed from the authorities' failure to respond adequately to the changing political environment surrounding East Asia, especially their inability to come to terms with the People's Republic of China at a time when the latter was increasingly opening up its economy while seeking political accommodation with Hong Kong and Taiwan.[22] This failure was significant, considering Taiwan's impending yet untested political succession and the atmosphere of political unrest in neighboring South Korea and the Philippines. These problems, combined with certain local political and financial scandals, cast a long shadow over Taiwan's long-term investment prospects.[23]

South Korea's vigorous policy actions

South Korea was in a difficult situation not only because of the worsened economic conditions but also because of the political uncertainty surrounding the assassination of its president in October 1979. In 1979, Korea's current account deficit expanded to $4.5 billion or 22 percent of its exports of goods and services. The sharp worsening in the Korean external balance resulted not only from the renewed terms of trade loss caused by the second oil shock, but also from a severe overheating in the economy and increased erosion of its international competitive position. During the period from 1976 to 1978, amid stepped-up domestic economic expansion and increased diversion of workers for overseas construction projects, Korea's manufacturing real wages increased by 18 percent per year compared with 11 percent in Taiwan, and its manufacturing unit labor costs increased by nearly 19 percent per year compared with only 3 percent in Taiwan. During this period the Korean exchange rate remained fixed with the U.S. dollar, resulting in increasing overvaluation (Table 3.4 and Charts 3.13, 3.15, and 3.17).

In January 1980, less than three months after the assassination of its president, the new Korean government undertook strong measures to correct the imbalances in the economy. The won was initially devalued by 17 percent against the U.S. dollar, and then under a flexible exchange rate system the devaluation continued through the year. (Chart 3.15) Fiscal and monetary policies were tightened. The 1980 budget was revised and its deficit reduced in relation to GDP by cutting real current expenditures and by deferring public investments. Interest rates were raised by an average of 6 percentage points. The expansion of real domestic credit was sharply reduced from 16.5 percent in 1979 to only 5 percent in 1980 (Charts 3.9 and 3.14).

These demand management policies were supplemented by measures to improve industrial efficiency and financial intermediation. Investment strategy shifted from capital-intensive industries toward highly skilled labor-intensive products, and certain key heavy industries were reorganized to promote efficiency. Steps were taken to denationalize the banking system, to liberalize financial markets, and to eliminate interest subsidies. Meanwhile, the government launched a long-term energy plan focusing on developing nuclear power and encouraging energy conservation. In addition, domestic prices of petroleum products were raised above the international level.[24]

The restrictive financial policies, combined with the depressive effect of a 13 percent loss in trade, resulted in a sharp decline in real domestic demand of nearly 13 percent in 1980 (Table 3.3 and Chart 3.14). As a consequence, export volume increased by 11 percent in 1980 compared with a decline of 1 percent in 1979, and import volume declined by 13.6 percent compared with a growth of 11.8 percent. Because of these changes in the real trade balance, the expansion of the trade deficit stopped despite further large losses in terms of trade, but the current account deficit nevertheless expanded further in 1980 because of increased interest payments (Chart 3.17). In addition, despite the recovery in export growth, real GDP declined by more than 6 percent in 1980 because of a disastrous harvest and a continued weakening in manufacturing and construction activities. Meanwhile, inflation accelerated to nearly 30 percent because of the combined effects of import cost-push, currency depreciation, and crop failures.

During 1981 the authorities continued efforts to reduce the external deficit and to lower inflation but somewhat relaxed the demand management policies to relieve the domestic recession. Fiscal stimulus was provided by increasing public expenditures and cutting tax rates, while monetary policy turned accommodative. The exchange rate against the U.S. dollar was maintained in real terms through further currency depreciation (Chart 3.13). Meanwhile, the structural and financial reforms initiated in 1980 were continued. These policies helped sustain the improvement in the trade balance, while inflation decelerated markedly from the second half of 1981. By 1982, despite a slowdown in export demand caused by the deepening world recession, South Korea managed to reduce its current account deficit from 24 percent of exports of goods and services in 1980 to less than 10 percent (Table 3.1 and Charts 3.3 and 3.17). Helped by falling import costs, improved food supplies, and a slowdown in the growth of unit labor costs, the rate of CPI inflation declined to only 7 percent per year. The stabilizing prices, combined with continued won depreciation against the U.S. dollar, further strengthened Korea's competitive export position (Chart 3.13).

In 1983, helped by a recovery in the U.S. markets, Korea's exports rebounded strongly, its current account deficit was reduced to less than 6 percent of exports of goods and services, manufacturing and construction continued to recover strongly, and real GDP expanded by more than 9 percent. Meanwhile, the government continued to tighten fiscal operation by raising indirect taxes (including a 5 percent oil import tariff) and cutting back capital outlays. These measures resulted in a significant reduction of fiscal deficit in relation to GNP, sharply reducing the public sector's financing needs. The latter in turn enabled the banking system to steadily reduce the rate of domestic credit expansion while satisfying the private sector's credit requirements. These developments, in addition to the continued decline of import costs, helped reduce inflation to less than 4 percent in 1983 (Table 3.1). These favorable economic developments continued into 1984, with the growth of real GDP sustained at nearly 8 percent and the CPI inflation falling to a mere 2.3 percent. Meanwhile, both domestic investment and savings also picked up, but the external deficit declined to less than 2 percent of GDP.[25]

Divergent evolution of the trade systems

The divergence in external payments and adjustment efforts in the three countries inevitably resulted in divergent evolution of their trade systems. In Brazil the deepening external payments problems compelled the authorities to increasingly resort to exchange and import controls to the detriment of economic efficiency, whereas in Taiwan and South Korea, the rapid adjustment of external deficits enabled the authorities to increasingly liberalize imports to improve resource allocation.

In Brazil at the beginning of 1979 the authorities made an attempt to reverse the increasingly restrictive and protective trends of the trade system that began in 1973. However, this attempt was soon sidetracked by the expansion of payments deficit and the resurgence of inflation after the second oil shock. Instead, the overvaluation of the cruzeiro became serious during 1980 along with the experiment of pre-announced exchange rate devaluations and monetary correction, until this policy was called off in February 1981. Meanwhile, the prior deposit requirement for imports imposed in 1975 was removed in December 1979, but restrictions on the use of foreign exchange were intensified by limiting public sector imports, by establishing firm-specific import budgets for the private sector, and by requiring specific foreign financing for most imports. Also, the export tax credit, abolished in late 1979 in conjunction with the maxidevaluation, was reintroduced in April 1981 in a modified form, with the rate of credit to be reduced over time. Nevertheless, the termination of the system was repeatedly postponed until April 1985. Except for the abolition of prior import deposits, these developments resulted in an increasing restrictiveness of the trade system.

In fact, it was not until 1984, after the strong improvement of the trade balance and the normalization of relations with external creditors, that the Brazilian authorities were able to resume their liberalization efforts. During that year, significant progress was made in relaxing the exchange and import restrictions imposed during the previous years. In addition, the surcharges on tariffs imposed in the mid-1970s were removed in September 1984. Instead of surcharges of 30 and 100 percentage points respectively on specific imports, the basic tariff rates were raised by 10 and 30 percentage points on the applicable items. These changes resulted in the reduction of the average (unweighted) tariff rate from 79 percent to 51 percent, even though the basic tariff structure was left largely unchanged.

Compared to Brazil, Taiwan has made much more progress in reducing import controls and import tariffs. Following the massive decontrols in the early 1970s, only 2 to 3 percent of Taiwan's import items remained in the controlled list, except for those with specified sources of imports for the purpose of reducing trade imbalances with the U.S. and Japan. Many tariff rates, which were raised in 1971 in lieu of import control, were significantly reduced in 1977 and 1980, with even lower rates for countries with the most favored status (Table 3.8).

South Korea's trade liberalization lagged far behind Taiwan, but major progress was made in more recent years. In 1978 the Korean authorities began to relax the management of imports that had become

Table 3.8

Taiwan: The Share of Restricted Import Items and the Frequency of Tariff Rates, Selected Years, 1956–84 (In percent)

	The share of restricted import items[1]	The share of items with a tariff rate of[2]		
		0–30%	31–60%	61–165%
1956	46.0	46.6*	34.7*	18.7*
1960	40.5	39.5**	45.0**	15.5**
1966	41.9	58.7***	28.0***	13.3***
1970	41.0			
1972	17.9	39.8†	34.1†	26.2†
1974	2.3			
1975	2.4			
1976	2.7	46.0††	31.1††	22.9††
1979	2.3			
1980	2.5	58.1(65.1)	25.8(25.3)	16.1(9.6)
1981	3.1			
1982	3.4	58.1(63.9)	25.7(26.9)	16.2(9.2)
1983	3.5			
1984	2.8			

Sources: Based on Tables 2–4 attached to S. C. Tsaing and Wen Lang Chen, "Developments Toward Trade Liberalization in Taiwan" (mimeo, December 24, 1984).
    *Effective January 1955.
   **Effective August 1959.
  ***Effective September 1965.
    †Effective August 1971.
   ††Effective August 1977.
[1]The share of controlled items in the 1970s exclude those whose imports are limited by sources of origin or importing agencies.
[2]The parenthetical figures for 1980 and 1982 apply to most favored nations.

more restrictive after the first oil shock. Except for luxury items, the advance import deposits in effect since 1961 were abolished, and the pace of import liberalization was accelerated. In 1979 the nominal tariffs were reduced to an average of around 25 percent from nearly 39 percent in the previous year. However, because of the ensuing worsening in the external payments situation, the liberalization of imports did not resume until the second half of 1981. By 1982 the share of restricted import items was reduced to 25 percent, and further progress was made in the following years to liberalize imports and reduce tariff rates (Table 3.9).

Table 3.9

**South Korea: The Share of Imports Under Average Control and the
Average Tariff Rate, 1978–85 (In percent)**

	Share of restricted import items[1]	Average nominal tariff rate
1978	46.1	38.7
1979	31.8	24.9
1980	30.9	24.9
1981	30.6	24.9
1982	25.3	23.7
1983	23.4	23.7
1984	19.6	21.9
1985	12.3	21.3

Sources: The Korean Ministry of Commerce and Industry and Ministry of Finance, as cited in Suh Sang-Mok, "The Evolution of the Korean Economy in Historical Perspective," presented to the World Bank Conference on Structural Adjustment in a Newly Industrialized Country: Lessons from Korea (Washington, D.C.: World Bank, mimeo, June 1986), p. 35.
[1]At the beginning of the year.

Conclusions

This comparative review indicates the importance of speedy price stabilization and external adjustment in a world of sharp fluctuations in economic activity, prices, and key financial variables. Under the changed circumstances of the 1970s and the early 1980s, it was necessary for the national authorities to adjust their policy emphasis in favor of short-term price stabilization and external adjustment in order to attain long-term growth objectives through the improvement of international competitiveness while avoiding persistent inflation and balance of payments difficulties. Partly because of the greater openness of their economies, the authorities in Taiwan and South Korea were quicker than their Brazilian counterparts in making the necessary policy adjustments in response to changes in external environment both after the first and the second oil shocks. In addition, the absence of rigid indexing arrangements in Taiwan and South Korea facilitated their stabilization and adjustment process at a time when short-term wage flexibility was needed in order to restrict the inflationary impact of the external price shocks.

By contrast, the existence of comprehensive indexing arrangements in Brazil distracted the authorities from undertaking adequate stabilization and adjustment measures, thereby prolonging inflation and balance of payments difficulties. It is ironical but inevitable that countries such as Taiwan and South Korea, which did not try to protect real wages in the short run but were more anxious to undertake serious stabilization and adjustment measures, should attain a rate of growth of real output and real wages over time higher than countries such as Brazil, which tried to protect real wages in the short run through formal indexation while delaying the undertaking of adequate stabilization and adjustment measures. This is so because the speedy attainment of price stabilization and external adjustment in Taiwan and South Korea enabled the authorities to subsequently relax monetary policy in order to facilitate the resumption of economic growth while the attendant strengthening of the domestic industry's international competitiveness also helped remove the external constraint for this growth. By contrast, the persistence of inflation and large external deficit in Brazil constricted the conduct of monetary policy and the expansion of real domestic demand, thereby resulting in lower economic growth over time. In the end Brazil was compelled, after the second oil shock, to undertake even greater deflation of domestic demand than Taiwan and South Korea. Even then the authorities failed to control inflation because of continuing widespread indexation. In fact, they lost control of credit expansion even after they had managed to partially de-index wage adjustments because of the continuing fiscal deficit caused by the indexation of public debts.

While both Brazil and South Korea relied heavily on external finance to sustain a high rate of domestic investment and economic growth, South Korea was much more successful than Brazil in maintaining a rapid growth of export earnings (of both goods and services), thus controlling the rise of the debt service burden. In comparison, Brazil was less successful in achieving rapid export growth commensurate with the growth of its mounting external debt, thereby encountering severe liquidity squeezes in the early 1980s amid disruptions in the international financial markets. This raises the question of whether it is advisable to rely so heavily on external finance to sustain a high rate of domestic growth in a world of protracted sluggish economic growth and enhanced uncertainty. It also questions whether the economic policies pursued by the Brazilian authorities were consistent with the need to prevent the occurrence of short-term liquidity problems once they had committed themselves to massive external financing.

It is true that being a much larger country with rich natural re-

Table 3.10

Debt and Debt Service Ratios of Selected Developing Countries, 1982 (In percentages)

	External public debt in relation to GDP	Debt service in relation to exports of goods and services
Brazil	16.9	42.1
Ivory Coast	74.3	36.9
Morocco	60.8	36.8
Peru	33.5	36.7
Ecuador	34.3	30.8
Mexico	31.1	29.5
Bolivia	39.1	28.2
Algeria	31.9	24.6
Argentina	29.5	24.5
Malawi	48.8	22.8
Uganda	8.0	22.3
South Korea	28.3	13.1
Philippines	22.5	12.8
Costa Rica	111.7	12.5
Malaysia	30.5	5.1
Taiwan	12.0	4.7

Sources: World Bank, *World Development Report, 1984*, pp. 248–249; and the Central Bank of China (Taiwan), *Balance of Payments: Taiwan District* (September 1985).

sources, Brazil can absorb more foreign capital than many smaller countries in order to finance a high rate of economic development. In fact, even in 1982, when Brazil encountered a severe balance of payments crisis, its debt and debt service ratios were much lower than many other countries in relation to the size of the economy. This, however, is not true when these ratios are measured against the value of export earnings. On the latter basis, Brazil ranked among the highest in both debt and debt service ratios (Table 3.10).

Because the export earnings ultimately must be used to repay the maturing debt or to sustain credit worthiness, the crucial measure is the ratio in relation to export earnings, not to GDP. In fact, a country can carry a large external debt relative to its GDP and not encounter frequent balance of payments difficulties, so long as it manages its economic policies in a way that generates a sustained growth of export earnings. Conversely, a country may encounter frequent balance of payments difficulties even if its external debt is relatively small in relation to GDP, so long as it fails to pursue economic policies necessary to generate rapid export growth.

Thus the debt crisis experienced by Brazil is not just a matter of liquidity shortage; it is an economic policy problem. The debt problem will not disappear unless Brazil modifies its economic policies to significantly lower its debt service ratio in relation to export earnings.[26] For this purpose, Brazil should reverse its renewed inward-orientation of the 1970s and strengthen the international competitiveness of its export industries. In addition, Brazil should make serious efforts to control inflation, strengthen the domestic financial system, and attain a better utilization of domestic savings. Meanwhile, to restrict the undue growth of debt service obligations, Brazil should preferably use foreign credit only where foreign exchange is needed, instead of substituting such credit for domestic financing.[27] This is true particularly with respect to the financing of infrastructure projects with long gestation periods.

Similarly, the pressure on debt servicing can be lessened if more import-substituting projects (which do not generate foreign exchange earnings) are financed with foreign equity participation rather than with foreign credit. Even if the suggested reorientation of development policies is successful, there is a limit to the rate of export growth that a country can reasonably hope to attain without encountering severe resistance from the importing countries, particularly in the industrial world where protectionist sentiments have been running high because of the protracted high levels of unemployment. From this point of view, it is very risky to rely too heavily on external financing in order to sustain rapid economic development in a world of sluggish economic growth and enhanced uncertainty, even if the country is as large as Brazil.

Chapter 4

CONTROLLING RAPID INFLATION: EAST ASIA VERSUS LATIN AMERICA

Introduction and Summary

Most East Asian countries differ crucially from a number of Latin American countries in the control of rapid inflation. To begin, rapid inflation is not a monopoly of the Latin American countries. In fact, hyperinflations of up to several hundred or even several thousand percent yearly have been experienced by many countries outside Latin America, including several European countries in the 1920s and several Eastern European and East Asian countries in the late 1940s.[1] Yet the Latin American countries stand out for their reluctance to deal with rapid inflation firmly and for their tendency to devise elaborate arguments in order to justify their attitude.[2]

Why are the Latin American countries so reluctant to control rapid inflation? The Latin American attitude is understandable if it had resulted in higher economic growth or better income distribution over time. But this has not been the case, particularly in comparison with the East Asian countries which had stopped hyperinflation early in the postwar development process and have firmly dealt with occasional flare-ups of inflation since. The reasons long-term economic performance has diverged between the price-stable East Asian countries and the inflationary Latin American countries are not difficult to understand.

In the East Asian countries, particularly Taiwan and South Korea, the control of rapid inflation early in their postwar development process, combined with the successful reform of incentive systems in favor of export activity, enabled them to maintain the international competitiveness of their industry. This resulted in an enhanced international credit worthiness and an expanded import capacity, thereby removing the dual constraints of low domestic savings and foreign exchange shortage. Meanwhile, the attainment of domestic price stability encouraged the holding of domestic financial assets relative to real assets, thereby facilitating the financial intermediation of savings and investment. In turn, price and financial stability permitted the authorities to relax their monetary stance, thus facilitating the growth of domestic finances and economic activity. These beneficial forces or trends tended to interact and strengthen each other, accelerating the growth of the economy. The higher growth of income, combined with the rapid growth of employment enhanced by the expansion of labor-intensive manufactured exports, also led to more equitable distribution of income and consumption.[3]

In contrast, in Chile, Argentina, and several other Latin American countries the reluctance to control rapid inflation for fear of worsening the growth and distribution of income actually led to such outcomes over time despite the authorities' good intentions. This happened because the persistence of inflation, with the authorities' continued pursuit of inward-oriented development policies, restrained the improvement of international competitiveness of domestic industries. This lack of competitiveness, along with the cyclical fluctuation of primary exports, resulted in a relatively poor export performance over time. This, and the persistent inflationary pressure, caused balance of payments difficulties from time to time and compelled the authorities to frequently undertake stop-go demand management policies.

Meanwhile, the persistent inflation discouraged the holding of domestic financial assets relative to real assets, thereby restraining the development of domestic financial intermediation. The latter in turn constricted the conduct of monetary policy while inducing an excessive reliance on external financing. These unfavorable developments tended to interact and result in an unimpressive economic growth over time. The mediocre long-term economic growth, combined with the failure to develop sizable labor-intensive manufactured exports, led to an inadequate growth of employment relative to the growth of the labor force. Under the circumstances, income distribution could not improve and distributive equity remained an important political issue, further constricting the authorities' policy options of breaking the inflationary spirals.

Faced with this situation, the response of some Latin American countries has been to institute widespread indexing of key economic variables, including wages, exchange rates, government debt instruments, and banking deposits.[4] Such indexing helps reduce the distortions caused by inflation and makes rapid inflation relatively painless in the short run. However, it makes the control of rapid inflation even more difficult, particularly under the circumstances of external shocks or major crop failures. It also tends to distract the authorities from undertaking adequate measures to attain domestic price stability. Such stability is needed for cultivating a mentality compatible with the development of manufactured exports. To be competitive manufactured exports require constant product improvement and cost control. These tend to be neglected in an environment of rapid inflation, where marginal gains derived from product improvement and cost control are often dwarfed by large changes in costs and prices caused by the rapid inflation.

Thus, to attain long-term economic growth, Latin American countries should make an all-out effort to control rapid inflation. Such control is not costless as it often requires a sharp reduction in the fiscal deficit or a temporary loss of real wages. However, not to control rapid inflation is even more costly in the long run because it inevitably results in poor economic performance and widespread social discontent as the Latin American countries' own experiences indicate. Latin American opinion-makers must realize that the need for price stability transcends ideological disputes. This stability is needed regardless of whether the authorities pursue more or less market-oriented policies. For examples the governments can point to the successful development experience of the East Asian countries. The latter indicates that the attainment of domestic price stability, when combined with appropriate policies to develop a pattern of production and trade in line with the country's dynamic comparative advantage, inevitably leads to higher growth of the domestic economy and real incomes over time.

The remainder of this chapter is organized as follows. The next section reviews the divergence in the experiences of inflation and stabilization between East Asia and Latin America during the postwar decades. Then the chapter reviews the reform of trade policies and key institutions in the East Asian countries that helped them establish a sustainable pattern of economic growth, and the relative lack of such reforms in the Latin American countries, which led to the perpetuation of the vicious circle of balance of payments crises, persistent inflation, and sluggish economic growth. Another section examines the interactions between export growth and domestic price stability in selected East Asian and Latin American countries during the decade or so before the first oil shock. A discussion follows of the consequences of different policy responses to external shocks in the 1970s between the East Asian and the Latin American countries, which led to the further divergence of their economic conditions. The last two sections provide concluding remarks and a brief commentary on the latest stabilization efforts in Argentina, Brazil, and Bolivia.

Divergence in Inflation and Stabilization

In the 40 years after World War II, the East Asian countries differed crucially from a number of Latin American countries in their experiences with rapid inflation. Most East Asian countries initially suffered from a severe hyperinflation emanating from the chaotic economic conditions after the war, and they began their postwar development process by first controlling the rapid inflation. This was true not only in Japan, Taiwan, and South Korea, the three high-performing market economies, but also in the People's Republic of China, a socialist economy. In the subsequent decades until the present, the authorities in these countries have dealt with the occasional flare-ups of inflation firmly, thereby resulting in relatively stable prices over time.

By contrast, the Latin American countries, which were not directly involved in World War II, were spared the severe social and economic dislocations suffered by the East Asian countries. In fact, many Latin American countries benefited from the commodity booms both during World War II and the subsequent Korean War.[5] Because of this, the Latin American countries experienced only mild inflation during the 1940s and the early 1950s. However, since the late 1950s, a number of Latin American countries have experienced rapid and persistent inflation. The list originally included Argentina, Brazil, Chile, and Uruguay, and since the early 1970s, also Bolivia, Costa Rica, Mexico, and Peru (Table 4.1).

In Japan, Taiwan, and South Korea, the hyperinflation, which began at the end of the war in August 1945, had been preceded by several years of wartime price controls and rationing. In Japan, the period of open, rapid inflation lasted five years, until 1950. In Taiwan, it lasted for nine years, until 1954. In South Korea, it remained even longer— for 13 years until 1957. The inflationary process prevailed longer in Taiwan and South Korea than in Japan largely because of the intervention of the massive civil wars in both China and Korea after World War II. In mainland China, the hyperinflation, starting in 1937 with the

Table 4.1

Comparative Data on Rapid Inflation in East Asia and Latin America

	Period of rapid inflation	Peak annual CPI inflation rate		Years before inflation returned to the pre-acceleration rate[1]
		Year	Percent	
East Asian countries				
Japan	1945–49	1946	—[2]	7
	1973–77	1974	24	5
Taiwan	1945–53	1949	3,400[3]	9
	1959–61	1960	19	3
	1973–74	1974	48	2
	1979–81	1980	19	3
South Korea	1945–57	1945	1,894[4]	13
	1963–65	1964	30	3
	1974–76	1975	25	3
	1978–82	1980	29	5
Mainland China	1937–50	1949	582,000[5]	14
Latin American countries				
Argentina	1957–61	1959	114	5
	1971–86	1985	672	16 +
Brazil	1959–68	1964	92	10
	1974–86	1985	227	12 +
Chile	1951–59	1955	76	9
	1963–66	1964	46	3
	1968–70	1970	33	3
	1972–81	1974	505	10
Uruguay	1958–62	1959	39	5
	1963–69	1968	125	7
	1971–81	1973	97	11
	1983–	1985	72	3 +
Bolivia	1951–57 .	1956	179	7
	1973–74	1974	63	2
	1979–86	1985	1,750	7
Costa Rica	1973–76	1974	30	4
	1980–83	1982	90	4
Mexico	1973–	1983	102	13 +
Peru	1971–	1985	163	15 +

Sources: International Monetary Fund, *International Financial Statistics Yearbook* (various issues), and various national sources.
[1]14 + indicates that inflation still has not returned to the pre-acceleration rate after 14 years.
[2]An increase of 953 percent between August 15, 1945, and March 31, 1946.
[3]Based on wholesale price index in Taipei.
[4]Based on changes in Seoul WPI from December 1944 to December 1945.
[5]Changes in April 1949 over December 1948. In addition, there was an increase of 2,900 percent between April and December 1949.

outbreak of the Sino-Japanese War, endured for an extended period of 15 years, until it was suppressed by the new Chinese government in 1950 (Table 4.1).

The severity of the inflation experienced by the East Asian countries in the early postwar years far exceeded any experienced by the Latin American countries in the postwar decades. The peak annual rate of inflation reached nearly 1,000 percent in Japan, more than 3,000 percent in Taiwan, about 2,000 percent in South Korea, and more than 500,000 percent in mainland China. In comparison, the peak CPI inflation in Latin America did not exceed 130 percent yearly in the 1960s, but then it worsened to 500 to 600 percent yearly in the 1970s and more than 1,000 percent in the 1980s (Table 4.1).

Control of postwar hyperinflation in East Asia

The severity of the inflation experienced by the East Asian countries and the associated massive economic and social dislocations explain why the control of rapid inflation has subsequently been considered an urgent task in East Asia, regardless of whether the government pursues capitalist or socialist economic policies. All hyperinflations in East Asia stemmed from massive supply/demand disequilibria in goods and services caused by wartime disruptions and rapid monetary expansion related to wartime finance and postwar reconstruction. In all the countries mentioned, the eventual contraction of the inflationary process required the restoration of political stability and productive capacity, with the injection of massive foreign commodity aid and the restriction of deficit financing by the central bank.

Japan, 1944–1951

Japan faced massive problems of demobilization and reconstruction after World War II. In 1946 the Japanese economy was in a shambles. Industrial output fell to less than 30 percent of the 1934 to 1936 average and import capacity was practically nil, while population increased by 10 percent despite the large wartime attrition (Table 4.2). Meanwhile, as many as 13 million people, approximately 23 percent of the adult population, required relocation and reabsorbtion into peacetime activities.[6] Under the circumstances, fiscal deficit and money supply expanded sharply in order to finance the relocation of manpower and the restoration of productive facilities. The sudden increase in purchasing

Table 4.2

Japan: Selected Economic Data, 1944–51

	1944	1946	1947	1948	1949	1950	1951
1. *Real output and external trade* (Index, 1934–36 = 100)							
Real GNP[1]	152.6	85.3	93.3	105.2	107.4	119.3	134.8
Industrial output[2]	158.7	27.7	34.6	45.8	59.5	72.7	100.7
Agricultural output	84.0	78.1	80.0	92.0	93.1	100.3	105.9
Real exports and factor incomes	56.1	2.4	4.9	9.8	19.5	39.0	53.7
Real imports and factor incomes	58.5	12.2	19.5	22.0	29.3	31.7	43.9
2. *Fiscal and external balances* (percent of GNP)							
Fiscal deficit[3]	−35.7	−4.4	−4.0	−1.3	−1.4	0.5	0.3
Current account balance	−0.5	−4.1	−4.1	−4.1	−3.3	2.7	3.8
3. *Money and prices* (percentage changes)							
Currency in circulation	73.6	148.2	128.1	133.0	62.2	18.7	20.0
Wholesale prices	13.3	365.5	195.9	165.4	63.3	18.2	38.8
Consumer prices	—	—[4]	115.0	82.7	32.0	−6.9	16.4
4. *Population* (Index, 1934–36 = 100)	106.9	110.4	113.8	116.6	119.1	121.2	123.1

Source: Bank of Japan, *Hundred Year Statistics of the Japanese Economy* (Tokyo: Bank of Japan, 1966).
[1]Fiscal year (April through March) for 1946–51.
[2]Mining and manufacturing.
[3]The fiscal deficit is approximated by net changes in the outstanding amount of national bonds. For the latter, see Saburo Shiomi (translated by Shotaro Hasegawa), *Japan's Finance and Taxation, 1940–56* (New York: Columbia University Press, 1957), p. 14.
[4]An increase of 953 percent from August 15, 1945, to March 31, 1946. See Shigeto Tsuru, *Essays on Japanese Economy* (Tokyo: Kinokuniya, 1958), pp. 25–26.

power, combined with severe shortages of daily essentials and basic industrial goods, led to rapid inflation in the immediate postwar years. To check excess demand, the authorities implemented a compulsory conversion of currency in February 1946 to freeze excess cash balances in bank deposits while imposing a heavy property tax.

A priority production system was established to expand the production of key industrial goods (such as coal, steel, and fertilizers) and

Table 4.3

Taiwan: Selected Economic Data, 1946–53

	1946	1947	1948	1949	1950	1951	1952	1953
I. *Real output* (1937 = 100)								
Gross output[1]	39.9	47.1	63.9	80.3	90.3	95.5	107.4	139.9
Manufacturing output	19.8	20.9	39.6	58.2	68.7	73.1	86.8	115.9
Agricultural output								
Export volume	2.3	22.5	22.8	—	16.8	18.5	20.3	25.3
Import volume	4.0	18.3	23.3	—	34.2	35.7	43.4	43.4
II. *External deficit and foreign aid*								
Current account deficit as percent of imports	—	—	—	—	−47.4	−34.9	−44.4	−37.7
U.S. aid as percent of current account deficit	—	—	—	—	22.9	109.4	92.6	104.2
III. *Money and prices* (percentage changes)								
Money supply[2]	131[3]	22[3]	1,188[3]	—	139	61	42	26
Wholesale prices (Taipei)	945[3]	680[3]	1,040[3]	3,400	306	66	23	9
IV. *Population and per capita real output* (1937 = 100)								
Population	108.6	117.6	124.9	137.2	146.1	151.0	155.6	161.1
Per capita real output	36.7	40.1	51.2	58.5	61.8	63.2	69.0	86.8

Source: Ching-yuan Lin, *Industrialization in Taiwan, 1946–72* (New York: Praeger, 1973), pp. 32, 37, 46, and 72.

[1]Goods only.
[2]Currency in circulation, 1946–48.
[3]Changes from December to December.

electric power, with a new Reconstruction Finance Bank providing the financing.[7] These efforts led to a substantial improvement of the supply situation by 1949. The improved supply capacity combined with the fiscal discipline imposed by the Dodge Plan finally led to the stabilization of domestic prices in 1950.[8]

Taiwan, 1945–1953

In Taiwan the latent inflationary pressures that had been building up during the war years were aggravated by heavy deficit financing for reconstruction, as well as by the detrimental impact of the civil war then raging in mainland China. Because of wartime destruction and the shift in trade relationships after the war, both industrial and agricultural production declined sharply from the peacetime capacity during the immediate postwar years while population increased rapidly because of a massive influx of refugees from the mainland (Table 4.3). While the local currency was kept separate from the rapidly depreciating mainland legal tender, the worsening military situation on the mainland nevertheless caused a massive capital flight into Taiwan during the last quarter of 1948. This led to a galloping expansion of the money supply and domestic prices in Taiwan of more than 1,000 percent per year in 1948.

Faced with the worsening economic situation, the authorities implemented a monetary reform in June 1949 while strengthening the administrative machinery for the development of Taiwan as an independent economy. Meanwhile, following the fall of Shanghai in May 1949, U.S. commodity aid, detoured to Taiwan, helped relieve the supply shortages and restrict government deficit financing. The presence of the U.S. Navy's Seventh Fleet in the Taiwan Strait following the outbreak of the Korean War in June 1950 further helped Taiwan's political stability. During the years from 1950 to 1952, domestic output continued to recover while monetary expansion continued to decelerate, the latter helped by the introduction of a special deposit scheme with a positive interest rate. These situations led to a rapid stabilization of domestic prices, with the rate of increase of wholesale prices declining from 3,400 percent in 1949 to 66 percent in 1951, 23 percent in 1952, and 9 percent in 1953[9] (Table 4.3).

South Korea, 1945–1958

South Korea suffered severe economic disruptions from the partition of the country in 1945 and the outbreak of the Korean War in 1950. The separation from the industrial north and the massive influx of refugees caused severe shortages of foodstuffs and industrial products, while the shift of trade relationships also adversely affected the production of many goods hitherto exported to Japan. Based on an official estimate,

Table 4.4

South Korea: Selected Data on Inflation, 1945–58 (In percent)

	Changes in WPI	Growth of money supply	Trade deficit as percent of imports	Rice output (1940–44 = 100)	Population (1940 = 100)
1945	1894	179	—	93.4	—
1946	358	133	−69	88.3	124.4
1947	82	134	−47	101.5	127.6
1948	63	66	−19	113.1	128.2
1949	37	59	−24	107.3	129.5
1950	56	—	—	106.6	—
1951	530	246	−62	82.5	—
1952	117	98	−72	67.9	131.4
1953	25	115	−82	102.9	137.8
1954	28	93	−80	109.5	139.6
1955	81	64	−82	113.1	142.0
1956	35	32	−90	93.4	146.6
1957	16	24	−95	114.5	150.3
1958	−7	26	−95	120.8	154.6

Sources: International Monetary Fund, *International Financial Statistics Yearbook* (1983); Bank of Korea, *Economic Statistics Yearbook* (1949 and 1960); and David C. Cole and Yung Chul Park, *Financial Development in South Korea, 1945-1978* (Cambridge, Mass: Council on East Asian Studies, Harvard University, 1983).

manufacturing output in 1948 dropped to only one fifth of the level attained in 1940, while population increased by 28 percent. Whereas many imports were financed with foreign aid in conjunction with the stationing of the U.N. troops, inflationary pressures remained strong because of rapid credit expansion to the public sector for financing reconstruction. Nevertheless, by 1949, the hyperinflation that erupted at the end of World War II had largely dissipated, with the rate of price inflation slowing down to around 40 percent yearly. This stabilizing trend was reversed by the outbreak of the Korean War in June 1950, with a large part of the country becoming battlegrounds. Thereafter, the financial need for reconstruction as well as the supplying of local currency funds to the U.N. forces kept the monetary expansion at high rates, thereby causing the inflation to persist until the mid-1950s. From 1956 onward, rigorous monetary and fiscal restraints were enforced, and these restraints, combined with a massive influx of commodity aid and a favorable turn in the food harvest, finally put an end to more than a decade of surging inflation[10] (Table 4.4).

Mainland China, 1937–1953

The Chinese hyperinflation began with the Sino-Japanese War in 1937 and ended shortly after the establishment of the People's Republic of China in 1949. Except for a brief period after the end of World War II, the entire period was dominated by massive warfare covering most of the country, with attendant severe disruptions in economic activity and the financial system. The driving force of the inflation was massive government deficit financing, which accounted for 50 to 85 percent of government expenditures throughout the period. The fiscal situation worsened as defense expenditures soared while tax revenues from the northern and coastal regions diminished because of enemy occupation. However, while inflation accelerated year after year, the annual rate had remained below 300 percent per year until 1947, partly because further worsening of the government's finances were spared by the suspension of servicing the old external debts in conjunction with the loss of customs revenue pledged for such a purpose, and partly because of the infusion of U.S. aid after the Pacific War broke out in late 1941. From 1947 through 1949, the inflation accelerated rapidly along with the worsening of the civil war and the ultimate collapse of the Nationalist government. By 1948, inflation rose to 21,000 percent per year and then jumped to 582,000 percent in the following four months before the fall of Shanghai in May 1949[11] (Table 4.5).

To slow down the rapid inflation, the Nationalist government introduced two abortive monetary reforms (in August 1948 and July 1949) and offered bond sales or special deposits redeemable in gold or foreign exchange. These attempts failed quickly under the deteriorating political and economic situation and the government's finances. Thus it was left to the People's Republic of China, which came into being in October 1949, to suppress the hyperinflation by means of draconian measures, namely through the compulsory depositing and freezing of private funds, the compulsory purchase of government bonds, and eventually the socialization of private enterprises and distribution networks as well as sharp curtailment of the market mechanism.[12]

The severity of the inflation and economic and social disruptions experienced by the East Asian countries in the early postwar years

Table 4.5

Mainland China: Selected Data on Inflation, 1938–49
(In percentage changes)

	Inflation[1]	Note issue	Fiscal deficit as percent of expenditure	Output[2] Rice	Wheat	Cotton yarn
1938	31	41	−67.3	8.3	54.4	—
1939	68	86	−73.5	2.2	−2.4	12.2
1940	133	83	−74.9	−19.0	1.6	77.8
1941	153	92	−86.8	4.0	−17.9	82.0
1942	201	128	−77.0	−1.2	26.9	15.2
1943	222	119	−65.0	−4.1	−4.9	24.8
1944	244	152	−77.6	10.7	24.7	−5.4
1945	278	446	−47.1	−12.8	−11.6	−43.0
1946	147	261	−62.0			
1947	797	691	−67.6			
1948	21,000	(1,079)[3]	−66.3[4]			
1949	(582,100)[5]					

Source: Chang Kia-Ngau, *The Inflationary Spiral: The Experience in China, 1939–1950* (Cambridge, Mass.: The Technology Press of MIT; and New York: John Wiley & Sons, 1958), pp. 371–374.
[1]Price index for 1938–45 is based on that compiled by the Director-General of Budgets, Accounts, and Statistics. That for 1946–49 is based on that compiled by the Central Bank of China.
[2]For Free China (13 provinces) only.
[3]First half 1948 over 1947.
[4]First half of the year only.
[5]April 1949 over December 1948.

explain a great deal about their subsequent aversion to rapid inflation and the national authorities' resolute pursuit of anti-inflation policies whenever price inflation, for whatever reasons, appeared to gather steam. These policies apparently enjoyed popular support and succeeded in controlling the inflationary forces. In the two decades from the early 1950s to the early 1970s, each of the four East Asian countries considered here either experienced an average inflation of 3 to 5 percent per year or experienced a rapidly stabilizing price situation. Even after the first oil shock (1973/1974), when inflationary pressures again emerged because of the combination of strong excess demand and sharp import cost-push, these countries managed to quickly control the resurgence of inflation in 1973 and 1974 and again in 1979 and 1980. This resulted in a relatively low average rate of inflation over time (Table 4.6 and Chart 4.1).

Table 4.6

Selected Countries in East Asia and Latin America: CPI Inflation before and after the First Oil Shock
(In annual percentage changes)

	Before the first oil shock			After the first oil shock		
	1946–52	1953–60	1961–73	1974–78	1979–83	1984
East Asian countries						
Japan	61.0	2.4	6.1	11.3	4.2	2.2
Taiwan (China)	546.0[1]	9.7	3.7	12.5	9.9	—
South Korea	117.0[2]	24.7	12.7	17.8	15.4	2.3
Latin American countries						
Argentina	24.8	25.5	27.5	170.2	162.7	626.7
Brazil	11.3	23.7	36.6	36.0	94.0	196.7
Chile	20.8	39.4	42.9	199.4	24.7	19.9
Uruguay	7.7	17.4	48.1	61.7	45.4	55.3
Costa Rica	2.9	1.8	3.3	11.8	34.8	12.0
Mexico	13.5	6.0	3.8	20.1	43.7	65.5
Peru	16.1	9.6	9.0	33.2	74.5	110.2
World trade indicators						
World import volume	—	7.4	8.4	4.1	1.9	8.7
World import unit value (U.S.$)	—	−0.5	3.4	13.3	5.0	−2.4

Sources: International Monetary Fund, *International Financial Statistics Yearbook* (various issues); James W. Wilkie and Stephen Haber (eds.), *Statistical Abstract of Latin America*, vol. 23 (Los Angeles: University of California, 1983); and Council for Economic Development and Planning (Taiwan), *Taiwan Statistical Data Book, 1984*. Also, see notes to Tables 2, 3, and 4.
[1]Wholesale prices in Taipei.
[2]Excludes 1950.

Sluggish stabilization efforts in Latin America

Before the oil shocks

Compared with the East Asian countries, the Latin American countries experienced relatively moderate inflation during the early postwar years. These inflations, at 5 to 25 percent per year, may have resulted both from the wartime supply shortages and the economic policies pursued by the national authorities in response to this situation. In most countries, these supply-related inflations subsided after World War II

CHART 4.1

CPI INFLATION IN JAPAN, TAIWAN, AND SOUTH KOREA,1948-83

(In annual percentage changes)

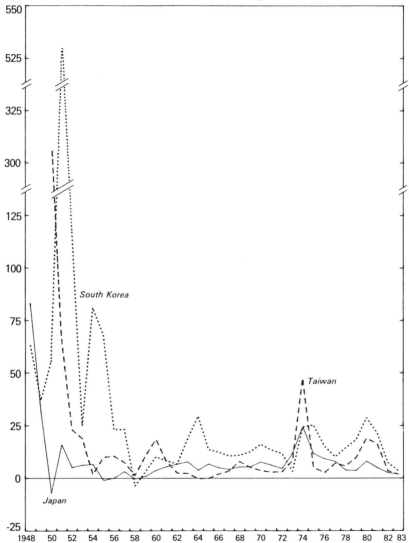

when foreign trade returned to normal. However, in Argentina, Brazil, Chile, and Uruguay recurrent bouts of rapid inflation occurred through the 1950s and the 1960s. In Argentina, these occurred from 1951 to

CHART 4.2

CPI INFLATION IN CHILE AND ARGENTINA, 1949-83

(In annual percentage changes)

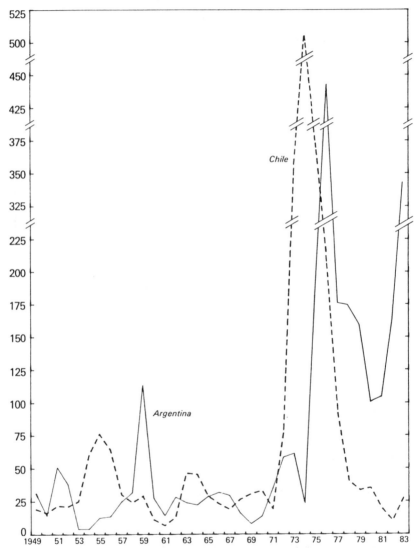

1952, 1957 to 1960, and 1965 to 1967; in Brazil from 1952 to 1968; in Chile fron 1953 to 1959 and 1963 to 1965; and in Uruguay from 1958 to 1961 and 1963 to 1968. In these countries, the annual rate of the CPI inflation rarely slowed down to less than 20 percent per year, with

CHART 4.3

CPI INFLATION IN BRAZIL, MEXICO, AND PERU, 1949-83

(In annual percentage changes)

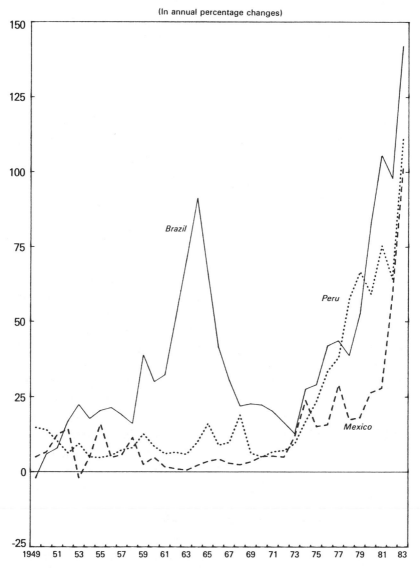

periodic upsurges ranging from 40 to 100 percent. These inflations occurred at a time when world trade was expanding rapidly at more than 7 percent yearly while import costs were relatively stable, falling by a half percent per year in U.S. dollars during 1953 to 1960, and rising by only 3 percent per year from 1960 to 1973 (Charts 4.2 and 4.3, and Table 4.6). These developments suggest that whatever the origins of inflation during World War II, its persistence at high rates after the war must be explained largely in terms of domestic factors.

After the oil shocks

In the decade after the first oil shock the Latin American inflation worsened considerably. Not only did the traditionally hyperinflationary countries experience much higher rates of inflation, but several others whose price situations were stable or stabilizing during the 1960s joined the ranks of the hyperinflationary countries. In Chile, following a brief socialist experiment under President Allende and subsequent liberalization attempts under the junta, the CPI inflation exploded to exceed 500 percent per year in 1975. Not until 1981 was inflation brought back to the 20 percent rate of 1971. In Argentina, the CPI inflation worsened to exceed 440 percent per year in 1976 in the transition from the labor-based Peronist government and the subsequent liberalization attempts under the junta. Since then, the Argentinean inflation slowed down briefly to the 100 percent level in 1980 and 1981 before rebounding to exceed 600 percent in 1984, despite the authorities' repeated stabilization efforts (Chart 4.2 and Table 4.1). Meanwhile, the stabilizing trend of inflation in Brazil was reversed after 1973 with the CPI inflation worsening dramatically after the second oil shock (1979/1980) to outstrip the previous peak of 1975.

Similar worsening in inflation was experienced by Bolivia, Costa Rica, Mexico, and Peru. During the 1960s, these four countries experienced only mild to moderate inflation. Following the disturbances caused by the two oil shocks, all experienced an inflation rate ranging from 90 to 300 percent in the early 1980s (Chart 4.3 and Table 4.6).

Disparity in Policy and Institutional Reforms

The divergence in experiences with respect to inflation and economic development during the war and early postwar years apparently contributed to the formation of different attitudes toward the control of inflation in East Asia and Latin America. In East Asia, the majority of the population had suffered from severe inflation and economic disruptions, and this made them more willing to accept the short-run defla-

Table 4.7

Selected Countries in East Asia and Latin America: Population, Population Density, Proportion of Primary Exports, and Per Capita Primary Exports and Manufactured Exports, 1982

				Per capita exports	
			Proportion	Primary	Manufactured
	Population	Population density	of primary exports	products	goods
	(millions)	(per sq. km)	(percent)	(U.S. $)	
Japan	118.4	318	3	35	1,134
Taiwan	18.5	514	8	97	1,118
South Korea	39.3	401	8	44	512
Chile	11.5	15	92	297	26
Argentina	28.4	10	76	204	64
Brazil	126.8	15	61	97	62
Mexico	73.1	37	88	255	35
Peru	17.4	14	86	163	26

Sources: International Monetary Fund, *International Financial Statistics: 1985 Yearbook*; World Bank, *World Development Report, 1984 and 1985.*

tionary effects of the stabilization policies, while reducing the national authorities' political costs in pursuing these policies. By contrast, most Latin American countries did not suffer from the ravages of hyperinflation during the war and early postwar years, making the general public and the national authorities less inclined to accept the short-run deflationary costs of the stabilization policies.

In addition, differences in population pressure and natural resource endowments between most countries in the two regions also contributed to the formation of different attitudes toward the management of trade and industrial policies. Most East Asian countries suffered from strong population pressure and a paucity of natural resources (Table 4.7), generating a strong need for export expansion to finance the necessary imports. Such a need in turn induced the national authorities to undertake major policy reforms in order to shift policy incentives in favor of export activity relatively early in their postwar development process. By contrast, most Latin American countries experienced less acute population pressure while having much greater potential for expanding primary exports (Table 4.7). This enabled them to escape from the constraint of foreign exchange shortage from time to time, and thus reduce the need for strong export promotion efforts.

Intensive export promotion and policy reforms in East Asia

In addition to controlling hyperinflation, the East Asian countries undertook important policy and institutional reforms that helped improve the performance of the economy. All three countries under review—Japan, Taiwan, and South Korea—carried out land reforms in the early postwar years that helped relieve social tensions and provided work incentives for the tenants and owner-cultivators. In addition, the governments provided technical services, modern inputs, and agricultural credit. These measures contributed to the rapid improvement of agricultural productivity in Japan and Taiwan during the 1950s, and later also in South Korea.[13] The higher productivity, in turn, enabled the subsequent release and transfer of rural surplus labor to the urban-centered industrial activity.

Another source of cheap labor was young females, following the expansion of public education. In both Taiwan and South Korea, as in Japan during the early period of industrialization, an ample supply of young female workers provided the backbone of the work force for the export-oriented light industries, chiefly textiles and apparel during the early years and subsequently electronics.

The ample supply of educated manpower, combined with the establishment of enterprise labor unions and a ''lifetime'' employment system in the modern corporate sector (that led to the formation of more cooperative labor-management relations), greatly reduced the chances of wage-push as a leading cause of inflation in postwar Japan. In Taiwan and South Korea similar results were obtained because of the lack of strong labor unions under the authoritarian political system, the orderly social relations based on the Confucian ethic, and the increased availability of employment opportunities under the successful export promotion efforts.

In all three countries strong population pressure and poor natural resources generated a strong need for export expansion. In fact, this led the national authorities to emphasize export expansion and industrial efficiency relatively early in their development process. It also induced the manufacturing firms to strive for product improvements and cost reduction as a means of increasing their international competitiveness.

In Japan active export promotion was started in the early 1950s, following the end of the Korean War boom. In 1954, various organizations for export promotion were consolidated into the Japan External Trade Organization (JETRO), and an Export Conference was established with the participation of various government agencies and industrial representatives. The Prime Minister served as chairman. JETRO conducted overseas market research, established trade centers in major foreign cities, and organized participation in international trade fairs. In addition to JETRO, special organizations were established for the promotion of exports of manufacturing plant and machine tools. Through these organizations, the government encouraged the development of good product designs; held overseas exhibits of outstanding products and handicrafts; enforced the inspection of specific export products; and took measures to prevent exports of products infringing on foreign designs or patents. Meanwhile, it also strengthened various export insurances; established various export financing schemes at favorable rates; and provided tax allowances for export incomes and depreciation of export-related facilities.[14]

In addition to the promotion of exports and industrial efficiency, the Japanese government strove to maintain macroeconomic balance through an effective use of monetary policy. Partly because of fiscal reforms undertaken during the late 1940s and because of rapid revenue growth enabled by rapid income growth, the government maintained fiscal discipline and achieved noninflationary government finance most of the time during the following two decades.[15]

Also, because of wartime destruction and isolation from Western technological development, Japan experienced strong investment demand after the war, with the business enterprises relying heavily on external funds. This enhanced the role of financial institutions in intermediating between savings and investment, while increasing the efficacy of monetary policy in influencing economic activity. Through the two decades before the oil shocks, the Bank of Japan closely regulated credit expansion by the commercial banks while imposing monetary restraints frequently in order to correct the imbalances in external payments caused by excessive domestic investments. These restraints were largely successful in restoring internal and external balances while avoiding protracted recessions.[16]

In Taiwan, following a decade of import-substituting industrialization, the authorities undertook major policy reforms from the late 1950s to shift policy incentives in favor of export activity. These reforms started initially with a substantial currency devaluation and the unification of exchange rates in 1958, which were followed by the strengthening of various export and investment incentives and the liberalization of discretionary controls in the early 1960s. In addition, the authorities took strong measures to stop the resurgence of inflation that resulted from the occurrence, all in 1958 and 1959, of sizable devaluations, hostilities in the offshore islands, and a major typhoon disaster. These policy efforts were successful in shifting the focus of entrepreneurial activity from domestic to export markets, thereby enabling Taiwan to take advantage of the favorable external environment in order to establish a sustainable growth pattern.[17]

In South Korea also, intensive policy reforms took place in favor of export activity. These reforms, which began in the late 1950s, were intensified in 1964 to 1965 with a massive currency devaluation and the strengthening of various export incentives.[18] In addition, the authorities tightened bank credit to stop the inflation that flared up in 1963 and 1964. These reforms paralleled those effected in Taiwan several years earlier. In addition, the Korean authorities experimented with a high interest rate policy for bank deposits while putting into effect a repayment guarantee scheme for foreign loans.[19] These measures induced a sharp expansion in quasi-money deposits in relation to GNP and large inflows of foreign credit particularly from Japan, the latter in conjunction with the normalization of diplomatic relations in 1965.[20] The sharply increased export incentives, combined with increased financing for foreign trade, led to a sharp expansion of both exports and bank credit during the second half of the 1960s. These developments enabled South Korea to achieve a rapid growth of investment and imports, although its domestic prices remained much more volatile than in Taiwan and Japan partly because of the much faster monetary expansion.

Sluggish policy reforms and excessive reliance on indexing in Latin America

In contrast with the East Asian countries' intensive efforts at price stabilization and export promotion, many Latin American countries' efforts in this regard were clearly inadequate. Much of the inflation experienced by the Latin American countries during the early postwar years apparently stemmed from the inward-oriented development policies pursued by the national authorities to sustain economic growth.

Table 4.8

Selected Countries in East Asia and Latin America: Estimates of Effective Protection and Bias against Exports for Selected Years in the 1960s (In percent)

	Effective protection				Bias against exports[3]	
	Without exchange rate adjustment[1]		With adjustment for the effects of protection on the equilibrium exchange rate[2]			
	Primary	Manufacturing[4]	Primary	Manufacturing[4]	Primary	Manufacturing[4]
Taiwan (1969)	—	14	−8	9	4	26
South Korea (1968)	9	13	1	−11	16	10
Chile (1961)	21	182	−28	68	—	324
Argentina (1969)	—	112	−29	38	24	241
Brazil	52	113	20	68	—	122
Mexico (1960)	1	26	−7	16	13	87

Source: Bela Balassa, *Change in Challenge in the World Economy* (London: MacMillan Press, 1985), p. 27.

[1]Estimated as $z_i = (t_i - \sum_j A_{ji} t_j)/(1 - \sum_j A_{ji})$, where t is the nominal rate of protection, representing the effects of tariffs (subsidies) or the tariff-equivalent of import restrictions and export subsidies (taxes) on the price of the product. Subscripts i and j, respectively, refer to the product and its tradeable inputs. A_{ji} denotes input-output coefficients under free trade.

[2]Estimated as $z_i = r_i/r_o(1 + z_i) - 1$, where r_i and r_o refer to the exchange rate under protection and under free trade, respectively.

[3]Estimated as $x_i = (z_i^m - z_i^x)/z_i^x - 1$, where m and x refer to domestic and export sales of a particular product.

[4]Excluding food processing, beverages, and tobacco.

These policies tended to generate inflationary pressures through various channels, including the deficit financing of increased government expenditures for development; the proliferation of industrial inefficiencies resulting from the prolonged protection of import substituting industries; and the shortage of foreign exchange caused by the policy bias against export activity. These inflationary pressures were also present in Taiwan and South Korea, but the authorities took decisive measures to control inflation and to shift policy emphasis in favor of export activity. By contrast, the aversion to the deflationary impact of stabilization policies and the potentials for expanding primary exports made several Latin American countries reluctant to pursue effective stabilization policies while undertaking only halfhearted policy reforms for promoting exports. The latter was indicated by the continuing high rates of effective protection on domestic industry in the 1960s estimated for several countries in the region and by the significant biases of their incentive systems against export activity[21] (Table 4.8).

Because of this deficiency in economic policy management, countries such as Chile and Argentina failed to generate a rapid growth of export earnings in order to enhance their credit worthiness and to satisfy their higher import needs. The latter, in turn, sustained the inflationary pressures through the periodic currency devaluations, the ensuing adjustment of wages and material costs, and the deepening of the import substituting process. As the growth of labor productivity and per capita income remained modest under this pattern of economic development, real wages could not grow rapidly and this further restricted the authorities' policy options in controlling inflation. Instead, the authorities tended to devise various indexation schemes in order to make the inflation less painful and to sustain the domestic financial system.

In Chile, which pioneered the use of indexation and where its use was pervasive, indexation was first applied to wages in 1942. By 1953, as the financial markets withered following a decade of rapid inflation, the indexation was extended to bonds issued by the State Bank and subsequently to savings accounts offered by various financial institutions. Meanwhile, corporations were required to revalue their total capital and inventories annually. Furthermore, in 1965 the indexation was applied to the trade segment of the dual exchange market through a system of minidevaluations.[22]

In Brazil the indexation was started by the junta, which took over the government in 1964 following a severe worsening of inflation and a prolonged recession. As in Chile, the Brazilian indexation scheme was comprehensive, encompassing wages, financial instruments, the tax system, and the exchange rate. In 1964, a National Wage Policy Council was established with the authority to approve or reject all wage increases. Under the guidance of the Council, real wages initially declined significantly, thereby contributing to the deceleration of inflation. Meanwhile, the government started to market treasury bonds that yielded about 6 percent plus a compensatory inflation premium. Subsequently the authorities added various features to increase the attractiveness of these bonds, such as adding the option of calculating monetary correction on the basis of the exchange rate vis-à-vis the U.S. dollar and allowing commercial banks to satisfy reserve requirements by holding these bonds. In addition, indexation was applied to both mortgages and rental contracts in order to stimulate housing construction. In fact, its use was expanded to many other types of financial assets (including state government bonds, corporate bonds, bills of exchange, promissory notes, and loan contracts). But the government's attempts to encourage indexation in the private sector met with resistance, particularly by commercial banks.

With respect to the tax system, the indexation was applied to the adjustment of personal income tax brackets and exemptions; the revaluation of corporate capital assets for calculating depreciation allowances; the taxation of capital gains; and the adjustment of delinquent taxes. Lastly, with respect to the exchange rate, the authorities adopted a "crawling peg" system in 1968 in order to maintain a purchasing power parity between the cruzeiro and the U.S. dollar.[23]

While both the Chilean and Brazilian indexations were quite comprehensive, the development of the two economies was very different during the 1960s and the early 1970s. The Chilean inflation did not slow down during the 1960s and even worsened sharply during the early 1970s in the aftermath of President Allende's socialist experiment. Its economic growth, following a favorable performance during the first half of the 1960s, also worsened considerably during the second half before turning sharply negative during the early 1970s.

In contrast, the Brazilian inflation continued to decline from more than 90 percent in 1964 to around 15 percent in 1972 and 1973, while the rate of economic growth continued to accelerate from 2 to 3 percent in 1964 and 1965 to 10 to 11 percent in 1971 through 1973. What caused this divergence? Apparently it was not due to any major differences in the indexation schemes because both systems were compre-

Table 4.9

Chile and Brazil: Growth of Export Earnings, Money Supply, and Real GDP, and Fiscal Deficit in Relation to GDP, 1961–73 (In percent)

	1961	1962	1963	1964	1965	1966	1967	1968	1969	1970	1971	1972	1973
1. Chile													
Export earnings (US$)	3.7	4.7	−1.5	13.4	7.6	28.3	3.7	1.3	25.3	16.3	−20.2	−14.2	44.0
Money supply (M2)	16.7	42.9	20.0	50.0	61.1	41.3	29.3	45.3	41.6	46.1	76.8	101.6	330.8
Inflation[1]	5.7	27.3	45.4	41.2	25.7	18.3	20.8	30.5	34.4	34.3	21.8	153.4	827.6
Real money supply (M2)	10.4	12.3	−17.5	6.2	28.2	19.4	7.0	11.3	5.4	8.8	45.2	−20.4	−53.6
Real GDP	6.1	4.6	5.1	4.3	5.1	3.8	4.9	11.2	9.9	2.4	12.0	11.1	13.6
Fiscal deficit/GDP ratio	4.0	5.4	5.7	4.9	5.7	5.7	4.1	3.4	4.3	5.6	8.3	12.6	23.1
2. Brazil													
Export earnings (US$)	10.6	15.8	1.7	11.6	9.1	−5.0	13.7	22.9	18.5	25.7	6.0	37.4	55.3
Money supply (M2)	44.2	52.5	57.5	85.6	83.3	40.7	36.2	43.0	32.6	29.4	31.7	34.2	45.6
Inflation[1]	32.3	51.2	70.8	91.4	65.9	41.3	30.4	22.0	22.7	22.3	20.2	16.5	12.7
Real money supply (M2)	6.8	−6.2	−8.6	−3.0	15.6	1.2	6.5	16.3	8.3	6.8	10.3	15.0	26.8
Real GDP	10.3	5.2	1.6	2.9	2.7	3.8	4.9	11.2	9.9	2.4	12.0	11.1	13.6
Fiscal deficit/GDP ratio	3.4	4.3	4.2	3.2	1.6	1.1	1.7	1.2	0.6	0.4	0.3	0.1	0.1

Sources: International Monetary Fund, *International Financial Statistics Yearbook* (various issues); James W. Wilkie and Adam Perkal (eds.), *Statistical Abstract of Latin America*, vol. 23 (Los Angeles: University of California, 1983); and Gustav Donald Jud, *Inflation and the Use of Indexing in Developing Countries* (New York: Praeger Publishers, 1978)

[1]Average of changes in the CPI and WPI.

hensive. Rather, the divergence must be attributed chiefly to other policies and developments, particularly with respect to external trade and fiscal and monetary policies (Charts 4.2 and 4.3 and Table 4.9).

First, while the Chilean exports and imports continued to fluctuate during the 1960s and the early 1970s, the Brazilian exports and imports expanded sharply from 1966 and 1967 onward, thereby removing the foreign exchange constraint on the development process. Secondly, while the Chilean fiscal deficit remained as large as 4 to 5 percent of GDP during the 1960s and expanded sharply during the early 1970s, the Brazilian deficit declined steadily from 3 to 4 percent to nearly zero, thereby eliminating a major source of inflationary finance.[24] Thirdly, in conjunction with these developments, the Chilean money supply which expanded sharply from time to time (particularly during 1963 to 1964 and 1971 to 1972) continued to sustain the inflationary process, while the Brazilian monetary growth, despite a slowdown in nominal terms, actually increased steadily in real terms during the second half of the 1960s in order to support a higher growth of economic activity (Table 4.9).

These contrasting developments attest to the importance of effective trade policy reforms and stabilization efforts, regardless of whether or not the government uses indexation. While the Brazilian export expansion followed intensive policy reforms in favor of export activity, the continued fluctuation of the Chilean exports reflected the authorities' inadequate policy efforts in this regard.[25] Despite the institution of tax rebates and other export incentives, the Chilean incentive systems remained heavily biased in favor of domestic markets during the 1960s because of the high rates of effective protection. This situation was worsened by the nationalization-cum-redistributive measures and the lack of fiscal and monetary discipline under President Allende's socialist regime, which further unsettled the system and led to a sharp acceleration of inflation and a major decline of economic activity in the early 1970s.[26]

While the improvement in the Brazilian economic performance occurred in conjunction with the use of various indexation schemes, it is debatable whether such indexation was helpful in the long run. The indexation of public debt instruments, while enabling the government to reduce the shrinkage of domestic finances, cumulatively twisted the financial system in favor of the public sector, thereby restraining the growth of private financial institutions and the deepening of the financial process. Coupled with other biases in the system, this led to the private sector's over dependence on foreign credit and sowed the seeds of the external debt problem. The indexation of wages and public debt instruments, while helpful in sustaining economic activity, also tended to prolong the inflationary process, thereby delaying the undertaking of the necessary adjustment efforts. This was true particularly during the 1970s when the inflationary impulse originated from abroad and when there was a strong need for adjustment because of the severe losses in terms of trade.

Interactions between Export Growth and Domestic Price Stability

During the decade or so before the first oil shock (1973/1974), the world economy was growing rapidly and the rise in world trade prices was relatively mild (Table 4.6, lowest panel). During this period, the less advanced countries could have participated in the growth of world trade and achieved a relatively high rate of economic growth while maintaining relatively stable domestic prices, as long as they undertook the necessary policy reforms to encourage exports and industrial efficiency. Under such conditions, the growth of export earnings and the attendant enhancement of credit worthiness enabled a country to remove the dual constraints of low savings ratio and foreign exchange shortages that existed in the 1950s. These conditions, in turn, led to higher investment and faster income growth, resulting in the expansion of productive capacity and the enlargement of domestic markets. These developments brought about substantial improvements in the operating efficiency of business enterprises and a rapid growth of productivity. Meanwhile, excessive demand for wage growth was restrained by the rapid growth of educated manpower and the still large potential for transferring labor out of the low productivity activities, particularly agriculture and household work. The rapid productivity growth and the moderate wage growth, combined with the relative stability of fuel and raw material import costs, facilitated the maintenance of relatively stable domestic prices.

Moreover, the faster growth of real income enabled a rise in the savings ratio, particularly in the household sector. The latter, combined with the stabilization of domestic prices, led to increased holding of financial assets (particularly bank deposits) relative to income. This holding of assets in turn facilitated increased intermediation by the financial institutions in the savings and investment activities. Such intermediation indirectly contributed to the improvement of the overall economic efficiency, by speeding up the growth of investments in large-scale modern operations. Under the circumstances, domestic credit expanded rapidly in order to support the rapid growth of economic activity without stimulating inflationary expectations.[27]

Virtuous circle between export expansion and domestic price stability in East Asia

These favorable developments, in fact, occurred in most East Asian countries in the period before the first oil shock. From 1960 to 1973 export earnings (in U.S. dollars) increased yearly by 18.5 percent in Japan, 29 percent in Taiwan, and 42 percent in South Korea. This rapid export growth, combined with the enhanced credit worthiness, enabled the three countries to attain an accelerated growth of imports, investment and real output (Table 4.10).

The acceleration of economic growth in the East Asian countries occurred in conjunction with a rapid growth in labor productivity and a stabilizing trend of unit labor costs. In Japan, real output per man-hour in manufacturing increased 10.3 percent per year from 1961 to 1973. This offset to a large extent the rise of 15.1 percent per year in hourly compensation and resulted in a rise of unit labor costs of 4.4 percent yearly. During the same period, the growth of manufacturing labor productivity in Taiwan, 9.3 percent yearly, was nearly as great as in Japan, while the rise of nominal wages was much slower, resulting in an even lower growth of unit labor costs—less than 2 percent per year.

In South Korea, however, the growth of labor productivity was slower than in Taiwan and Japan while the rise of nominal wages was faster, resulting in a higher increase of unit labor costs. However, at less than 13 percent per year, the underlying rate of inflation in South Korea had slowed down considerably from the 1950s, and this reduction, combined with the lower rate of increase in import costs, enabled the authorities to restrain inflation to a manageable level (Table 4.11).

Meanwhile, in conjunction with the acceleration in the growth of per capita GDP, gross domestic savings in Japan increased from less than 25 percent of GNP in the early 1950s to nearly 40 in the late 1960s. In both Taiwan and South Korea, the savings ratios in the early 1950s were much lower than in Japan, less than 10 percent, because of the lower per capita income, but their growth during the 1960s was even faster than in Japan because of the sharper acceleration in the growth of per

Table 4.10

Selected Countries in East Asia and Latin America: Export Earnings, Import Unit Value, Import Purchasing Power, Import Volume, Real Output, Money Supply, Inflation, and Real Money Supply, 1954–60, 1960–73, 1973–78, 1978–83 (In annual percentage changes)

	1954–60	1960–73	1973–78	1978–83
1. *Export earnings* (US$)				
Japan	18.0	18.5	21.5	8.4
Taiwan	4.3	29.2	22.3	14.0
South Korea	−2.7	42.3	31.6	14.0
Argentina	−0.6	8.9	14.4	4.1
Chile	2.6	7.4	15.0	9.1
Brazil	−2.7	13.0	15.3	11.6
Mexico	3.8	8.7	21.4	28.8
2. *Import unit value* (US$)				
Japan	−1.4	3.2	14.7	8.8
Taiwan	−0.3	3.5	12.0	9.8
South Korea	−0.3*	2.5	11.1	6.5
Argentina**	0.2**	3.7	11.2	3.3
Chile***	0.2	3.2	13.2	6.3
Brazil	0.2**	3.2	12.7	9.2
Mexico**	0.2	3.7	11.2	3.3
3. *Import purchasing power*				
Japan	19.7	14.8	5.9	−0.4
Taiwan	4.6	24.8	9.9	4.4
South Korea	−2.4	38.8	18.5	7.0
Argentina	−0.8	5.0	2.9	0.8
Chile	2.4	4.1	1.6	2.6
Brazil	−2.9	9.5	2.3	2.2
Mexico	3.6	4.8	9.2	24.7
4. *Import volume*				
Japan	10.9	14.2	1.0	0.7
Taiwan	4.4	22.4	10.5	2.9
South Korea	0.3	18.3	15.8	5.0
Argentina	6.5	0.9	0.2	—
Chile	6.5	2.5	8.0	−7.5
Brazil	1.3	9.3	3.5	−6.4
Mexico	5.4	5.5	3.1	5.2

5. *Real GDP or GNP*

Japan	8.2	9.6	5.1	6.3
Taiwan	7.3	10.4	8.4	6.1
South Korea	3.8	8.9	10.3	5.1
Argentina	4.8	2.6	1.5	−0.8
Chile	2.8	3.4	1.6	(1.4)
Brazil	7.3	8.5	7.8	1.9
Mexico	7.0	7.0	5.5	3.9

6. *Money supply* (M2)

Japan	8.9	18.9	12.7	8.5
Taiwan	23.9	25.1	29.6	19.8
South Korea	32.0	38.7	31.5	24.2
Argentina	25.1	25.4	149.0	174.9
Chile		36.2	305.5	36.2
Brazil	27.1	46.0	40.1	88.0
Mexico	12.4	11.3	50.4	50.5

7. *Inflation* (average of CPI and WPI)

Japan	0.9	4.1	9.3	5.0
Taiwan	8.6	3.6	10.2	9.0
South Korea	20.9	12.3	18.8	15.7
Argentina	30.8	27.0	167.3	167.7
Chile		44.5	226.8	26.8
Brazil	23.0	36.6	35.3	98.6
Mexico	6.6	3.7	21.1	43.3

8. *Real money supply* (M2)

Japan	7.9	14.2	3.1	3.3
Taiwan	14.1	20.8	17.6	9.9
South Korea	9.2	23.5	10.7	7.3
Argentina	−4.4	−1.3	−6.8	2.7
Chile		1.2	24.1	7.4
Brazil	3.3	6.9	3.5	−5.3
Mexico	5.4	7.3	24.2	5.0

Sources: International Monetary Fund, *International Financial Statistics Yearbook* (various issues); Council for Economic Planning and Development, *Taiwan Statistical Data Book, 1984* (Taipei, 1984).

*Approximation, based on Taiwan data.
**Based on changes in the export unit value of industrial countries.
***Based on changes in the aggregate import unit value of all non-oil developing countries.

Table 4.11

Selected Countries in East Asia and Latin America: Growth of Labor Productivity and Unit Labor Costs in Manufacturing, 1960–73 (In annual percentage changes)

	Real output	Labor productivity[1]	Nominal wages[1]	Unit labor costs
East Asia				
Japan	12.5	10.3	15.1	4.4
Taiwan	18.1	9.3	11.4	1.9
South Korea	17.9	5.8	19.1	12.6
Latin America				
Argentina	6.8	4.9	29.0	23.0
Chile	4.2	3.3	45.5	40.9

Sources: International Labour Office, *Yearbook of Labour Statistics* (various issues); International Monetary Fund, *International Financial Statistics* (various issues); Economic Planning Agency, *Keizai Yoran* (Economic Handbook), 1982; and the Council for Economic Planning and Development, *Taiwan Statistical Data Book* (Taipei, 1983).

[1]Measured on per man-hour basis for Japan, and on per employee basis for the rest of the countries.

capita income. By the early 1970s, Taiwan's savings ratio far exceeded 30 percent of GDP while South Korea's reached 20 percent (Table 4.10 and Chart 4.4). The higher savings ratio combined with the stabilizing price situation induced a sharp increase in the holding of financial assets in relation to GNP. In Japan the ratio of the broad money supply (M2) increased from around 65 percent in the early 1960s to nearly 90 percent in the early 1970s. In Taiwan the ratio increased from 20-some percent to around 50 percent, while in South Korea it increased from about 12 percent to about 38 percent (Chart 4.5). In all three countries, the rise in the M2 ratio was dominated by the interest-bearing bank deposits, which served as the main instruments of household savings[28] (Charts 4.6, 4.7, and 4.8). This situation permitted a rapid expansion of domestic credit in real terms in order to support a rapid growth of economic activity.

Mixed economic performances in Latin America

In sharp contrast with the East Asian countries, several countries in Latin America continued to experience rapid inflation and sluggish

CHART 4.4

JAPAN, TAIWAN, AND SOUTH KOREA

GROSS DOMESTIC SAVINGS IN RELATION TO GNP, 1953-83

(In percentages)

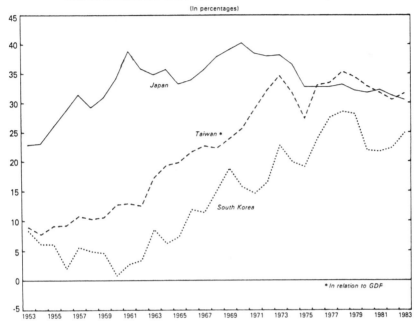

economic growth. In Argentina, real GDP increased only 2.6 percent per year from 1960 to 1973, compared to 4.8 percent from 1954 to 1960. In Chile, it increased 3.4 percent yearly compared to 2.8 percent. During this period, the CPI increased by 27 percent yearly in Argentina and 44 percent in Chile, not much different from the earlier period.

In both countries the poor macroeconomic performance in the 1960s was intimately related to the unimpressive growth of their exports. From 1961 to 1973, export earnings (in U.S. dollars) increased less than 9 percent per year in Argentina and slightly more than 7 percent in Chile (Table 4.10). These rates, while higher than in 1954 through 1960, were inadequate to inspire confidence. This, combined with the cyclical fluctuations of commodity exports (which continued to dominate the two countries' exports) and the lagging response of imports and investment to changes in export earnings, led to periodic external payments difficulties. The latter, combined with the continued rapid inflation, required frequent exchange rate devaluations. These devaluations were needed in order to keep domestic industry competitive, but they interacted with domestic factors to sustain the inflationary movements.

CHART 4.5

SELECTED COUNTRIES IN EAST ASIA AND LATIN AMERICA

THE RATIO OF M2 TO GNP, 1961-83

(In percent)

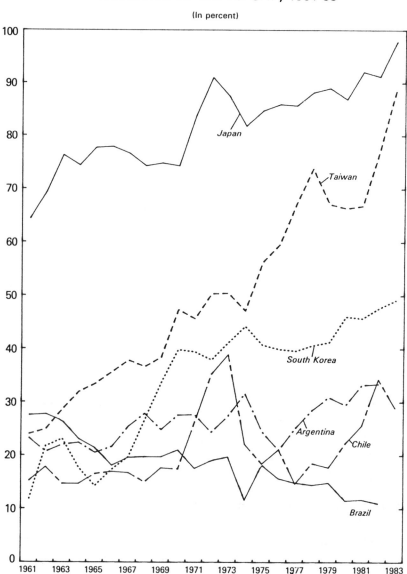

Another aspect of the poor economic performance in Argentina and Chile concerns the relatively slow growth of labor productivity and the rapid rise of unit labor costs. In Argentina, manufacturing labor pro-

CHART 4.6

JAPAN
M1, QUASI-MONEY, BONDS, AND OTHER
MONETARY LIABILITIES IN RELATION TO GNP, 1960-83
(In percent)

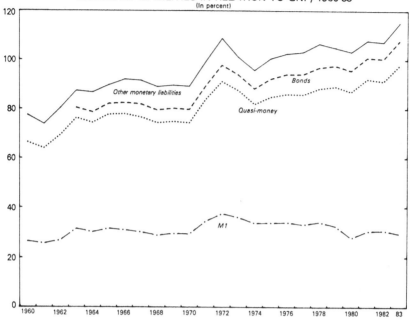

ductivity increased 4.9 percent yearly from 1961 to 1973, but nominal wages increased 29 percent per year, leading to a yearly increase
of unit labor costs of 23 percent. In Chile, the productivity growth
was even lower and the nominal wage growth even higher, creating an
increase in manufacturing unit labor costs of 41 percent per year
(Table 4.11).

In both Argentina and Chile, per capita real GDP increased slowly
at about 1.5 percent per year from 1961 to 1973, thereby restricting the growth of domestic savings. The Argentine savings ratio
remained flat at less than 20 percent of GNP throughout the 1960s,
while the Chilean ratio, following a strong gain in the first half
of the 1960s, fluctuated during the second half before declining steeply
during the early 1970s. The slow growth of domestic savings, combined with the persistent inflation, impeded the growth of financial
intermediation in both countries. During the 1960s, the ratio of quasi-
money to GNP remained flat at 6 to 7 percent in both Argentina and
Chile (Charts 4.9, 4.10, and 4.11). Both the higher inflation and the
slower growth of quasi-money hindered the expansion of the real

CHART 4.7
TAIWAN
M1, QUASI-MONEY, AND
OTHER MONETARY LIABILITIES IN RELATION TO GNP, 1961-83
(In percent)

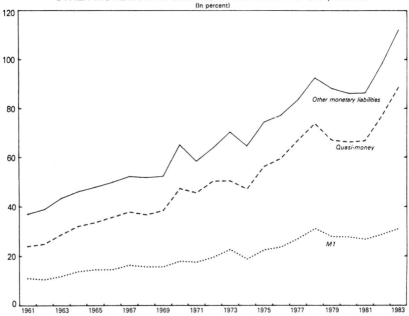

money supply and economic activity in both countries (Table 4.10).

Compared with Argentina and Chile, the economic performances of Mexico and Brazil were much more favorable. During 1960 to 1973 real GDP grew by 7 percent per year in Mexico, and by 8.3 percent in Brazil. In Mexico, the rapid economic growth was accompanied by stable domestic prices. The latter was achieved by prudent fiscal and monetary policies as well as exchange rate parity with the U.S. dollar. [29] However, due to an increased bias against exports in the Mexican incentive systems during the 1960s, export earnings (in U.S. dollars) increased by only 9 percent per year from 1960 to 1973. [30] Moreover, Mexico's savings ratio increased only moderately over time (from around 15 percent of GDP in the early 1960s to 18 to 19 percent in the early 1970s) because of rapid population growth and hence a moderate growth of per capita income. [31] Nevertheless, the growth process was helped by a sustained net inflow of foreign capital, while the stable domestic prices also permitted the authorities to provide an adequate growth of real money supply to support the expanding economic activity (Table 4.10 and Charts 4.12 and 4.13).

In Brazil the growth process accelerated in the second half of the

CHART 4.8
SOUTH KOREA
M1, QUASI-MONEY, AND
OTHER MONETARY LIABILITIES IN RELATION TO GNP, 1961-83
(In percent)

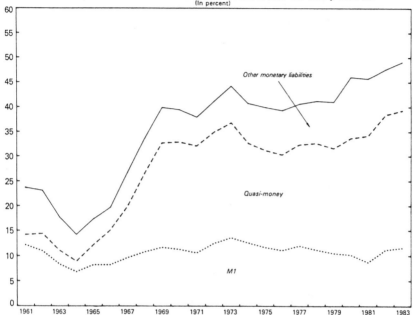

1960s in conjunction with a gradually stabilizing price trend. As distinct from the situation in Mexico, both net capital inflow and rapid export growth (particularly of manufactures) played a key role in raising the growth of domestic investment and real output. During the period from 1961 to 1973 the Brazilian export earnings increased by 13 percent yearly in dollar terms (18.5 percent during 1965 through 1973) while its per capita real output increased by 5.5 percent. This enabled a rise of the savings ratio from 15 percent in 1960 to nearly 25 percent in the early 1970s. The latter, combined with the stabilizing price trend, contributed to a sharp improvement in the domestic financial situation. (Tables 4.9 and 4.10 and Charts 4.12 and 4.14).

Consequences of Divergent Policy Responses to the Worsening in the Global Environment

Divergent policy responses to the worsening in the global environment

The weakness of the Latin American policy approach to economic

CHART 4.9

ARGENTINA AND CHILE

GROSS DOMESTIC SAVINGS AND GROSS DOMESTIC INVESTMENT IN RELATION TO GNP, 1953-83

(In percent)

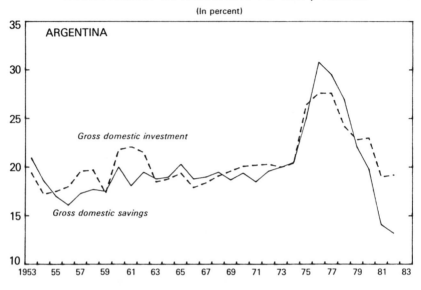

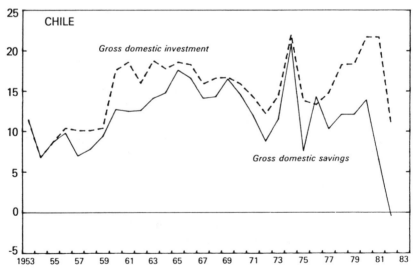

development and price stabilization became even more evident in the decade following the first oil shock of 1973/1974 when the world economic environment was generally less favorable. For the oil

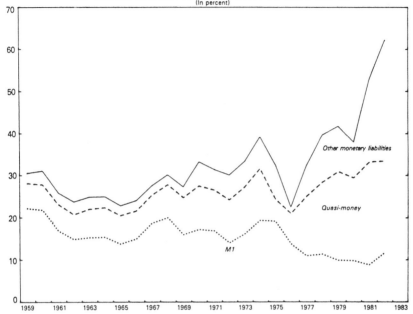

CHART 4.10

ARGENTINA
M1, QUASI-MONEY, AND OTHER
MONETARY LIABILITIES IN RELATION TO GNP, 1959-83
(In percent)

importing countries this worsening in the environment included a sharp rise in import costs (particularly of oil) and severe losses in terms of trade, a sharp slowdown and wide fluctuation in export demand, and, after the second oil shock (1979/1980), a sharp rise in real interest rates on external debt (Table 4.12). Taken together, these developments represented a sharp break in the global environment for the non-oil developing countries from the relatively predictable and steadily growing world economy of the 1960s. These changes made it more difficult to attain rapid economic growth while avoiding severe inflation and external payments difficulties. Faced with this situation, how should the national authorities have reacted—by maintaining their existing policy approach to sustain economic development, or by adjusting their policy emphasis in favor of short-term price stabilization in order to restore their external competitiveness and attain long-term economic growth?

The evidence indicates that the East Asian and the Latin American countries reacted quite differently to the worsening in their external

CHART 4.11

CHILE
M1, QUASI-MONEY, LONG-TERM EXTERNAL BORROWING, AND
OTHER MONETARY LIABILITIES IN RELATION TO GNP, 1960-83
(In percent)

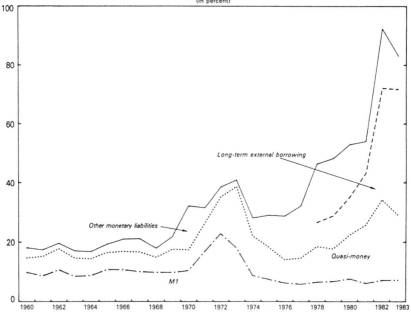

environments, thereby creating a further divergence in their economic performances. Specifically, the East Asian countries tended to respond to the ramifications of the first oil shock by adjusting their policy emphasis in favor of short-term price stabilization. This was achieved primarily by tightening monetary policy. Such an approach, while exacerbating the deflationary impact of the large losses in terms of trade, enabled these countries to stop the surging inflation resulting from the strong excess demand that existed in 1972 and 1973 and the sharp rise in import costs. The swift control of inflation, in turn, permitted them to recover their international competitiveness quickly, thereby attaining a rapid expansion of exports in the subsequent world economic recovery led by the U.S. economy. This pattern of development was most evident in Japan and Taiwan. Both countries recovered domestic price stability and eliminated the oil-related external deficit by 1976/1977[32] (Tables 4.13, 4.14, and 4.15 and Charts 4.1, 4.15, and 4.16).

Compared to Japan and Taiwan, South Korea was more aggressive in the use of foreign credit to sustain economic development and was

CHART 4.12

BRAZIL AND MEXICO

GROSS DOMESTIC SAVINGS AND GROSS DOMESTIC INVESTMENT IN RELATION TO GDP, 1960-83 AND 1953-83

(In percent)

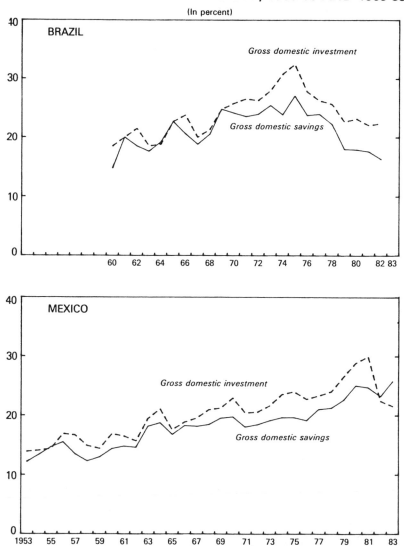

less vigorous in the pursuit of stabilization policies. Nevertheless, the Korean authorities maintained outward-looking policies despite severe worsening in the external environment, and they aggressively promoted

CHART 4.13

MEXICO

M1, QUASI-MONEY, LONG-TERM EXTERNAL BORROWING, AND OTHER MONETARY LIABILITIES IN RELATION TO GNP, 1962-83

(In percent)

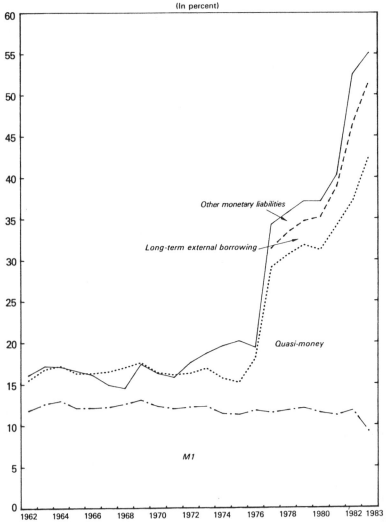

the sales of construction services to the Middle East. These efforts helped prevent the rise of the Korean debt-service ratio, despite the belated and less successful stabilization efforts (Tables 4.13, 4.14, 4.15 and Charts 4.1, 4.15, and 4.16).

In contrast with Japan and Taiwan, but similar to South Korea, many Latin American countries delayed pursuing stabilization policies while

Table 4.12

Evolution of World Trade Volume, Eurodollar Interest Rate, Non-Oil Developing Countries' Import Unit Value, Export Unit Value, and the Real Interest Rate of Their External Bank Debt, 1963–83 (In percent)

	Changes in world trade volume	Eurodollar rate (60–days)[1]	Non-oil developing countries			
			Changes in US$		Terms of trade	Real interest rate of Eurodollar credit[2]
			Import unit value	Export unit value		
1973	12.0	9.2	25.3	33.0	6.1	−17.9
1974	4.5	11.0	47.1	38.9	−5.6	−20.1
1975	−3.5	7.0	8.9	−1.0	−9.1	8.1
1976	11.0	5.6	0.9	7.1	6.1	−1.4
1977	5.0	6.0	7.5	14.5	6.5	−7.4
1978	5.5	8.9	9.6	5.4	−3.8	3.3
1979	6.5	12.1	18.6	19.5	0.3	−5.8
1980	2.0	14.2	20.5	16.0	−3.7	−1.6
1981	1.0	16.8	3.2	−1.8	−4.8	18.9
1982	−2.5	13.2	−3.2	−6.2	−3.1	20.9
1983	2.0	9.6	−4.3	−4.6	−0.3	14.9
Average:						
1963–72	8.5	6.1	2.1	2.2	0.1	3.8
1974–78	4.4	7.7	14.8	13.0	−1.6	−3.5
1979–83	1.8	13.2	7.0	4.5	−2.3	9.4

Sources: International Monetary Fund, *World Economic Outlook* (1982, 1984, and April 1986); *International Financial Statistics* (1983 Yearbook).

[1]At an annual rate.
[2]Figures in column 2 deflated by column 4, as an approximation.

relying on expanded external borrowing to sustain a higher rate of domestic demand. These policies enabled a stronger growth of the economy in 1974 and 1975, but they also resulted in the persistence of inflationary trends and the continuation of large current account deficits. Such a pattern of development was most evident in Brazil, whose terms of trade declined sharply but whose credit worthiness was high because of its great development potentials.[33] Similar policy behavior, to a lesser extent, was also discernible in Mexico and Peru, partly because of the availability of external credit in anticipation of rapid expansion in oil revenues. The latter, however, did not materialize until late in the 1970s and, as a consequence, both countries were compelled to pursue belated stabilization and adjust-

CHART 4.14

BRAZIL

M1, QUASI-MONEY, LONG-TERM EXTERNAL BORROWING, AND OTHER MONETARY LIABILITIES IN RELATION TO GNP, 1963-83

(In percent)

ment efforts in 1976 and 1977 in the aftermath of sharp deterioration in their external balances[34, 35] (Tables 4.13, 4.14, and 4.15 and Charts 4.2, 4.3, 4.17, and 4.18).

Moreover, as distinct from South Korea, which maintained outward-looking policies, both Brazil and Mexico relaxed their export promotion efforts and shifted their trade policies in favor of a renewed inward

CHART 4.15

JAPAN, TAIWAN, AND SOUTH KOREA

REAL DOMESTIC CREDIT EXPANSION, Q1 1965—Q4 1985

(Percentage change, current quarter over the corresponding quarter
in the previous year, deflated by average changes in the CPI and the WPI)

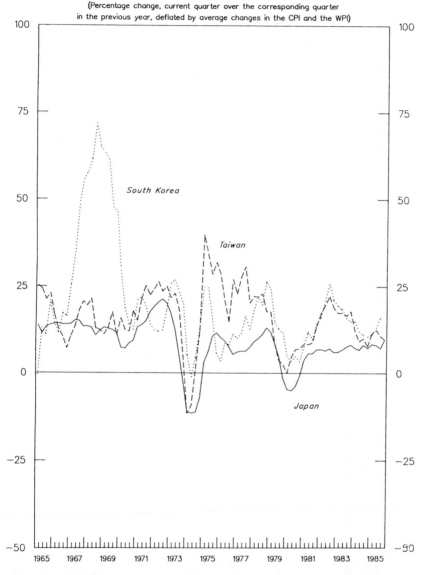

orientation. In Brazil this took the form of increased import controls, widespread tariff increases, and the establishment of a prohibitive prior deposit system.[36] In Mexico, also, import controls were tightened and tariffs increased while the exchange rate became increasingly overval-

Table 4.13

Selected East Asian and Latin American Countries: Real Output, Savings and Investment Ratios, Net Factor Income from Abroad, and Real Private Consumption, Selected Periods from 1965 through 1985 (Annual compound rate of changes, except ratios)

| | Before the oil shocks | | After the first oil shock | | | | After the second oil shock | |
	1965–70	1970–73	1973–74	1974–75	1975–78	1978–80	1980–82	1982–85
1. *Real output*								
Japan	11.2	7.5	-1.3	2.4	5.2	5.0	3.4	4.3
Taiwan	9.8	13.0	1.1	4.8	12.3	7.7	4.5	7.7
South Korea	12.5	9.8	7.9	7.5	11.2	2.0	6.2	8.4
Brazil	6.4	12.2	9.7	5.4	6.8	6.8	-0.4	8.6[2]
Mexico	6.8	7.0	6.1	5.6	5.3	8.8	3.6	0.5
Peru	4.4	5.7	6.9	2.4	0.4	3.5	2.0	-2.1
Chile	3.4	0.5	1.0	-12.9	7.2	8.0	-4.8	2.7
Argentina	4.5	3.7	6.3	-1.0	0.6	3.9	-5.4	0.3
2. *Gross savings ratio*[1]								
Japan	37.5	38.2	38.1	32.8	32.9	31.9	31.5	30.6[2]
Taiwan	23.2	31.9	31.7	27.3	33.8	33.8	31.4	32.0
South Korea	13.5	18.3	20.6	20.2	26.0	25.6	23.7	28.8
Brazil	22.5	24.9	24.6	28.1	24.7	20.3	20.8	19.3[3]
Mexico	19.6	19.7	21.0	21.0	21.6	26.0	27.4	28.8[2]
Peru	16.9	15.3	13.5	10.0	13.8	24.2	18.3	18.8
Chile	16.3	11.8	13.9	2.8	14.3	13.7	10.9	13.9
Argentina	20.3	22.2	22.7	19.0	29.6	23.6	19.5	21.2[3]

3. Gross investment ratio[1]								
Japan	36.3	36.5	37.3	32.8	31.4	32.8	30.6	28.3[2]
Taiwan	24.3	27.2	39.5	38.6	29.3	33.8	27.8	20.9
South Korea	25.0	24.2	31.4	29.6	27.8	33.2	27.5	28.8
Brazil	22.9	26.7	30.5	32.1	26.2	22.3	21.2	17.0[3]
Mexico	20.6	20.6	23.2	23.7	22.9	27.1	25.1	21.1
Peru	16.0	14.9	18.9	19.8	15.8	16.1	22.4	16.4[2]
Chile	15.9	13.9	13.5	6.3	16.0	19.6	17.0	12.0
Argentina	19.4	20.5	22.2	21.6	25.9	24.4	18.0	16.7[3]
4. Excess of savings ratio over investment ratio[1]								
Japan	1.2	1.7	0.8	—	1.5	-0.9	0.9	2.3[2]
Taiwan	-1.1	4.7	-7.8	-3.3	4.5	—	3.6	11.1
South Korea	-11.5	-5.9	-10.8	-9.4	-1.8	-7.6	-3.8	—
Brazil	-0.4	-1.8	-5.9	-4.0	-1.5	-2.0	2.5	2.3
Mexico	-1.0	-0.9	-2.2	-2.7	-1.3	-1.1	2.3	7.7
Peru	0.9	0.4	-5.4	-9.8	-2.0	8.1	-4.1	2.4
Chile	0.4	-2.1	0.4	-3.5	-1.7	-5.9	-6.1	1.9
Argentina	0.7	1.7	0.5	-2.6	3.7	-0.9	1.5	4.5
5. Net factor income from abroad[1]								
Japan	-0.3	—	-0.2	-0.1	—	—	-0.1	0.2[2]
Taiwan	-0.2	—	—	-0.5	-0.8	-0.2	-0.3	0.9
South Korea	1.0	-0.4	-0.9	-1.4	0.8	-0.8	-2.2	-3.4

Table 4.13 (continued)

	Before the oil shocks		After the first oil shock			After the second oil shock		
	1965–70	1970–73	1973–74	1974–75	1975–78	1978–80	1980–82	1982–85
Brazil	−0.9	−0.8	−0.8	−1.4	−1.8	−2.9	−4.6	−5.6[2]
Mexico	−0.9	−1.3	−1.7	−1.6	−2.2	−2.6	−4.5	−5.7
Peru	−2.1	−0.9	−0.8	−0.9	−2.6	−3.8	−2.9	−3.3[2]
Chile	−2.6	−0.9	−1.3	−3.2	−2.8	−3.2	−4.9	−8.6[3]
Argentina	−1.3	−1.2	−2.6	−2.6	−1.2	−0.9	−6.6	−8.8[3]
6. *Real private consumption*								
Japan	9.0	8.3	−2.8	3.9	3.8	3.0	3.8	2.9
Taiwan	8.2	10.7	5.0	6.4	7.5	9.9	4.0	7.1
South Korea	10.9	10.9	15.6	7.8	12.5	4.7	4.0	6.0
Brazil	4.2	15.9	18.8	3.4	12.9	15.3	−3.6	0.3[3]
Mexico	7.0	7.1	18.5	4.5	5.2	7.3	3.4	0.6
Peru	5.3	6.6	9.6	2.2	−1.3	5.6	0.6	−1.8[2]
Chile	1.7	23.7	28.3	4.2	16.7	10.3	−3.5	−1.4
Argentina	1.6	6.8	10.4	−2.3	−6.1	10.4	0.1	8.5[3]

Sources: International Monetary Fund, *International Financial Statistics* (various issues), except Taiwan, based on Council for Economic Planning and Development, *Taiwan Statistical Data Book, 1983* (Taipei, CEPD, 1983).

[1] As percent of GDP.
[2] For 1982–84.
[3] For 1982–83.

ued.[37] These policies contributed to the worsening of export performance and the persistence of balance of payments difficulties.

These differences in policy developments between the East Asian and the Latin American countries apparently largely stemmed from the divergent perceptions of the changes in the external environment that occurred in the 1970s. To the resource-poor, over-crowded East Asian countries, which must compete successfully in the international markets in order to grow, the sharp increase in energy costs and the marked slowdown in world export demand constituted a double squeeze, which had to be overcome through a further strengthening of their competitive positions. This explains why, in the aftermath of the first oil shock, there was a moderation of wage behavior in both Japan and Taiwan. In Japan, which had developed cooperative labor-management relations after the war, this moderation occurred without first involving large unemployment.[38]

In Taiwan, where organized labor activity had been severely restricted, wage moderation occurred also largely because of the slackening in labor demand. The moderation of wage behavior after the first oil shock not only helped domestic industry control the rise of unit labor costs and restore its export competitiveness, it also enabled the authorities to subsequently relax monetary policy in order to support the recovery of economic activity. For the same reasons, household savings were maintained at a high level in both Japan and Taiwan despite the slowdown in the growth of per capita income. In both countries, in response to the severe loss in the terms of trade, there was a marked slowdown in the growth of real private consumption, while the elasticity of exports rose relative to the reduced rate of growth in world export demand. These developments, helped by the recovery of export demand during 1976 and 1978, led to a quick elimination of the large external deficits (Tables 4.13, 4.14, and 4.15.).

By contrast, in the Latin American countries, which were well endowed with natural resources and whose exports were dominated by primary commodities, the upsurge of inflationary pressure in the world economy did not constitute a serious problem so long as their export prices rose. In fact, the market prices of non-oil primary commodities continued to surge in 1974, consonant with the jumps in oil prices, thus enabling many Latin American countries to realize large gains in export receipts. Moreover, to business enterprises in many of these countries whose domestic finances had been constricted by the persistence of inflation, the sharply increased availability of external credit after

Table 4.14

Selected East Asian and Latin American Countries: Terms of Trade, Nominal and Real Export Earnings, Export and Import Volumes, Export and Import Elasticities, Selected Periods from 1965 through 1985 (Annual compound rate of changes, except elasticities)

	Before the oil shocks		After the first oil shock			After the second oil shock		
	1965–70	1970–73	1973–74	1974–75	1975–78	1978–80	1980–82	1982–85
1. *Terms of trade*								
Japan	1.8	1.2	-23.2	-5.3	5.0	-18.0	3.1	4.0
Taiwan	1.3	-4.5	-10.9	-1.1	-1.5	-6.4	-5.7	0.8
South Korea	2.8	-2.2	-18.6	-9.8	8.4	-7.8	1.0	3.6
Brazil	0.2	2.7	-13.8	-8.1	4.3	-12.9	-9.3	1.5
Peru	-2.9	4.1	-3.1	-37.9	0.1	23.2	-12.0	-2.5
2. *Export Earnings* (US$)								
Japan	18.0	24.2	49.8	0.6	20.7	15.2	3.0	8.6
Taiwan	26.0	44.5	25.8	-5.9	33.7	24.9	5.5	11.8
South Korea	36.7	56.9	38.3	13.9	35.7	17.3	11.7	11.5
Brazil	11.4	31.2	28.2	9.0	13.4	26.1	0.1	8.3
Mexico	4.6	17.3	31.6	-2.8	27.0	61.6	16.7	1.4
Peru	8.6	2.4	35.2	-14.1	14.5	41.7	-8.1	3.3
Chile	14.4	-0.5	101.5	-37.4	16.9	26.1	-10.9	0.8
Argentina	3.5	22.6	20.4	-24.7	29.3	11.9	-2.5	3.2
3. *Import unit value* (US$)								
Japan	0.8	11.0	62.7	6.4	4.7	29.5	-2.3	-3.8
Taiwan	1.8	13.3	47.6	-4.0	7.5	22.9	5.2	-2.0
South Korea	-0.1	10.5	55.5	2.9	2.0	21.2	-1.2	-2.6

Brazil	1.5	11.5	46.2	8.8	4.5	23.8	3.6	−4.6
Mexico[1]	2.0	11.8	24.5	3.8	6.7	14.5	−3.7	−2.2
Chile[1]	1.6	8.6	28.5	6.7	7.4	10.0	4.2	−1.6
4. Real export earnings								
Japan	17.1	11.9	−7.9	−5.5	15.3	−11.0	5.4	12.9
Taiwan	23.8	27.5	1.0	−2.0	24.4	1.6	0.3	14.1
South Korea	36.6	42.0	−11.1	10.7	33.0	−3.2	13.1	14.5
Brazil	9.8	17.7	−12.3	9.2	8.5	1.9	−3.4	13.5
Mexico	2.5	4.9	5.7	−6.4	19.0	41.1	21.2	3.7
Peru	6.5	−8.4	8.6	−17.2	7.3	23.8	−4.6	−1.1
Chile	9.6	−8.3	61.8	−39.7	9.6	10.1	−7.5	3.1
Argentina	1.5	9.7	−3.3	−27.5	21.2	−2.3	1.2	5.5
5. Export volume								
Japan	11.7	10.6	19.9	−0.2	9.8	8.5	2.3	8.6
Taiwan	23.5	30.8	−4.4	0.2	26.3	8.6	6.3	13.2
South Korea	32.7	45.1	9.2	22.7	22.7	5.0	11.9	10.5
Brazil	9.2	14.6	1.7	9.0	4.0	8.8	6.5	11.8
Peru	2.4	−12.0	12.1	24.5	7.2	0.4	8.5	1.4
6. Import volume								
Japan	17.3	14.1	−0.9	−12.2	6.4	2.7	−1.2	3.6
Taiwan	20.5	17.1	24.5	−11.0	14.2	8.9	−8.3	3.1
South Korea	33.3	16.7	3.9	3.2	24.7	0.7	5.6	11.6
Brazil	19.3	20.9	38.5	−11.8	−1.1	4.0	−11.3	−7.9
Mexico[1]	7.4	3.5	27.6	4.5	−1.8	40.3	−8.5	−0.4
Peru[1]	−5.0	5.5	20.7	60.5	−14.2	−1.3	24.6	−18.4
Chile[1]	7.6	−4.4	35.4	−34.3	21.8	18.7	−20.3	−6.6
Argentina[1]	5.1	−2.0	30.9	−2.4	−7.2	44.8	−26.2	−8.6

Table 4.14 (continued)

	Before the oil shocks		After the first oil shock			After the second oil shock		
	1965–70	1970–73	1973–74	1974–75	1975–78	1978–80	1980–82	1982–85
7. *Export elasticity* (with respect to the growth of world import volume)[2]								
Japan	1.2			2.2			2.3	
Taiwan	2.9			3.3			3.4	
South Korea	4.1			4.6			3.2	
Brazil	1.2			1.0			3.2	
Peru	−0.1			2.7			1.1	
8. *Import elasticity* (with respect to the growth of real output)[2]								
Japan	1.6			0.3			0.5	
Taiwan	1.7			1.3			0.2	
South Korea	2.3			1.6			1.1	
Brazil	2.2			0.1			−1.2	
Mexico	0.9			0.7			1.3	
Peru	−0.3			1.2			−4.7	
Chile	1.4			6.3			−2.3	
Argentina	0.6			0.3			−4.8	

Sources: Author's estimate based on International Monetary Fund, *International Financial Statistics* (various issues), except Taiwan, which is based on Council for Economic Planning and Development, *Taiwan Statistical Data Book, 1983* (Taipei: CEPD, 1983).

[1] Changes in the import unit value of Argentina, Mexico, and Peru are approximated by changes in the export unit value of the industrial countries. Those of Chile are approximated by changes in the import unit value of Colombia.

[2] For the periods 1965–73, 1973–78, and 1978–85, respectively.

Table 4.15

Selected Countries in Asia and Latin America: Current Account Balance in Relation to Exports of Goods and Services, before and after the Oil Shocks[a] (In percent)

	Before the oil shocks		After the first oil shock			After the second oil shock		
	1967–73	1971–73	1974–75	1976–78	1979–80	1981	1982	1983
Japan	9.9	13.7	−3.6	10.5	−6.4	3.3	4.9	12.1
Taiwan	2.6	12.9	−13.1	15.1	−1.5	2.0	8.8	15.4
South Korea	−43.6	−27.7	−36.1	−3.9	−22.7	−17.2	−9.5	−5.6
Chile	−14.3	−29.4	−20.0	−16.9	−29.0	−84.3	−43.6	−21.7
Argentina	−3.3	−3.0	−16.7	18.8	−23.4	−39.4	−24.1	−25.0
Brazil	−29.4	−39.5	−74.9	−46.4	−57.7	−43.5	−69.4	−28.4
Mexico	−28.4	−26.8	−54.8	−32.1	−32.8	−45.8	−19.9	18.2

Source: International Monetary Fund.

[a] Current account includes goods, services, and private transfers.

CHART 4.16
BRAZIL, MEXICO, AND PERU
REAL DOMESTIC CREDIT EXPANSION, Q1 1965—Q4 1985
(Percentage change, current quarter over the corresponding quarter
in the previous year, deflated by average changes in the CPI and the WPI)

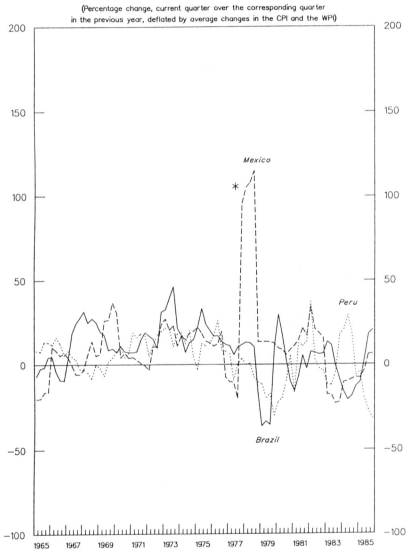

* Changes in the period from Q4 1977 through Q3 1978 are distorted by
expanded inclusion of private financial intermediaries in the data base,
beginning from December 1977.

the first oil shock might have appeared as a boon.[39] Besides, under the
circumstances then prevailing, the real interest cost of these credits
appeared negative or relatively low (Table 4.12). This explains why,

CHART 4.17
JAPAN, TAIWAN, AND SOUTH KOREA
REAL EFFECTIVE EXCHANGE RATE, 1965–85
(Index of national currency per unit of SDR, deflated
by the index of relative wholesale prices; 1970=100)

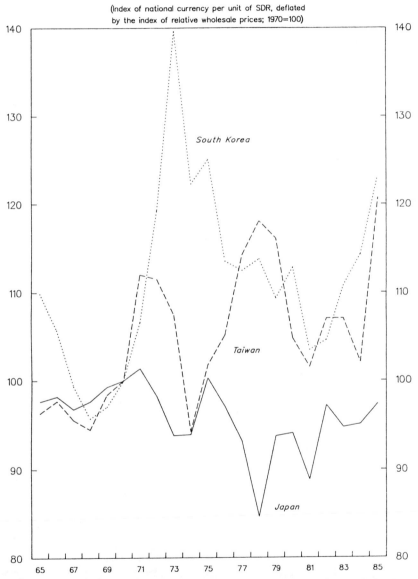

after the first oil shock, many governments in Latin America condoned or encouraged the expanded use of external credit in order to sustain a high rate of domestic investment and imports. It also explains why in countries such as Brazil and Mexico the growth of real wages and real

CHART 4.18

BRAZIL, MEXICO, AND PERU

REAL EFFECTIVE EXCHANGE RATE, 1965–85

(Index of national currency per unit of SDR, deflated
by the index of relative wholesale prices; 1970=100)

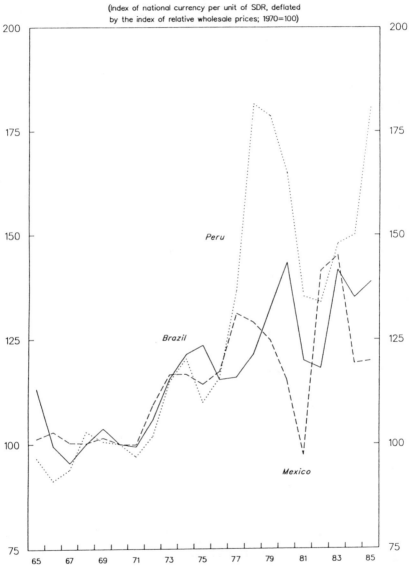

private consumption was not restrained in 1974 and 1975 despite the
severe loss in terms of trade (Brazil) or before the realization of the oil
bonanza (Mexico), thus contributing to the persistence of inflationary
pressure and balance of payments difficulties (Tables 4.13 and 4.14).

Further divergence in economic performance after the second oil shock

Unfortunately, this fortuitous situation did not last long. After the second oil shock, the world economy worsened as the major industrial countries pursued disinflation with much stronger monetary and fiscal restraints than before. As a consequence, in addition to the cumulatively large losses on terms of trade, many developing countries faced a sharp deterioration in their growth prospects because of the much worsened export demand and the sharp rise in real interest rates for external credit (Tables 4.12, 4.13, and 4.14). In particular, several Latin American countries suddenly found themselves saddled with ballooning service obligations on their large external debts, while their inflations accelerated to 100 or even several hundred percent per year (Tables 4.15 and 4.16 and Charts 4.2 and 4.3).

These economic difficulties, while exacerbated by the worsening of the global environment, were actually rooted in the authorities' failure to respond adequately to the ramifications of the first oil shock and to restore a sustainable pattern of economic growth. In several Latin American countries the reluctance to undertake adequate measures to control inflation for fear of depressing output and employment growth and the tendency to rely on indexation in order to ease the pains of inflation inevitably caused further deviations from equilibrium when the economy was subjected to repeated strong cost-push movements from abroad. Through exchange rate depreciations, wage adjustments, the revaluation of indexed public debt, and the resulting fiscal and monetary expansions, the exogenous and domestic inflationary factors tended to interact to cause a spiralling inflation after the two oil shocks. In Brazil, inflation, which did not subside following the first oil shock, accelerated sharply in 1979 when wage adjustments were changed from once to twice a year at a time when the economy was subjected to renewed import cost and balance of payments pressures.[40]

Even in Mexico and Peru, both benefiting from sharply rising oil revenues in the late 1970s, the ongoing inflation accelerated sharply in 1982 and 1983 when declining oil revenue and expanded external deficits compelled the authorities to increase recourse to deficit financing and sharp exchange depreciations (Tables 4.13, 4.14, and 4.15 and Charts 4.3 and 4.17). In Chile and Argentina also, where the worsening of inflation in the early 1970s stemmed from the expansion of fiscal deficit under the socialist or the labor-based regimes, subsequent ex-

Table 4.16

Debt and Debt Service Ratios of Selected Latin American and Asian Countries, 1970 and 1982 (In percentages)

	External public debt to GDP in relation to GDP		Debt service in relation to exports of goods and services	
	1970	1982	1970	1982
Brazil	7.1	16.9	12.5	42.1
Peru	12.6	33.5	11.6	36.7
Equador	13.2	34.3	2.5	30.8
Mexico	9.1	31.1	23.6	29.5
Boliva	47.1	39.1	11.3	28.2
Argentina	8.2	29.5	21.5	24.5
Chile	25.8	23.7	18.9	18.8
South Korea	20.4	28.3	19.4	13.1
Philippines	8.1	22.5	7.2	12.8
Thailand	4.9	7.4	3.4	8.4
Taiwan	—	12.0	2.6[1]	4.7

Sources: World Bank, *World Development Report, 1984*, pp. 248–249; and Central Bank of China (Taiwan), *Balance of Payments: Taiwan District* (September 1985).
[1] For 1974.

plosive movements (in Chile, 1973 to 1974, and in Argentina, 1975 to 1976, and again in 1982 to 1985) reflected both the unraveling of the accumulated economic disequilibria and the interactions between exchange depreciations and domestic wage and cost adjustments in the aftermath of external shocks[41] (Chart 4.2).

This persistence of rapid inflation was harmful. It encouraged speculative activity and hampered resource reallocation in favor of productive activity. It also discouraged the growth of financial assets, thereby inducing the Latin American authorities and businesses to overborrow in the 1970s when they were faced with easy credits in the international financial markets. During this period, several Latin American countries experienced capital inflows far in excess of the amount needed to finance their current account deficits. This occurred in Brazil and Mexico in most years of the 1970s and in Chile and Argentina in the second half of the decade.

In Chile and Argentina, these inflows were stimulated by the liberalization of capital flows and the sharp rise in the real domestic interest rates that occurred in conjunction with the authorities' experimentation with preannounced exchange rate devaluations as a means to influence inflationary expectations. Also, a significant part of these inflows was used to finance infrastructural projects, or, as in Chile, to purchase existing assets and enterprises in conjunction with the authorities' denationalization programs.[42] These activities, which contributed to a rapid expansion of external liabilities, did not help generate export earnings quickly. As a result, along with the worsening of export markets and the rise of international interest rates, the debt service burden increased rapidly, eroding the authorities' policy credibility and stimulating capital outflows.

In contrast with the worsened economic situations in many Latin American countries, both Japan and Taiwan had their inflation and external deficits well under control by the time of the second oil shock and so were able to absorb the adverse impacts of the renewed terms of trade losses and cost-push movements without suffering protracted economic difficulties. However, in both countries the growth of private investment stagnated despite stable domestic prices and high domestic savings and led to the accumulation of large trade surpluses and the intensification of protectionist pressures from their trading partners, particularly the United States (Chart 4.1 and Table 4.15).

Even South Korea, which was less vigorous in the pursuit of stabilization policies after the first oil shock, rapidly undertook strong stabilization and adjustment measures in 1980 and 1981 when it encountered serious internal and external imbalances as a result of the domestic overexpansion in 1977 and 1978 and the second oil shock. In addition to fiscal and monetary restraints, the government instituted a flexible management of the exchange rate while taking steps to liberalize financial markets, reduce import controls, and correct the biased investment strategy of the 1970s. By 1982 to 1983 these measures resulted in the stabilization of domestic prices, the improvement of the external balance, and the resumption of economic growth[43] (Tables 4.13, 4.14, and 4.15 and Charts 4.1, 4.15, and 4.16).

Thus, by 1983 and 1984, a decade after the first oil shock, economic conditions in the East Asian and the Latin American countries diverged even further. The East Asian countries, which had largely resolved the problems of inflation and external deficits caused by the two oil shocks, were poised to participate in the recovery in the world economy. By contrast, the Latin American countries, which had failed to resolve these problems, faced a difficult future. In fact, several of them were compelled to undertake strong stabilization and adjustment measures that resulted in severe declines of domestic absorption and economic growth. (Tables 4.13, 4.14, and 4.15, and Charts 4.17 and 4.18)

Conclusions

How can the Latin American countries break out of their present predicament and establish a sustainable pattern of economic growth? With inflation running at several tens or hundreds of percent per year and with heavy debt burdens, the tasks of stabilization and adjustment facing the national authorities are difficult indeed. It will be a miracle if these tasks are accomplished without incurring the heavy costs of economic slowdown or higher unemployment. In order to soften the adverse impacts of the stabilization and adjustment policies, it will be necessary to restructure and reschedule the Latin American countries' external debts in order to maintain the necessary imports. Such restructuring and rescheduling are needed not only to help the debtor countries, but also to help avoid a repetition of the isolationist and deflationary tendencies of the 1930s.

Meanwhile, to end the vicious circle of balance of payments crises, persistent inflation, and sluggish economic growth, the Latin American authorities need to undertake a thorough reexamination of their basic policy approaches to economic development and price stabilization. This comparative review of the development and stabilization experiences in East Asia and Latin America suggests that the differences in export expansion and price stabilization contributed crucially to the divergence of their economic performances both before and after the first oil shock. In the East Asian countries, the control of hyperinflation in the early postwar years and subsequent policy reforms in favor of export activity—along with the continuity of these policies—took advantage of the favorable external environment in the 1960s in order to attain rapid export growth and establish a sustainable pattern of economic growth. The faster export growth enabled higher investment and the attainment of economies of scale. The stabilization of domestic prices and the faster growth of per capita income facilitated the growth of domestic financial intermediation, thereby improving resource allocation and strengthening domestic price stability.

By contrast, the failure to control inflation and attain rapid export growth confined several Latin American countries to a vicious circle of balance of payments crises, persistent inflation, and sluggish economic growth even during the 1960s when the global environment was favorable. Such a pattern of development tended to constrict the growth of domestic savings and financial assets, thereby contributing to an excessive reliance on external credit. This pattern also induced several countries in the region to rely excessively on indexation arrangements which, while being helpful in reducing the pains of inflation, tended to distract the authorities from the urgency of undertaking the politically difficult stabilization policies.

These differences in the pattern of economic development and price stabilization were magnified in the decade after the first oil shock. While the East Asian countries, particularly Japan and Taiwan, acted strongly to control the resurgent inflation and restore their international competitiveness, many Latin American countries attempted to sustain domestic growth through expanded external borrowing and renewed inward-orientation of their development policies. The East Asian countries' successful stabilization and adjustment efforts after the first oil shock enabled them to surmount the economic problems caused by the second oil shock without protracted recessions. By contrast, the reliance on external credit and the increased use of indexing led the Latin American countries to serious debt-service problems and spiraling inflation after the second oil shock.

These contrasting developments indicate the importance of undertaking rapid stabilization and adjustment efforts in a world of increased uncertainty. It is ironical, but hardly surprising, that the Latin American countries, which had attempted to sustain domestic growth through enlarged external borrowing and renewed inward-orientation, should end with much worsened growth prospects, while the East Asian countries, which had placed more emphasis on controlling inflation and strengthening international competitiveness, should end with a brighter economic outlook.

In a longer term perspective, the contrasting developments between East Asia and Latin America during the postwar decades indicate the importance of the Latin American authorities undertaking fundamental policy reforms and sustained stabilization efforts to improve resource allocation and establish a viable pattern of economic growth. Without policy reforms, it is difficult to shift the entrepreneurial focus from inward-oriented to outward-oriented activity; without price stabilization, it is difficult to discourage speculative activity and to cultivate competitive attitudes compatible with the development of manufactured exports and the attainment of economic efficiency.

As the East Asian experiences indicate, the long-term beneficial effects of the improvement in the growth process far outweigh the temporary losses in output and employment that may be incurred by the stabilization programs and policy reforms. This is important because the resulting acceleration in the growth of income and employment enabled the East Asian countries to greatly improve the standards of living for the majority of the population while enabling the authorities to increasingly liberalize the economic system. Such liberalization, in turn, contributed to the improvement of resource allocation and the attainment of economic efficiency. By contrast, the failure to achieve a higher growth of income and employment made it more difficult for the Latin American countries to improve the standards of living for the majority of the population while impeding the reduction of government interventions and restrictions. The latter, in turn, restricted the authorities' choice of policy instruments for controlling inflation while hindering the attainment of economic efficiency.

These contrasting outcomes suggest the importance of stabilization efforts and policy reforms in the success of the East Asian economic development. This is a point that the Latin American countries cannot afford to ignore in their search for an alternate, workable model of economic development.

Epilogue

Following several years of unsuccessful stabilization attempts and facing new threats of runaway inflation, Argentina and Brazil finally moved to undertake more effective policy actions in June 1985 and February 1986. The new Argentine and Brazilian stabilization efforts, which coincided with those of Israel in July 1985 and of Bolivia in August 1985, are significant, considering their extraordinary policy mixes. The new policies, which were similar in the first three countries, combined fiscal and monetary stringency with wage-price controls and exchange rate fixing with the U.S. dollar.[44] These policies diverged not only from the conventional IMF approach, emphasizing strict fiscal and monetary controls, but also from the national authorities' past policy patterns aimed at maintaining real economic activity through widespread indexing. They therefore signified the authorities' new determination to do away with inertial inflation and to reestablish a pattern of economic growth based on stable domestic prices.

While the system of indexing enabled the authorities to maintain the real value of wages, exchange rates, financial instruments, and public debts, it tended to retard economic adjustment and cause further deviation from equilibrium when the economy was subjected to repeated price shocks and terms of trade losses. This, in fact, occurred in all three countries as inflation accelerated to the triple digit levels. Under the circumstances, the control of inflation through fiscal and monetary restrictions became costly and time-consuming because of inertial inflation under the widespread indexing. In fact, past attempts to use preannounced exchange devaluations to lower inflationary expectations in Argentina and Brazil failed because of incompatible policies on wages, public finance, and capital flows. Subsequent efforts by Brazil to reduce the fiscal deficit without the accompaniment of price control also proved difficult because of continued fiscal and monetary expansion necessitated by the indexed public debts.

The new policy approach is important. It attacked both the root cause and the mechanism of inflation. Nevertheless, both wage-price controls and exchange rate fixing can serve no more than a transitional purpose, because prolonged wage-price controls tend to create distortions in the factor and product markets while the fixed exchange rate tends to become overvalued under a basically unbalanced external payments situation. Over time, wage-price controls must be phased out and the exchange rate overvaluation corrected in order to improve market mechanism and resource allocation.

Compared with Argentina, Brazil, and Israel, Bolivia had little formal indexing, and its degeneration into hyperinflation and economic depression in the mid-1980s was caused by both stagnant commodity exports and the severe worsening of fiscal and monetary imbalances. As such, the Bolivian measures to control hyperinflation included strict fiscal and monetary controls, exchange rate determination through periodic auctions, decontrols of major commodity prices, and a public wage freeze.[45] Therefore, the Bolivian approach was more akin to the Chilean stabilization episode of 1973 to 1975. Both the Chilean and Bolivian stabilization efforts incurred heavy losses of real output and employment, although the Chilean process was more protracted because of inertial inflation under the indexed economy. In comparison, part of the Bolivian loss was associated with the retrenchment in the mineral sector and the paramilitary cocaine operation with the United States.

Compared with the Latin American experiences, the process of disinflation in Japan and Taiwan in the early postwar years was more rapid and less costly once the political situation settled down and serious stabilization efforts were initiated. This success was facilitated by the lack of formal indexing, the competitive functioning of the labor markets, and the availability of massive U.S. commodity aid. The last-mentioned item helped modify the shortage of daily essentials, the fiscal balance, and the slowdown of monetary expansion, whereas the first two helped reduce the output and employment costs of restrictive monetary policy. In addition, the control of monetary expansion in Taiwan was helped by the innovative creation of a special quasi-money deposit with a positive interest rate.[46]

Chapter 5

SUMMARY AND CONCLUSIONS

This chapter summarizes the divergent experiences of the East Asian and the Latin American countries with respect to export expansion, economic growth, and price stabilization, and discusses the policy implications for the Latin American countries from the perspectives of the East Asian countries.

Divergence in the Pattern of Economic Growth before the First Oil Shock

During the period before the first oil shock, the pattern of economic growth diverged widely between the East Asian and the Latin American countries. While the East Asian countries experienced a virtuous circle of rapid export expansion, higher economic growth, and stable domestic prices, several Latin American countries experienced a vicious circle of balance of payments crises, persistent inflation, and sluggish economic growth. A strategic link in the divergence of their growth patterns concerned the growth of export earnings that accelerated sharply in the East Asian countries during the 1960s while remaining relatively modest in many Latin American countries.

The Mechanism of the Virtuous Circle in the East Asian Growth Process

In the East Asian countries, the rapid growth of export earnings in the 1960s and the attendant improvement in their credit worthiness enabled them to remove the dual constraints of foreign exchange shortages and low domestic savings, thereby raising domestic investment and imports. This, and the development of manufactured exports in line with their dynamic comparative advantage, enabled the East Asian countries to raise productivity growth and overall economic efficiency. The higher productivity growth restrained the rise of unit labor costs, and this growth, plus the stable import prices then prevailing, facilitated the maintenance of domestic price stability. These developments were helped by the rising savings ratio resulting from the accelerated growth of per capita income, and by the improvement of domestic finances facilitated by the stable domestic prices.

The Mechanism of the Vicious Circle in the Latin American Growth Process

By contrast, in several Latin American countries, the failure to expand exports and the lagging response of domestic investment and imports to cyclical changes in primary exports caused periodic balance of payments difficulties. This, and the continued pursuit of inward-oriented development policies, sustained the inflationary pressure through frequent exchange depreciations, wage adjustments, and fiscal and monetary expansion. Under this pattern of development, the growth of labor productivity and per capita income remained modest, limiting the growth of real wages. The latter in turn restricted the authorities' policy option for controlling inflation. Instead, the authorities tended to devise various indexation schemes in order to ease the pains of inflation. Meanwhile, the slow growth of per capita income impeded the growth of domestic savings, and this, combined with the persistent inflation, tended to restrain the growth of domestic finances. These developments tended to interact and thus perpetuate the vicious circle.

The Control of Hyperinflation and the Reform of Key Institutions and Trade Policies in East Asia

The virtuous circle experienced by the East Asian countries, while helped by the favorable global environment in the 1960s, did not emerge by itself; it followed the authorities' success in controlling the rapid inflation that raged in the early postwar years. In addition, various institutional reforms were undertaken in Japan in order to defuse the social tensions in the rural areas, to develop more cooperative labor management relations, to institute fiscal discipline, and to improve financial intermediation between savings and investment. In

Taiwan and South Korea also, in addition to land reforms in the early 1950s, intensive reforms in trade policies were carried out in the late 1950s and the early 1960s to shift the overall thrust of policy incentives in favor of export activity. In both countries these reforms were supported by strong stabilization policies to control the resurgent inflation resulting from currency devaluations and other specific factors. These policy efforts enabled the East Asian countries to take advantage of the favorable global environment in order to establish a sustainable pattern of economic growth.

The Inadequacy of Stabilization Efforts and Trade Policy Reforms in Latin America

By contrast, in many Latin American countries both the stabilization efforts and trade policy reforms were inadequate because the rich natural resources and the cyclical expansion of primary exports permitted the removal of the foreign exchange constraint from time to time, thereby enabling the authorities to continue the pursuit of inward-oriented industrial development. Because of this, in both Chile and Argentina, the inflationary pressure remained strong and the incentive systems remained biased against exports. Consequently, both countries failed to establish a sustainable pattern of economic growth in the 1960s despite the favorable external environment.

Compared to Chile and Argentina, Brazil attained an accelerated growth of exports and real output in the second half of the 1960s while significantly reducing its inflation rate. The improvement in the Brazilian economic performance followed major policy reforms in the mid-1960s. These reforms included a significant strengthening of export incentives, a sharp reduction in fiscal deficit, and the institution of various indexation schemes, which initially helped reduce the wage adjustment rate while preventing the contraction of domestic finances.

However, the success of the Brazilian stabilization efforts in the late 1960s owed more to its trade and fiscal policies than to the indexations. This was evident from the poor economic performance of Chile in the same period, where the use of indexations was equally pervasive. In contrast with Brazil, however, Chile did not significantly strengthen its export incentives while its fiscal deficit remained large during the second half of the 1960s before expanding even further in the aftermath of the unsuccessful socialist experiment.

The Extensive Policy Reforms in Chile and Argentina during the 1970s and Their Outcomes

This failure to establish a sustainable pattern of economic growth over a long period induced the Chilean and the Argentine authorities to experiment with more comprehensive liberalization and stabilization measures in the 1970s. The Chilean program, which began in September 1973, initially attempted to control inflation by sharply reducing the large fiscal deficit. This was accompanied by extensive exchange devaluations, price decontrols, and the suppression of labor union activity. Meanwhile, the government gradually liberalized the financial market, sharply reducing the tariff rates, while returning the properties taken over by the previous government. As a result of these policies, the fiscal deficit was sharply cut back but the decline in the rate of inflation was slow and unemployment increased sharply.

These situations led to the experiment of preannounced exchange devaluations in June 1976 as a way of influencing inflationary expectations. This new approach was complemented by more drastic tariff reductions and a gradual deregulation of capital inflows. The rate of inflation then declined to around 40 percent in 1978 and a vigorous economic recovery occurred, partly because of a more favorable external environment. Meanwhile, large capital inflows occurred to finance growing imports of consumer goods and various domestic service activities. In June 1979 the authorities shifted to a passive monetary policy by fixing the peso to the U.S. dollar. This action, given the appreciation of the U.S. dollar and the expansion in the current account deficit associated with the second oil shock, led to increasing overvaluation of the Chilean currency. In addition, domestic interest rates and real wages rose sharply. These developments led to mounting business failures and sharply higher unemployment, thereby compelling the authorities to undertake repeated exchange rate devaluations and to reintroduce exchange controls, while intervening to rescue the faltering banks and businesses.

The Argentine program, which began in March 1976, placed more emphasis on opening up the economy than on controlling inflation. The measures included exchange rate devaluations through indexing, withdrawal of numerous quantitative restrictions and of the heavy taxes on traditional exports, and a step-by-step reduction of the high tariffs. Meanwhile, the authorities moved to decontrol the banking system and interest rates on time deposits, while significantly removing the barriers on international capital flows. Moreover, the government took steps to remove price controls, relax guidelines on minimum wages, and compel public enterprises to reduce operation deficits. These policies led to a significant reduction in fiscal and external payments deficits, but inflation continued at triple digit rates despite the stagnant economic conditions.

These situations led the authorities to experiment with the preannounced exchange devaluations in December 1978, as in Chile, while further relaxing the restrictions on capital flows and intensifying the tariff reduction program. As a consequence of these policies, inflation slowed down further, but the real interest rates shot up sharply, inducing massive capital inflows. Meanwhile, increased market competition and rising financial and wage costs led to mounting business failures and a financial crisis in early 1980. These developments prompted the central bank to intervene to rescue the failing banks, but the economic conditions continued to deteriorate, thereby inducing huge capital outflows and eventual currency devaluations. In 1982, six years after the stabilization and liberalization programs, the Argentine inflation was back to the situation existing before the new programs. The business sector was in deep financial difficulties, and the nation was saddled with huge external debts.

The Problems with the Southern Cone Reform Attempts in Light of the East Asian Reform Experiences

The operation of the Southern Cone reform programs was undoubtedly complicated by the worsening of the global environment after the second oil shock. In addition, both the policy mix and time sequence of these programs may have caused undue difficulties for the economy. This is evident when they are compared with the successful policy approaches of Taiwan and South Korea in the 1960s.

(1) In both Chile and Argentina the control of hyperinflation and the liberalization of the economy occurred largely at the same time. This greatly compounded the difficulties of the domestic industries by forcing them to cope with both the deflationary effects of the stabilization policies and the increased competition of foreign producers at the same time. This contrasted sharply with the situation in Taiwan and South Korea, where the control of hyperinflation preceded intensive trade policy reforms by several years.

(2) In both Chile and Argentina, the reform of trade policies consisted primarily of removing quantitative import restrictions and reducing import tariffs. By contrast, in both Taiwan and South Korea, the improvement of export incentives dominated the initial stage of the reform, while the removal of quantitative controls and the reduction of import tariffs followed the successful expansion of exports. In both countries, the initial relaxation of import controls applied mostly to the duty-free imports of intermediate products for use in the export products.

(3) In conjunction with the trade liberalization measures, both Chile and Argentina largely removed the restrictions on capital flows. This initially led to the overvaluation of the currency, thereby retarding the growth of exports. Subsequently, this removable of restrictions exacerbated the balance of payments deficits by permitting large speculative capital outflows. By contrast, in Taiwan and South Korea, the inflow of foreign capital, while actively solicited, was linked more directly to trade and productive activities.

Brazil's Policy Response to External Shocks in the 1970s Compared to Taiwan and South Korea

Following the two oil shocks in the 1970s, the divergence in economic conditions between the East Asian and the Latin American countries became even stronger. By the early 1980s, the East Asian countries had largely surmounted the economic difficulties posed by the oil shocks and the subsequent worsening in the world economy. By contrast, many more Latin American countries (including Brazil and Mexico) which were relatively successful in attaining rapid economic growth and stable domestic prices during the 1960s joined the ranks of countries with hyperinflation, burdensome external debt, and stagnant domestic growth.

The further divergence in economic performances between the East Asian and the Latin American countries stemmed mainly from the following factors.

(1) The East Asian countries were much faster than the Latin American countries in undertaking a restrictive monetary policy to stop the resurgent inflation resulting from the export boom of 1972 and 1973 and the oil shock of 1974. By contrast, Brazil and several other Latin American countries attempted to sustain domestic growth through increased external borrowing, while maintaining real wages

through indexation despite the sharp decline in terms of trade. In addition, while the East Asian countries maintained their outward-looking policies, Brazil placed a renewed emphasis on import-substituting industrialization by severely tightening import restrictions and raising import tariffs.

(2) These differences in policy response to the first oil shock resulted in a divergence of economic conditions between the East Asian and the Latin American countries. Because of the rapid control of inflation, the East Asian countries quickly regained their international competitiveness, thereby eliminating the oil related external deficits in the cyclical recovery of world export demand in 1976 through 1978. Even South Korea, relatively slow in controlling inflation while more aggressive in the use of external credit, participated in the export recovery, thereby restraining the rise of the debt service burden. By contrast, many Latin American countries lagged in the control of inflation while failing to fully participate in the world export recovery, thereby continuing to rely on large external borrowing in order to sustain domestic growth.

(3) With the outbreak of the second oil shock and the sharp rise in the real interest rate following the earnest pursuit of disinflation in the United States, both the inflation and external deficits of many Latin American countries inevitably worsened. The sharply increased debt burden under the much worsened export prospects led to a sudden change in the perception of credit worthiness in these countries, thereby compelling the national authorities to undertake the long-delayed stabilization and adjustment efforts. By contrast, the well-adjusted East Asian countries were able to surmount the economic difficulties posed by the second oil shock relatively quickly, and regain export and economic growth in the U.S.-led world economic recovery in 1983. Even South Korea, which experienced severe economic difficulties in 1979 through 1980 because of domestic overexpansion, quickly undertook strong stabilization and adjustment efforts, regained internal and external balances, and resumed economic growth during 1982 and 1983.

The Need for a Thorough Reexamination of Basic Policy Approaches to Economic Development and Price Stabilization in Latin America

The failure to achieve a sustainable pattern of economic growth under the favorable environment of the 1960s and the severe worsening of economic performance in the decade after the first oil shock indicate that many Latin American countries need to undertake a thorough reexamination of their basic policy approaches to economic development and price stabilization in order to break away from the vicious circle of balance of payments crises, persistent inflation, and sluggish economic growth. Both the experiences of the Latin American and the East Asian countries indicate that the achievement of rapid export growth is a prerequisite to the establishment of a sustainable pattern of economic growth. For this purpose, the Latin American countries must not only undertake various policy reforms in order to shift policy incentives in favor of export activity, but must also pursue intensive stabilization efforts in order to cultivate a mentality compatible with export and productivity growth and to establish a financial pattern conducive to the growth of domestic savings and financial intermediation. Instead of relying on various indexation schemes and excessive external borrowing, the authorities must undertake the necessary measures to improve the fiscal balance, to restrict excessive monetary expansion, and to promote short-term wage moderation in order to attain long-term real wage growth through lower inflation and higher income growth.

These policy prescriptions, by emphasizing the importance of price stabilization, support the basic tenets of the conventional stabilization program as practiced by the International Monetary Fund. In addition, the experiences of both the East Asian and the Latin American countries indicate the importance of achieving rapid export growth before proceeding with massive import liberalization in order to lessen the pains of adjustment. Similarly, it is important to link the encouragement of capital inflows more directly to export and investment activity in order to avoid undue fluctuations of the external balance and exchange rate.

NOTES

Chapter 2

1. For a similar point of view, see Gustav Ranis, "Challenges and Opportunities Posed by Asia's Superexporters: Implications for Manufactured Exports from Latin America," in Werner Baer and Malcolm Gillis (eds.), *Export Diversification and the New Protectionism: The Experiences of Latin America* (Champaign, Ill.: University of Illinois, 1981).

2. On the factor intensity and market orientation of Taiwan's manufactured exports, see Ching-yuan Lin, "Industrial Development and Changes in the Structure of Foreign Trade," *Staff Papers* (15:2, 1968). On Korea, see Wontack Hong, "Export Promotion and Employment Growth in South Korea," in Anne O. Krueger, et al. (eds.), *Trade and Employment in Developing Countries. I. Individual Studies* (Chicago: University of Chicago Press, for National Bureau of Economic Research, 1981).

3. Export earnings increased by about 12.5 percent per year in terms of U.S. dollars in both Australia and Canada from 1961 to 1973 while real GDP increased by 5.1 and 5.6 percent, respectively. For the much lower Chilean and Argentine growth rates, see Table 1.

4. While Chile and Argentina differed widely from Taiwan and South Korea in population density, natural resource base, and cultural heritage, they were much alike in the stage of their industrialization efforts and the quality of their labor forces.

5. On the early history of industrialization in Chile and Argentina, see Markos J. Mamalakis, *The Growth and Structure of the Chilean Economy: From Independence to Allende* (New Haven: Yale University Press, 1976); and Carlos F. Diaz-Alejandro, *Essays on the Economic History of the Argentine Republic* (New Haven: Yale University Press, 1970).

6. On the early history of industrialization in Taiwan and South Korea, see Ching-yuan Lin, *Industrialization in Taiwan, 1946–1972: Trade and Import-Substitution Policies for Developing Countries* (New York: Praeger Publishers, 1973); S. C. Suh, *Growth and Structural Changes in the Korean Economy, 1910–1940* (Cambridge, Mass.: Harvard University, 1978); and Paul W. Kuznets, *Economic Growth and Structure in the Republic of Korea* (New Haven: Yale University Press, 1977).

7. In Taiwan, the foreign exchange controls and so forth generated a "pull" effect, whereas the land reforms generated a "push" effect in the reallocation of rural financial resources and manpower. See Lin, ibid., p. 52.

8. On Chile, see Jere R. Behrman, *Foreign Trade Regimes and Economic Development: Chile* (New York: National Bureau of Economic Research, 1976); on Argenti-

na, see the article by Julio Berlinski and Daniel M. Schydlowsky in Bela Balassa and associates, *Development Strategies in Semi-Industrial Economies* (Baltimore: Johns Hopkins University Press, 1982); on Taiwan, see Lin, ibid.; on South Korea, see the article by Larry Westphal and Kwang Suk Kim in Bela Balassa and associates, op. cit.

9. For a sympathetic argument justifying the employment of these instruments during the transitional phase of import-substituting industrialization, see Douglas S. Pauuw and John C. Fei, *The Transition in Open Dualistic Economies* (New Haven: Yale University Press, 1973).

10. Such an argument was first presented in Ching-yuan Lin, "From Import Substitution to Development of Manufactured Exports: The Need for Policy Reorientation in the Process of Industrialization" (International Monetary Fund, DM/72/68, July 1972).

11. Such a sequence was first observed in Japan in K. Akamatsu's article, "A Historical Pattern of Economic Growth in Developing Countries," *The Developing Economies*, preliminary issue (May-August 1962).

12. In Argentina, from the fall of the first Peronist government in 1955 to the military coup of 1976, there were 11 presidents (five of them military); in Chile, from the mid-1950s to the fall of Allende in 1973, governments of different ideologies succeeded each other. On Argentina, see Gary W. Wynia, *Argentina in the Postwar Era: Politics and Economic Policy Making in a Divided Society* (Albuquerque, New Mexico: University of New Mexico, 1978). On Chile, see Barbara Stallings, *Class Conflict and Economic Development in Chile, 1958–1973* (Stanford, Stanford University Press, 1978).

13. Note that these changes in relative incentives were not just between tradables and nontradables, but, more importantly, between export and domestic sales among the tradables. These changes cannot be accomplished by exchange rate devaluations alone.

14. For details of these policy changes, see Lin, *Industrialization in Taiwan, op. cit.*, Chapter 5.

15. In the early 1950s, the domestic prices of many import substitutes exceeded the c.i.f. costs of comparable imports by 20 to 300 percent. By the early 1960s, this was reduced to a range of negative 50 percent and positive 100 percent, and by the mid-1960s, to a range of negative 100 and positive 70 percent. For these estimates, see the tables in Lin, *Industrialization in Taiwan, op. cit.*, pp. 51 and 112.

16. A manufacturer-cum-exporter of cotton yarn received NT$15.55 per US$ for his export earnings in the second half of 1953, compared to NT$22.13 for domestic sale of the same product. Because of the policy changes summarized in the text, however, in the first half of 1966, he received NT$66.35 per US$ of export earnings compared to NT$46.10 for domestic sales. For these estimates, see Lin, *Industrialization in Taiwan, op. cit.* pp. 113–115.

17. The delay in the Korean reform, compared to Taiwan, may be explained by the facts that (1) import-substituting industrialization started earlier in Taiwan than in South Korea; (2) the Korean price stabilization was achieved later than in Taiwan because of disruptions caused by the Korean war; and (3) the bigger size of the domestic markets for import substitutes in South Korea than in Taiwan.

18. Similar conferences or councils for export promotion were also established in Japan and Taiwan. In Japan, in addition to the Ministry of International Trade and Industry (MITI) and the semiautonomous Japan External Trade Organization (JETRO), an export conference, with the participation of concerned government agencies and industrial representatives and with the prime minister as chairman, was established in 1954 to expedite matters related to export promotion. In Taiwan, a cabinet-level Council (which underwent several changes of name over time), with the participation of concerned government agencies, existed from the early 1950s to serve similar

purposes. On South Korea, see Gilbert T. Brown, *Korean Pricing Policies and Economic Development in the 1960s* (Baltimore: Johns Hopkins University Press, 1973), p. 145. On Japan, see Japan External Trade Research Center, *Sengo-Nihon-no Boeki Nijiu-Nen Shi* (Twenty-Year History of Japan's Postwar External Trade) III (Tokyo: International Trade and Industry Research Association, 1961). On Taiwan, Foreign Trade Council, *Wai-Mao-Fei Shih-Shu-Nien* (Fourteen Years of Foreign Trade Council) (Taipei: Foreign Trade Council, 1969), II.

19. Jere R. Behrman, *op. cit.*, pp. 110–114.

20. Julio Berlinski and Daniel M. Schydlowsky, in Balassa and associates, *op. cit.*, pp. 88–90.

21. The rate of effective protection relates the joint effects of protective measures on the price of the product and the prices of its inputs to value added in the production process. The protective measures considered include, in addition to import duties, indirect taxes, quantitative restrictions, export taxes and subsidies, and advanced deposits for import payments. See Bela Balassa and associates, *Development Strategies in Semi-Industrial Economies* (Baltimore: Johns Hopkins University, 1982), pp. 3–4.

22. The shift in the relative incentive measures between all industries and manufacturing in Taiwan and South Korea resulted from the fact that agriculture and mining received negative incentives for domestic sales in Taiwan while agricultural production was heavily protected in South Korea.

23. These estimates are based on studies by Julian Berlinski and Daniel M. Schydlowsky on Argentina, T. H. Lee and Kuo-Shu Liang on Taiwan, and Larry E. Westphal and Kwang Suk Kim on South Korea, published in Bela Balassa and associates, *op. cit.* See also the summary chapters by Balassa.

24. See Teresa Jenneret, "Structure of Protection in Chile," in Bela Balassa, *The Structure of Protection in Developing Countries* (Baltimore: Johns Hopkins University Press, 1971), p. 159.

25. Jere R. Behrman, *op. cit.*, p. 138. For 1961, Behrman shows an alternative estimate of 133 percent for all goods production.

26. These high protection rates were partly responsible for inducing many U.S. and European automobile producers to establish production facilities in Argentina during the early 1960s. However, production costs were high owing to low labor productivity and the small scale of production caused by the large number of firms producing a wide variety of frequently changing models. See Rhys Jenkins, "The Rise and Fall of the Argentine Motor Vehicle Industry," in Rich Kronish and Kenneth S. Mericle (eds.), *The Political Economy of the Latin American Motor Vehicle Industry* (Cambridge, Mass.: The MIT Press, 1984).

27. On Taiwan's price stabilization efforts in the early 1950s and 1959–1960, see Lin, *Industrialization in Taiwan, op. cit.*, pp. 33–38 and 78–82. On South Korea's experience during the 1950s and the 1960s, see David C. Cole and Yung Chul Park, *Financial Development in Korea, 1945–1978* (Cambridge, Mass.: Council on East Asian Studies, Harvard University, 1983), Chapter 8.

28. For a more detailed discussion of this issue, see the author's "Controlling Rapid Inflation in East Asia versus Latin America" (Draft, International Monetary Fund, April 1986).

29. Such indexing was more widespread in Chile than in Argentina. In Argentina, formal indexing was limited to government bonds and the tax system. For details, see Gustav Donald Jud, *Inflation and the Use of Indexing in Developing Countries* (New York: Praeger Publishers, 1978), Chapters 2 and 3.

30. The real exchange rate is defined here as the index of national currency per unit of U.S. dollar, deflated by the index of relative wholesale prices.

31. For more details of Taiwan's agricultural performance, see Teng-hui Lee,

Intersectoral Capital Flows in the Economic Development of Taiwan, 1889–1960 (Ithaca: Cornell University Press, 1971); and Yih-Min Ho, *Agricultural Development of Taiwan, 1903–60* (Nashville, Tenn.: Vanderbilt University Press, 1966). On Korea, see Sung Hwan Ban, "Agricultral Growth in Korea, 1918–1971" in Y. Hayami, V.W. Ruttan, and H.M. Southworth (eds.), *Agricultural Growth in Japan, Taiwan, Korea, and the Philippines* (Honolulu: University of Hawaii, 1979).

32. This was led by the U.S. and China Joint Commission for Rural Reconstruction.

33. During this period, food prices were not a major contributing factor to the acceleration of inflation, except for two brief periods during the late 1960s and the mid-1970s.

34. For the Chilean government's neglect of the agricultural sector, see Markos Mamalakis and Clark Winston Reynolds, *Essays on the Chilean Economy* (New Haven: Yale University Press, 1965), pp. 138–141. On Argentina, see Eugenio A. Maffucci and Lucio G. Reca, "Agricultural Exports and Economic Development: The Case of Argentina," in Nurul Islam (ed.), *Agricultural Policy in Developing Countries* (New York: John Wiley and Sons, 1974), pp. 233–234.

35. In the table, the Korean agricultural value added per hectare of agricultural land was estimated to be somewhat higher in Taiwan, despite its lower labor productivity and per hectare cereals output. This bias may have resulted from the relatively high Korean agricultural prices.

36. Average female earnings in Taiwan's manufacturing industry ranged from 50 to 60 percent of average male earnings through the years in the 1960s. See for example, Walter Galenson, "The Labor Force, Wages, and Living Standards," in Walter Galenson (ed.), *Economic Growth and Structural Change in Taiwan* (Ithaca: Cornell University Press, 1979), p. 417.

37. In fact, based on a U.N. study in 1970, no country in Latin America had a female labor force participation rate more than 31 percent, compared to nearly 41 percent in both Taiwan and South Korea. See United Nations (CEPAL), *Five Studies on the Situation of Women in Latin America* (Santiago, Chile: United Nations, 1983), p. 160.

38. In this work, productivity growth is measured against labor input instead of total factor inputs in order to explain the movement of unit labor costs. Available estimates of economy-wide total factor productivity growth show similar divergence between Taiwan and South Korea on the one hand and Chile and Argentina on the other. For the period 1955–1970, this growth is estimated at 4.3 and 5.0 percent per year for Taiwan and South Korea, and 1.2 and 0.5 percent per year for Chile and Argentina. See E. K. Chen, "Factor Inputs, Total Factor Productivity, and Economic Growth: The Asian Case," in *The Developing Economies* (15:121–143, 1977); V. Elias, "Sources of Economic Growth in Latin American Countries," in *Review of Economics and Statistics* (60:363–370, 1978); and Jaime de Melo, "Sources of Growth and Structural Change in Korea and Taiwan: Some Comparisons" in Vittorio Corbo, Anne O. Krueger, and Fernando Ossa (eds.), *Export-Oriented Development Strategies: The Success of Five Newly Industrializing Countries* (Boulder, Col.: Westview Press, 1985).

39. The efficiency of capital as defined here relates the growth of real output to the growth of capital stock. Its relation with labor productivity is shown as $Y/L = (K/L)(Y/K)$, where Y/L, K/L, and Y/K indicate, respectively, real output per employee, capital stock per employee, and real output per unit of real capital stock.

40. The inverse relationship between the ICOR and the growth rate of real output was first observed by Ohkawa and Rosovsky with regard to Japan and was later confirmed by other researchers in many other countries. See K. Ohkawa and H.

Rosovsky, "Economic Fluctuations in Prewar Japan," *Hitotsubashi Journal of Economics* (October 1962); H. Leibenstein, "Incremental Capital-Output Ratios and Growth Rates in the Short-Run," *Review of Economics and Statistics* (February 1966); and K. Sato, "Incremental Variations in the Capital-Output Ratio," *Economic Development and Cultural Change* (July 1971).

41. For evidence on Chile, see Vittorio Corbo and Patricio Meller, "Alternative Trade Strategies and Employment Implications: Chile," in Anne 0. Krueger, et al. (eds.), *Trade and Employment in Developing Countries, op. cit.*

42. There is a large and growing literature on the Chilean experience since 1974. An incomplete list includes the following: Bela Balassa, "Policy Experiments in Chile, 1973-83" in Gary M. Walton (ed.), *The National Economic Policies of Chile* (Greenwich, Conn.: JAI Press, 1985); Sebastian Edwards, "Stabilization with Liberalization: An Evaluation of Ten Years of Chile's Experiment with Free Market Policies, 1973-1983" (University of California, Los Angeles: revised May 1984); Gonzalo Falabella, *Labour in Chile Under the Junta, 1973-1979* (London: Institute of Latin American Studies, University of London, 1980); Ricardo French-Davis, "The Monetarist Experiment in Chile: A Critical Survey," in *World Development* (11:1983); "The External Debt, Financial Liberalization, and Crisis in Chile," in Miguel S. Wionczek (ed.), *Politics and Economics of External Debt Crisis: The Latin American Experience* (Boulder, Col.: Westview Press, 1985); Alejandro Foxley, "Economic Stabilization and Structural Change: The Chilean Economy After 1973," in Moshe Syrquin and Simon Teitel (eds.), *Trade, Stability, Technology, and Equity in Latin America* (New York: Academic Press, 1982); "Towards a Free Market Economy," *Journal of Development Economics* (February 1982); and *Latin American Experiments in Neoconservative Economics* (Berkeley, Cal.: University of California Press, 1983); Garcia H. Alvaro and John Wells, "Chile: A Laboratory for Failed Experiments in Capitalist Political Economy," *Cambridge Journal of Economics* (7:1983); Arnold C. Harberger, "The Chilean Economy in the 1970s: Crisis, Stabilization, Liberalization, Reform," in Karl Brunner and Allan H. Meltzer (eds.), *Economic Policy in a World of Change* (Amsterdam: North-Holland Publishing Co., Carnegie-Rochester Conference Series on Public Policy, 1982); Ronald I. McKinnon, "The Order of Economic Liberalization: Lessons from Chile and Argentina," in Brunner and Meltzer (eds.), ibid.; Vincent Parkin, "Economic Liberalism in Chile, 1973-82: A Model for Growth and Development or a Recipe for Stagnation and Impoverishment?" *Cambridge Journal of Economics* (7:1983); Joseph R. Ramos, "The Economics of Hyperstagflation: Stabilization Policy in Post-1973 Chile," in *Journal of Development Economics* (7:1980); Larry A. Sjaastad, "Liberalization and Stabilization Experiences in the Southern Cone," in Nicholas Ardito Barletta, Mario I. Blejer, and Luis Landau (eds.), *Economic Liberalization and Stabilization Policies in Argentina, Chile, and Uruguay: Applications of Monetary Approach to the Balance of Payments* (Washington, D.C.: World Bank, 1983); Laurence Whitehead, "Inflation and Stabilization in Chile, 1970-77," in Rosemary Thorp and Laurence Whitehead (eds.), *Inflation and Stabilization in Latin America* (New York: Holms and Meier Publishers, 1979); World Bank, *Chile: An Economy in Transition* (Washington, D.C.: January 1980).

43. President Allende's socialist government came to power with a plurality (36.6 percent) of the vote, not a majority. On the evolution of social, economic, and political forces which led to the emergence of the socialist regime in Chile, see Barbara Stallings, *Class Conflict and Economic Development in Chile, 1958-73, op. cit.,* Chapters 3 through 6; Gary W. Wynia, *The Politics of Latin American Development* (London: Cambridge University Press, 1984), Chapter 7; and David Lehmann, "The Political Economy of Armageddon: Chile, 1970-1973," *Journal of Development Economics* (5:107-123, 1978)

44. This was accompanied by the country's withdrawal from the Andean Pact with the neighboring countries on mutual tariff actions.

45. The reasons for the extraordinarily high real interest rates in Chile are not well understood, considering the large net capital inflows and the long period of fixed parity with the U.S. dollar. In retrospect, there may have been a deep-seated doubt about the sustainability of the external sector policies governing capital inflows, consumer goods imports, and the exchange rate. However, Arnold C. Harberger attributed the persistence of the high real interest rate largely to the Chilean banks' poor loan structure. See his "Observations on the Chilean Economy, 1973–1983," *Economic Development and Cultural Change* (April 1985) for a detailed analysis.

46. Between 1975 and 1981, the real exchange rate per U.S. dollar (measured by the movement of relative wholesale prices between Chile and the United States) declined by 30 percent while manufacturing product wages (manufacturing wage deflated by the wholesale price index, as an approximation) rose by more than 160 percent. Measured against the relative consumer prices, the real exchange rate declined by 29 percent, while the real manufacturing wages rose by more than 180 percent.

47. Some details of the Argentine experience in the 1970s can be found in the following: L. Beccaria and R. Caiofi, "The Recent Experience of Stabilizing and Opening Up the Argentinian Economy," *Cambridge Journal of Economics* (2: 1982); Guillermo A. Calvo, "Trying to Stabilize: Some Theoretical Reflections Based on the Case of Argentina," in P.A. Armella, Rudiger Dornbusch, and M. Obsfeld (eds.), *Financial Policies and the World Capital Market: The Problem of Latin American Countries* (Chicago: University of Chicago Press, 1983); and "Fractured Liberalism: Argentina Under Martinez de Hoz," *Economic Development and Cultural Change* (April 1986); Adolfo Canitrot, "Discipline as the Central Objective of Economic Policy: Economic Programme of the Argentine Government Since 1976," *World Development* (8:913–928, 1980); Marcelo Diamond and Daniel Naszewski, "Argentina's Foreign Debt: Its Origin and Consequences," in M.S. Wionczek (ed.), *op. cit.*; B. Fischer, U. Hiemenz, and P. Trapp, "Economic Development, Debt Crisis, and the Importance of Domestic Policies—The Case of Argentina," *Economia Internazionale* (February 1985); Arthur J. Mann and Carlos E. Sanchez, "Monetarism, Economic Reform and Socio-Economic Consequences: Argentina, 1976–1982," in *Festschrift in Honour of George F. Rohrlich, II* (Bradford, West Yorkshire: MCB University Press, 1984), compiled by J.C. O'Brien; Morgan Guaranty Trust Company of New York, "Argentina," *World Financial Markets* (February 1985); Jose Maria Dagnino Pastore, "Assessment of an Anti-Inflationary Experiment: Argentina in 1979–81," in Barletta, Blejer, and Landau (eds.), *op. cit.*: "Progress and Prospects for the Adjustment Program in Argentina," in John Williamson (ed.), *Prospects for Adjustment in Argentina, Brazil, and Mexico: Responding to the Debt Crisis* (Washington, D.C.: Institute for International Economics, 1983); Guido Di Tella, "The Economic Policies of Argentina's Labour-Based Government 1973–77," in Thorp and Whitehead (eds.), *op.cit.*; Ronald I. McKinnon, *op. cit.*; Larry A. Sjaastad, *op. cit.*; and World Bank, *Argentina: Economic Memorandum* (Washington, D.C.: World Bank, 1985).

48. Price controls were reimposed for a period from February to July 1977, whereas wage controls were relaxed after 1977. See Julio Nogues, "The Nature of Argentina's Policy Reforms During 1976–81" (Washington, D.C.: World Bank Staff Working Paper No. 765, 1986), pp. 10–13.

49. Except for a uniform 10 percent duty on goods not domestically produced.

50. The real lending rate, which was negative in the first half of 1979, jumped to 25 percent and rose further during 1980.

51. Between 1977 and 1980, the real exchange rate per U.S. dollar (measured by the movement of relative wholesale prices between Argentina and the United States)

declined by 42 percent while manufacturing product wages (manufacturing wage deflated by the wholesale price index as an approximation) rose by more than 55 percent.

52. It should be noted that the Chilean and Argentine experiments were not without their successes. In particular, for Chile, the growth of new exports was most impressive, as indicated by the trade data shown in Tables 2.1 and 2.2.

53. For the patterns of the developing countries' responses to multicurrency realignments and subsequent generalized floating, and for the differences in their saving and investment behaviors, output and inflation performances, and external account developments following the first oil shock, see Ching-yuan Lin, *Developing Countries in a Turbulent World: Patterns of Adjustment Since the Oil Crisis* (New York: Praeger Publishers, 1981), Chapters 3, 5, 6, and 7. For a more detailed analysis of policy response to external shocks, see Bela Balassa, *The Newly Industrializing Countries in the World Economy* (New York: Pergamon, 1981).

54. For more details on the time sequence of tariff reductions and import decontrols in Taiwan and South Korea, see Lin, *Industrialization in Taiwan*, Chapter 5; Frank, Kim and Westphal, *op. cit.*, Chapters 4 and 5; and Chong Hyun Nam, "Trade and Industrial Policies, and the Structure of Protection in Korea," in Wontack Hong and Lawrence B. Krause (eds.), *Trade and Growth of the Advanced Developing Countries in the Pacific Basin* (Seoul: Korea Development Institute, 1981).

55. On the pros and cons of the preannounced exchange rate model, see Mario I. Blejer and Donald J. Mathieson, "The Preannouncement of Exchange Changes as a Stabilization Instrument," *Staff Papers* (28:4, December 1981), and various papers and discussions in Barletta, Blejer, and Landau (eds.), *op. cit.* On the adverse effect of hasty liberalization of capital inflows, see McKinnon, "The Order of Economic Liberalism," *op. cit.*, and Jacob A. Frenkel, "Economic Liberalization and Stabilization Programs," in Barletta, Blejer, and Landau (eds.), *op. cit.* For a simulation analysis of the effects of alternative trade and capital liberalization, see Mohsin S. Khan and Robert Zahler, "The Macroeconomic Effects of Changes in Barriers to Trade and Capital Flows: A Simulation Analysis," *Staff Papers* (30:2, 1983).

56. Such a cautious attitude toward foreign short-term capital flows was demonstrated not just by Taiwan, but also by Japan. Despite its much more advanced state of industrialization, Japan did not start to seriously dismantle capital controls until the 1970s.

57. This is particularly evident in the period after the first oil shock. For details of Korean policy behavior in comparison with Brazil, see Lin, "Policy Response to External Shocks: Brazil Versus Taiwan and South Korea" (Draft, December 14, 1984).

58. On the excess and abuses of the liberalization and denationalization measures in Chile, see for example Alejandro Foxley, *Latin American Experiments in Neoconservative Economics* (Berkeley, Calif.: University of California Press, 1983).

59. This is true also of Japan and Singapore. In fact, the only East Asian market economy which has followed the laissez-faire approach to economic development is Hong Kong, whose success as a processing and commercial center has depended critically on an ample supply of refugee workers and entrepreneurs, many of whom have gone through tremendous hardships and who are therefore eager to work hard to reestablish themselves.

60. For details on the income distributive mechanism in Taiwan, see John C. Fei, Gustav Ranis, and Shirley W. Y. Kuo, *Growth with Equity: The Taiwan Case* (London: Oxford University Press, 1979); on South Korea, see Irma Adelman and Sherman Robinson, *Income Distribution Policies in Developing Countries: A Case Study of Korea* (Oxford: Oxford University Press, 1978).

Chapter 3

1. This phase of the Taiwanese experience was like that of Japan, which also quickly restored price stability and international competitiveness. For details on Japan, see the author's *Japanese and U.S. Inflation: A Comparative Analysis* (Lexington, Mass.: Lexington Books, 1984), Chapters 2–4.

2. In 1973, imports of goods and nonfactor services in relation to GDP amounted to 41 percent in Taiwan and 25 percent in South Korea, compared to only 8.4 percent in Brazil.

3. The inventory decumulation, in turn, was prompted by a sharp fall in export demand and world commodity prices and the intensified credit restraint.

4. John R. Wells, "Brazil and the Post–1973 Crisis in the International Economy," in Rosemary Thorp and Laurence Whitehead (eds.), *Inflation and Stabilization in Latin America* (New York: Holmes and Meier, 1979).

5. See Shirley W. Y. Kuo, *The Taiwan Economy in Transition* (Boulder, Col.: Westview Press, 1983), pp. 214–215.

6. For econometric evidence in this regard, see William R. Cline, "Brazil's Aggressive Response to External Shocks," in William R. Cline and associates, *World Inflation and the Developing Countries* (Washington, D.C.: Brookings, 1981), pp. 111–112.

7. Bank of Korea, *Annual Report, 1974*.

8. The extraordinarily high investment ratio in 1974 resulted entirely from the large stock investment that amounted to 10 percent of GDP in that year.

9. The debt service ratio is defined as the sum of amortization and interest payments as percent of the exports of goods and services.

10. See World Bank, *Brazil: Economic Memorandum, op. cit.*, pp. 2–4, and Bela Balassa, *The Newly Industrializing Countries in the World Economy* (New York: Pergamon Press, 1981), Chapter 10. According to William G. Taylor, there was a nominal antiexport bias of 43 percent on average in the Brazilian tariff and incentive systems governing the manufacturing industry in 1977. See Taylor's "The Anti-Export Bias in Commercial Policies and Export Performance: Some Evidence from the Recent Brazilian Experience," *Weltwirtschaftliches Archiv* (119:1, 1983), p. 106.

11. For various years in the late 1960s the nominal rate of protection on manufacturing was estimated at 13 percent in Taiwan and 11 percent in South Korea, compared with 48 percent in Brazil. The effective rate (on value added) was estimated at 19 perent and –1 percent, compared with 94 percent. For the estimates on Taiwan and South Korea, see the chapters by T. H. Lee and Kuo-shu Liang on Taiwan and by Larry E. Westphal and Kwang Suk Kim on Korea in Bela Balassa and associates, *Development Strategies in Semi-Industrial Economies* (Baltimore: Johns Hopkins University Press, 1982). For the estimates on Brazil, see Joel Bergsman and Pedro S. Malan, "The Structure of Protection in Brazil," in Bela Balassa and associates, *The Structure of Protection in Developing Countries* (Baltimore: Johns Hopkins University Press, 1971).

12. The percentage of items under import control declined from 17.9 in 1972 to 2.3 in 1974. See Table 9 attached to Ching-yuan Lin, "Policy Reforms, International Competitiveness, and Export Expansion: Chile and Argentina Versus Taiwan and South Korea," mimeo (March 1985).

13. See Bela Balassa, *The Newly Industrializing Countries in the World Economy*, *op. cit.*, Chapter 16.

14. It also introduced differential wage adjustment factors in favor of lower paid workers, while keeping the productivity factor subject to annual collective bargaining between labor unions and employers' associations. The formula applied to permanent workers in the private urban (formal) sector and in public enterprises (excluding civil

servants and the military)—about 55 percent of the nonagricultural labor force. See World Bank, *Brazil: Economic Memorandum* (Washington, D.C., 1984), pp. 91–92. Also, see Mario Henrique Simonsen, "Indexation: Current Theory and the Brazilian Experience," and Roberto Macedo, "Wage Indexation and Inflation: The Recent Brazilian Experience," in Rudiger Dornbusch and Mario Henrique Simonsen (eds.), *Inflation, Debt, and Indexation* (Cambridge, Mass.: The MIT Press, 1983).

15. World Bank, *Brazil: Economic Memorandum, op. cit.*, pp. 6–7. Excluding the effect of changes in the fiscal subsidy and import deposit requirement, this occurred despite the fact that there was a depreciation in the average real exchange of the cruzeiro against the U.S. dollar from 1979 to 1980. See Chart 3.6.

16. In comparison, the real rates of 1979 to 1980 were deeply negative. See Edmar L. Bacha, "Vicissitudes of Recent Stabilization Attempts in Brazil and the IMF Alternative," in John Williamson (ed.), *IMF Conditionality* (Washington, D.C.: Institute for International Economics, 1983), p. 331, Table 14.1.

17. On the slow turnaround in the Brazilian policy stance, see Edmar L. Bacha, ibid., and Carlos F. Diaz-Alejandro, "Some Aspects of the 1982–83 Brazilian Payments Crisis," *Brookings Papers on Economic Activity* (2:1983).

18. See Morgan Guaranty Trust Company of New York, *World Financial Markets* (July 1984); and Edmar L. Bacha, "The IMF and the Prospects for Adjustment in Brazil," in John Williamson (ed.), *Prospects for Adjustment in Argentina, Brazil, and Mexico: Responding to the Debt Crisis* (Washington, D.C.: Institute for International Economics, 1983).

19. The base for import duty assessment was reduced from 120 percent of the c.i.f. value to 115 percent. Separately, import duties on capital goods were reduced by 50 percent, and productive enterprises that had merged were allowed duty free imports of machinery and equipment for two years to encourage raising the scale of operation.

20. Initially, the exchange rate was determined daily by the representatives of six banks, including the Central Bank. Since March 1980, the rate has been determined by the representatives of the commercial banks alone, without the participation of the Central Bank.

21. This occurred despite a 4.8 percent devaluation in Taiwan's currency against the U.S. dollar in August 1981.

22. Despite its geographic proximity to the Chinese mainland, Taiwan's economic development during the past three decades was based on increasing trade with the United States, Japan, and many other countries across the ocean, while there was little trade with the nearby Chinese mainland. This abnormality in the geographic pattern of trade and economic development was made possible by China's political and economic seclusion from the nonsocialist world. This situation began to change in the early 1970s when the People's Republic of China established normal relations with the United States and Japan. Thus Taiwan's external trade has been increasingly conducted on a private basis. The issue came to the fore in the late 1970s, when China began to institute various political and economic reforms while seeking closer trade and investment relations with the Western countries. This put China in direct competition with Hong Kong, Taiwan, and other East Asian economies with regard to the development of export markets and the acquisition of trading partners, technology, and foreign capital. This new situation required certain political and economic adjustments on the part of Taiwan in order to reestablish a political base for stable long-term economic development. The reestablishment of a political base has been delayed owing to the difficulty of Taiwanese authorities in coming to terms with the People's Republic of China.

23. In May 1985 the authorities convened an Economic Reform Committee to examine Taiwan's basic economic issues and problems, but the resolution of the impasse awaits the undertaking of effective political actions.

24. See G. Russell Kincaid, "Korea's Major Adjustment Effort," *Finance and Development* (December 1983); Morgan Guaranty Trust Company of New York, *World Financial Markets* (March 1984); Bijan Aghevli and Jorge Marquez-Ruarte, *A Case of Successful Adjustment: Korea's Experience During 1980–84* (Washington, D.C.: International Monetary Fund, Occasional Paper No. 39, August 1985); and Yung Chul Park, "Economic Stabilization and Liberalization in Korea, 1980–1984," in Bank of Korea, *Monetary Policy in a Changing Financial Environment* (Seoul: Bank of Korea, 1985).

25. For more details on policy developments in South Korea, see B. Aghevli and J. Marques-Ruarte, *op. cit.*, Sec. 5.

26. The rescheduling of debt services is helpful, but to be successful, must be accompanied by the adaptation of economic policies since the rescheduling can only reduce the short-term liquidity pressure, not the long-term debt service obligations.

27. For a more detailed discussion of the Brazilian financial system and suggestions for reform, see World Bank, *Brazil: Financial Systems Review* (Washington, D.C.: World Bank, 1984), Chapters 7–10.

Chapter 4

1. The Chinese inflation of 1939 to 1949 reached 152 (10^{12}) percent, compared with the Weimar German inflation of 1.26 (10^{12}) percent from 1914 to 1923. See Shun-hsin Chou, *The Chinese Inflation, 1937–1949* (New York: Columbia University Press, 1963), p. 261. On the European hyperinflation, see for example Thomas J. Sargent, "The End of Four Big Inflations," in Robert E. Hall (ed.), *Inflation: Causes and Effects* (Chicago: University of Chicago Press, for National Bureau of Economic Research, 1982); and G. D. Feldman, et al. (eds.), *The Experience of Inflation: International and Comparative Studies* (Berlin: de Gruyster, 1984).

2. On the monetarist-structurist controversy in Latin America, see for example Werner Baer and Isaac Kerstenetzky (eds.), *Inflation and Growth in Latin America* (Homewood, Ill.: Richard D. Irwin, 1964).

3. On the beneficial effect of domestic price stability and financial deepening, see Ronald I. McKinnon, *Money and Capital in Economic Development* (Washington, D.C.: Brookings, 1973). For a systematic study of the favorable impact of the East Asian countries' pattern of economic growth on income distribution, see John C. H. Fei, Gustav Ranis, and Shirley W. Y. Kuo, *Growth with Equity: The Taiwan Case* (London: Oxford University Press, 1979) and Irma Adelman and Sherman Robinson, *Income Distribution Policies in Developing Countries: A Case Study of Korea* (Oxford: Oxford University Press, 1978).

4. See Gustav Donald Jud, *Inflation and the Use of Indexing in Developing Countries* (New York: Praeger Publishers, 1978) for a survey of indexation in the developing countries, and Herbert Giersch, et al., *Essays on Inflation and Indexation* (Washington, D.C.: American Enterprise Institute, 1974) for a discussion of its pros and cons.

5. For details, see Carlos F. Diaz-Alejandro, "The 1940s in Latin America," in Moshe Syrquin, Lance Taylor, and Larry E. Westphal (eds.), *Economic Structure and Performance* (Orlando, Fl.: Academic Press, 1984).

6. 7.6 million from the disbanding of the military forces, 4 million from the closing of the defense industries, and 1.5 million from repatriation of former overseas territories. For this estimate, see Takafusa Nakamura, *The Postwar Japanese Economy: Its Development and Structure* (Tokyo: University of Tokyo Press, 1981), p. 21.

7. The Reconstruction Bank obtained its funds by issuing bonds which were then accepted by the Bank of Japan. For this and other details of the Japanese postwar reconstruction and stabilization process, see T. Nakamura, ibid., Chapter 2, and

Shigeto Tsuru, *Essays on Japanese Economy* (Tokyo: Kinokuniya, 1958), Chapters 1 and 2.

8. However, because prices already started to stabilize in 1949, Japanese opinions are divided as to whether the Dodge Plan was necessary to stop the inflation. At any rate, the deflationary impact of the Dodge Plan was softened by the Japanese monetary authorities which mobilized financial institutions to bail out insolvent businesses impacted by the elimination of fiscal subsidies. See Nakamura, ibid., p. 39, and Tsuru, ibid., pp. 28–29.

9. For more details on Taiwan's postwar hyperinflation and stabilization process, see Ching-yuan Lin, *Industrialization in Taiwan, 1946–72* (New York: Praeger Publishers, 1973), pp. 29–38.

10. For more details on the Korean hyperinflation, see David C. Cole and Yung Chul Park, *Financial Development in Korea, 1945–1978* (Cambridge, Mass.: Council for East Asian Studies, Harvard University, 1983), pp. 215–224.

11. For more details on the Chinese hyperinflation, see Shun-hsin Chou, *The Chinese Inflation, 1937–1949* (New York: Columbia University Press, 1963) and Chang Kia-Ngau, *The Inflationary Spiral: The Experience in China, 1939–1950* (New York: The Technology Press of MIT and John Wiley & Sons, 1958).

12. For details of the stabilization measures adopted by the People's Republic of China in its early years, see Hsin Ying, *The Price Problems of Communist China* (Hong Kong: Union Research Institute, mimeo, 1954).

13. See Yujiro Hayami, Vernon W. Ruttan, and Herman M. Southworth (eds.), *Agricultural Growth in Japan, Taiwan, Korea, and the Philippines* (Honolulu: University of Hawaii, 1979), Chapters 1–4.

14. Following Japan's participation in the GATT in 1964, the tax allowance for export incomes was replaced by various tax deductible reserves for the development of export markets and for undertaking overseas investment, and so forth. For more details of Japan's export promotion measures, see Japan External Trade Research Center, *Sengo Nihon no Boeki Nijiu-Nen Shi* (Twenty-Year History of Japan's Postwar External Trade), Part III (Tokyo: International Trade and Industry Research Association, 1961); and Lawrence B. Krause and Sueo Sekiguchi, "Japan and the World Economy," in Hugh Patrick and Henry Rosovsky (eds.), *Asia's Giant: How the Japanese Economy Works* (Washington, D.C.: Brookings, 1976), pp. 411–417.

15. The government was not permitted to issue marketable bonds until 1965. For more details on Japanese fiscal performance, see Gardner Ackley and Hiromitsu Ishi, "Fiscal, Monetary, and Related Policies," in Hugh Patrick and Henry Rosovsky (eds.), *Asia's Giant: How the Japanese Economy Works*, ibid., Chapter 3, pp. 212–215.

16. These monetary restraints took place in 1951, 1954, 1961 to 1962, 1964, 1967, and 1968 to 1970. See T. Nakamura, *op. cit.,* Chapters 2 and 4. On the Bank of Japan's policy behavior, see Yoshio Suzuki, *Money and Banking in Contemporary Japan* (New Haven: Yale University Press, 1980).

17. For details of Taiwan's policy reforms in the 1950s and the 1960s, see Ching-yuan Lin, *Industrialization in Taiwan, op. cit.,* Chapter 5.

18. On South Korea's trade policy reforms, see Charles R. Frank, Jr., Kwang Suk Kim, and Larry E. Westphal, *Foreign Trade Regimes and Economic Development: South Korea* (New York: National Bureau of Economic Research, 1975), Chapters 4 and 5.

19. While the commercial banks' time deposit rates were doubled in 1965, the central bank's low export loan rate was kept unchanged.

20. On the Korean financial reforms, see Ronald I. McKinnon, *Money and Capital in Economic Development* (Washington, D.C.: Brookings, 1973), Chapter 8; David C.

Cole and Yung Chul Park, *Financial Development in Korea, 1945-1978* (Cambridge, Mass.: Council on East Asian Studies, Harvard University, 1983), pp. 224-231; and Akira Kohsaka, "The High Interest Rate Policy Under Financial Repression," *The Developing Economies* (December 1984).

21. On Brazil, see Joel Bergsman and Pedro S. Malan, "The Structure of Protection in Brazil," in Bela Balassa and associates, *The Structure of Protection in Developing Countries* (Baltimore: Johns Hopkins University Press, 1971); and William G. Taylor, "The Anti-Export Bias in Commercial Policies and Export Performance: Some Evidence from the Recent Brazilian Experience," *Weltwirtschaftliches Archiv* (119:1, 1983). On Chile, see Jere R. Behrman, *Foreign Trade Regimes and Economic Development: Chile* (New York: National Bureau of Economic Research, 1976) and Teresa Jenneret, "Structure of Protection in Chile," in Bela Balassa and associates, ibid. On Argentina, see Julio Berlinski and Daniel M. Schydlowsky, "Argentina," in Bela Balassa and associates, *Development Strategies in Semi-Industrial Economies* (Baltimore: Johns Hopkins University Press, 1982).

22. For details of the indexation schemes used in Chile, Brazil, and Argentina, see Gustav Donald Jud, *op. cit.,* Chapters 2 and 3.

23. For more details of the Brazilian indexation schemes, see Albert Fishlow, "Indexing Brazilian Style: Inflation Without Tears?" *Brookings Papers on Economic Activity* (1:1974); G. D. Jud, *op. cit.*; Alexandre Kafka, "Indexing for Inflation in Brazil," in Herbert Giersch, et al., *Essays on Inflation and Indexation* (Washington, D.C.: American Enterprise Institute, 1974).

24. For details of Brazilian fiscal and financial reforms, see World Bank, *Brazil: Financial Systems Review* (Washington, D.C., 1984), Chapters 2 and 3.

25. On the reform of the Brazilian incentive systems during the second half of the 1960s, see for example Bela Balassa, *The Newly Industrializing Countries in the World Economy, op. cit.,* Essay 10. On Chile, see Jere R. Behrman, *Foreign Trade Regimes and Economic Development: Chile, op. cit.*

26. For details of Allende's socialist experiment, see Barbara Stallings, *Class Conflict and Economic Development in Chile, 1958-1973* (Stanford: Stanford University Press, 1978), Chapter 6.

27. For an early exposition of a similar view, see Hugh T. Patrick, "Financial Development and Economic Growth in Underdeveloped Countries," *Economic Development and Cultural Change* (14: January 1966).

28. In addition to commercial banks and nonbank cooperatives, the ubiquitous postal offices in the countryside served as major institutions for absorbing household savings.

29. See E.V.K. Fitzgerald, "Stabilization Policy in Mexico: The Fiscal Deficit and Macroeconomic Equilibrium, 1960-77," in Rosemary Thorp and Laurence Whitehead (eds.), *Inflation and Stabilization in Latin America* (New York: Holms & Meier, 1979), pp. 34-39.

30. The percentage of import categories under control increased from 44 percent in 1962 to 65 percent in 1970, while the effective protection rate for durable consumer goods increased from around 65 percent to 77 percent. See Bela Balassa, "Trade Policy in Mexico," *World Development* (11:9, 1983).

31. At 3.4 percent per year from 1961 to 1973, the growth of per capita real income was much higher than in Chile and Argentina, but much lower than in Taiwan and South Korea.

32. In addition, the restoration of Japanese external balance was helped by the downward floating of its exchange rate, but the Taiwanese currency was tied to the appreciating U.S. dollar through 1974 to 1976. On Japan's macroeconomic policy response to the first oil shock, see the author's *Japanese and U.S. Inflation: A Com-*

parative Analysis (Lexington, Mass.: Lexington Books, 1984), Chapter 3. For an insider's analysis of Japanese monetary policy, see Yoshio Suzuki, *Money, Finance, and Macroeconomic Performance in Japan* (New Haven: Yale University Press, 1986), Chapter 5. On Taiwan's experience compared to Brazil, see the author's "Policy Response to External Shocks: Brazil versus Taiwan and South Korea," Chapter 3 in this book.

33. On the Brazilian policy response, see John R. Wells, "Brazil and the Post-1973 Crisis in the International Economy," in Rosemary Thorp and Laurence Whitehead (eds.), *Inflation and Stabilization in Latin America* (New York: Holms & Meier, 1979); William R. Cline, "Brazil's Aggressive Response to External Shocks," in William R. Cline and associates, *World Inflation and the Developing Countries* (Washington, D.C.: Brookings, 1981); Edmar L. Bacha, "Vicissitudes of Recent Stabilization Attempts in Brazil and the IMF Alternative," in John Williamson (ed.), *IMF Conditionality* (Washington, D.C.: Institute for International Economics, 1983); Carlos F. Diaz-Alejandro, "Some Aspects of the 1982–83 Brazilian Payments Crisis," *Brookings Papers on Economic Activity* (2:1983); and World Bank, *Brazil: Economic Memorandum* (Washington, D.C.: World Bank, 1984).

34. On the Mexican stabilization problems in the 1970s, see E.V.K. Fitzgerald, "Stabilization Policy in Mexico: The Fiscal Deficit and Macroeconomic Equilibrium, 1960–77," in Rosemary Thorp and Laurence Whitehead (eds.), *Inflation and Stabilization in Latin America, op. cit.*; Sidney Weintraub, "Case Study of Economic Stabilization: Mexico," in William R. Cline and Sidney Weintraub (eds.), *Economic Stabilization in Developing Countries* (Washington, D.C.: Brookings, 1981); and Francisco Gil Diaz, "Mexico's Path from Stability to Inflation," in Arnold C. Harberger (ed.), *World Economic Growth* (San Francisco: Institute for Contemporary Studies, 1985), Chapter 12.

35. Whether there was a condition of excess demand in Peru during the mid-1970s has been a matter of controversy, particularly in light of the existence of severe unemployment and idle capacity. Nevertheless, it remains true that the economic difficulties encountered by Peru, while exacerbated by external shocks, resulted from the cumulative effects of the negligence of price incentives, economic efficiency, and macroeconomic balances during the first phase (1968 to 1975) of the military government. For discussions of the Peruvian situation before the shortlived oil bonanza, see Rosemary Thorp, "The Stabilization Crisis in Peru, 1975–78," in Rosemary Thorp and Laurence Whitehead, (eds.), *Inflation and Stabilization in Latin America, op. cit.*; William R. Cline, "Economic Stabilization in Peru, 1975–78," in William R. Cline and Sidney Weintraub, ibid.; and Daniel M. Schydrowsky, "The Anatomy of an Economic Failure: Peru, 1968 to 1978," in A. Lowenthal and C. McClintock (eds.), *The Peruvian Experiment Reconsidered* (Princeton: Princeton University Press, 1983). For an insightful analysis of the Peruvian experiment, in comparison with Allende's Chile and Peron's Argentina, see John Sheahan, "The Economics of the Peruvian Experiment in Comparative Perspective" in A. Lowenthal and C. McClintock, *op cit.*

36. See Bela Balassa, *The Newly Industrializing Countries in the World Ecoonomy* (New York: Pergamon, 1981), Essay 10.

37. See Bela Balassa, "Trade Policy in Mexico," *World Development* (11:9, 1983), p. 802.

38. For evidence in this regard and for a comparison with U.S. wage behavior, see the author's *Japanese and U.S. Inflation, op. cit.*, Chapter 4.

39. This provided a sharp contrast with the situation in the early 1930s, when the supply of external credit quickly dried up in conjunction with the collapse of the international capital market. For this and other developments in comparison with the 1930s, see Angus Maddison, *Two Crises: Latin America and Asia, 1929–38 and 1973–*

83 (Paris: OECD Development Center, 1985), pp. 13–16.

40. On the effect of the indexation in prolonging inflation in Brazil after the first oil shock, see Mario Henrique Simonsen, "Indexation: Current Theory and the Brazilian Experience," and Roberto Macedo, "Wage Indexation and Inflation: The Recent Brazilian Experience," both in Rudiger Dornbusch and Mario Henrique Simonsen (eds.), *Inflation, Debt, and Indexation* (Cambridge, Mass.: The MIT Press, 1983).

41. On Argentina, see Guido Di Tella, "The Economic Policies of Argentina's Labour-Based Government, 1973–76," in Rosemary Thorp and Laurence Whitehead (eds.), *Inflation and Stabilization in Latin America, op. cit.*; Jose Maria Dagnino Pastore, "Assessment of an Anti-Inflationary Experiment: Argentina in 1979–81," in Barletta, Blejer, and Landau (eds.), *Economic Liberalization and Stabilization Policies in Argentina, Chile, and Uruguay* (Washington, D.C.: World Bank, 1983); and World Bank, *Argentina: Economic Memorandum* (Washington, D.C.: 1985)

42. On the Chilean policy reform experience in the 1970s, see, for example, Alejandro Foxley, *Latin American Experiments in Neoconservative Economics* (Berkeley: University of California Press, 1983); Ricardo French-Davis, "The Monetary Experiment in Chile: A Critical Survey," *World Development* (11:1983); Sebastian Edwards, "Stabilization with Liberalization: An Evaluation of Ten Years of Chile's Experiment with Free Market Policies, 1973–1983," *Economic Development and Cultural Change* (33:2, 1985); Arnold C. Harberger, "Observations on the Chilean Economy, 1973–83," *Economic Development and Cultural Change* (33:2, 1985); Carlos Diaz-Alejandro, "Goodbye Financial Repression, Hello Financial Crash," *Journal of Development Economics* (19:1–24, 1985); and Larry A. Sjaastad, "Liberalization and Stabilization Experiences in the Southern Cone" and other papers in Nicholas Ardito Barletta, Mario I. Blejer, and Luis Landau (eds.), *Economic Liberalization and Stabilization Policies in Argentina, Chile, and Uruguay* (Washington, D.C.: World Bank, 1983).

43. See G. Russell Kincaid, "Korea's Major Adjustment Effort," *Finance and Development* (December 1983); Yung Chul Park, "Korea's Experience with External Debt Management," in Gordon W. Smith and John T. Cuddington (eds.), *International Debt and the Developing Countries* (Washington, D.C.: World Bank, 1985); and Bijan Aghevli and Jorge Marques-Ruarte, *A Case of Successful Adjustment: Korea's Experience During 1980–84* (Washington, D.C.: International Monetary Fund, Occasional Paper No. 39, August 1985). For a comparison with Brazil and Taiwan, see Chapter 3 in this book, "Policy Response to External Shocks: Brazil versus Taiwan and South Korea."

44. On Argentina, see Rudiger Dornbusch, "A New Chance for Argentina," *Challenge* (January-February 1986) and Rudiger Dornbush and Stanley Fischer, "Stopping Hyperinflations Past and Present," *Weltwirtschaftliches Archiv*, Band 122 (1986), Heft 1. On Brazil, see Morgan Guaranty Trust Company of New York, "Brazil: Beyond the Cruzado Plan," *World Financial Markets* (August 1986); on Israel, see Michael Bruno, "Sharp Disinflation Strategy: Israel 1985," *Economic Policy* (April 1986) and Dornbush and Fischer, *op. cit.* For a comparative analysis of the above three countries, see Peter T. Knight, F. Desmond McCarthy, and Sweder van Wijnbergen, "Escaping Hyperinflation," *Finance and Development* (December 1986).

45. "Hyperinflation: Taming the Beast," *The Economist* (November 15, 1986).

46. C. Lin, *Industrialization in Taiwan, op. cit.*, pp. 33–38 and 196–197; and S. C. Tsiang, "Exchange Rate, Interest Rate, and Economic Development," in L. R. Klein, M. Nerlove, and S. C. Tsiang (eds.), *Quantitative Economics and Development: Essays in Memory of Ta-Chung Liu* (New York: Academic Press, 1980).

SELECTED BIBLIOGRAPHY

Adelman, Irma, and Sherman Robinson. *Income Distribution Policies in Developing Countries: A Case Study of Korea.* Oxford: Oxford University Press, 1978.

Aghevli, Bijan, and Jorge Marques-Ruarte. *A Case of Successful Adjustment: Korea's Experience During 1980–84.* Washington, D.C.: International Monetary Fund, Occasional Paper No. 39 (August 1985).

Akamatsu, K.. "A Historical Pattern of Economic Growth in Developing Countries." *The Developing Economies.* Preliminary issue (May-August 1962).

Alvaro, Garcia H., and John Wells. "Chile: A Laboratory for Failed Experiments in Capitalist Political Economy." *Cambridge Journal of Economics* 7 (1983).

Angell, Alan, and Rosemary Thorp. "Inflation, Stabilization and Attempted Redemocratization in Peru, 1975–1979." *World Development* (November 1980).

Armella, P. A., Rudiger Dornbusch, and M. Obsfeld, eds. *Financial Policies and the World Capital Market: The Problem of Latin American Countries.* Chicago: University of Chicago Press, 1983.

Bacha, Edmar L. "Vicissitudes of Recent Stabilization Attempts in Brazil and the IMF Alternative." In *IMF Conditionality*, edited by John Williamson. Washington, D.C.: Institute for International Economics, 1983.

————. "The IMF and the Prospects for Adjustment in Brazil." In *Prospects for Adjustment in Argentina, Brazil, and Mexico: Responding to the Debt Crisis*, edited by John Williamson. Washington, D.C.: Institute for International Economics, 1983.

Baer, Werner, and Paul Berkerman, "The Trouble with Index-Linking: Reflections on the Recent Brazilian Experience." *World Development* (September 1980).

Baer, Werner, Paul Berkerman, and Malcolm Gillis, eds. *Export Diversification and the New Protectionism: The Experiences of Latin America.* Champaign, Ill.: University Press, 1981.

Baer, Werner, Paul Berkerman, and Isaac Kerstenetzky, eds. *Inflation and Growth in Latin America.* Homewood, Ill.: Richard D. Irwin, 1964.

Balassa, Bela. *Policy Reform in Developing Countries.* New York: Pergamon, 1977.

————. *The Newly Industrializing Countries in the World Economy.* New York: Pergamon, 1981.

————. *Change and Challenge in the World Economy.* London: Macmillan Press, 1985.

Balassa, Bela, and Associates Staff. *The Structure of Protection in Developing Countries.* Baltimore: Johns Hopkins University Press, 1971.

Barletta, Nicholas Ardito, Mario I. Blejer, and Luis Landau, eds. *Economic Liberalization and Stabilization Policies in Argentina, Chile, and Uruguay: Applications of Monetary Approach to the Balance of Payments*. Washington, D.C.: World Bank, 1983.

Beccaria, L., and R. Caiofi. "The Recent Experience of Stabilizing and Opening Up the Argentinian Economy." *Cambridge Journal of Economics* 2 (1982).

Behrman, Jere R. *Foreign Trade Regimes and Economic Development: Chile*. New York: National Bureau of Economic Research, 1976.

―――. *Macroeconomic Policy in a Developing Country: The Chilean Experience*. Amsterdam: North-Holland Publishing Co., 1977.

Behrman, Jere R., and James A. Hanson, eds. *Short-Term Macroeconomic Policy in Latin America*. Cambridge, Mass.: Ballinger, for National Bureau of Economic Research, 1979.

Bergsman, Joel. *Brazil: Industrialization and Trade Policies*. Paris: Organization for Economic Cooperation and Development, 1970.

―――. "Growth and Equity in Semi-Industrialized Countries." Washington, D.C.: World Bank Staff Working Paper No. 351, 1979.

Berlinski, Julio. "Dismantling Foreign Trade Restrictions: Some Evidence and Issues on the Argentine Case." In *Trade, Stability, Technology, and Equity in Latin America*, edited by Moshe Syrquin and Simon Teitel. New York: Academic Press, 1982.

Berlinski, Julio, and Daniel M. Schydlowsky. "Argentina." In *Development Strategies in Semi-Industrial Economies*, edited by Bela Balassa and Associates Staff. Baltimore: Johns Hopkins University Press, 1982.

Bhagwati, Jagdish, *Anatomy and Consequences of Exchange Control Regimes* (New York: National Bureau of Economic Research, 1978)

―――. "Rethinking Trade Strategy." In *Development Strategies Reconsidered*, edited by John P. Lewis and Valeriana Kallab. New Brunswick: Transaction Books, for Overseas Development Council, 1986.

Blejer, Mario I., and Donald J. Mathieson. "The Preannouncement of Exchange Changes as a Stabilization Instrument." *Staff Papers* 28 (December 1981).

Bradford, Colin I. "East Asian 'Models': Myths and Lessons." In *Development Strategies Reconsidered*, edited by John P. Lewis and Valeriana Kalla. New Brunswick: Transaction Books, for Overseas Development Council, 1986.

Brown, Gilbert T. *Korean Pricing Policies and Economic Development in the 1960s*. Baltimore: Johns Hopkins University Press, 1973.

Calvo, Guillermo A. "Fractured Liberalism: Argentina Under Martinez de Hoz." *Economic Development and Cultural Change* (April 1986).

Canitrot, Adolfo "Discipline as the Central Objective of Economic Policy: Economic Programme of the Argentine Government Since 1976." *World Development* 8 (1980): 913–928.

Chang, Kia-Ngau. *The Inflationary Spiral: The Experience in China, 1939–1950*. New York: The Technology Press of MIT and John Wiley & Sons, 1958.

Chen, E. K. "Factor Inputs, Total Factor Productivity, and Economic Growth: The Asian Case." *The Developing Economies* 15 (1977): 121–143.

Chenery, Hollis, and Moshe Syrquin. *Patterns of Development, 1950–1970*. Oxford: Oxford University Press for the World Bank, 1975.

Cheng, Hang-Sheng. "Financial Policy and Reform in Taiwan, China." In *Financial Policy and Reform in Pacific Basin Countries*, edited by Hang-Sheng Cheng. Lexington, Mass.: Lexington Books, 1986.

Chou, Shun-hsin. *The Chinese Inflation, 1937–1949*. New York: Columbia University Press, 1963.

Chung, Jae Wan. "Inflation in a Newly Industrialized Country: The Case of Korea." *World Development* 10 (1982).

Cline, William R. "Brazil's Aggressive Response to External Shocks." In *World Inflation and the Developing Countries*, edited by William R. Cline et al. Washington, D.C.: Brookings, 1981.

―――――. "Economic Stabilization in Peru, 1975–78." In *Economic Stabilization in Developing Countries*, edited by William R. Cline and Sidney Weintraub. Washington, D.C.: Brookings, 1981.

―――――. "Economic Stabilization in Developing Countries: Theory and Stylized Facts." In *IMF Conditionality*, edited by John Williamson. Washington, D.C.: Institute for International Economics, 1983.

―――――. *Exports of Manufactures from Developing Countries*. Washington, D.C.: Brookings, 1984.

―――――. "Can the East Asian Export Model of Development Be Generalized." *World Development* 10 (1982).

Cole, David C., and Yung Chul Park. *Financial Development in Korea, 1945–1978*. Cambridge, Mass.: Council on East Asian Studies, Harvard University, 1983.

Collier, David, ed. *The New Authoritarianism in Latin America*. Princeton: Princeton University Press, 1979.

Corbo, Vittorio, and Patricio Meller. "Alternative Trade Strategies and Employment Implications: Chile." In *Trade and Employment in Developing Countries: I. Individual Studies*, edited by Anne O. Krueger, et al. Chicago: University of Chicago Press, for National Bureau of Economic Research, 1981.

Corbo, Vittorio, Jaime de Melo, and James Tybout, "What Went Wrong with the Recent Reforms in the Southern Cone." *Economic Development and Cultural Change* (April 1986).

Corbo, Vittorio, Anne O. Krueger, and Fernando Ossa, eds. *Export-Oriented Development Strategies: The Success of Five Newly Industrializing Countries*. Boulder, Col.: Westview Press, 1985.

Cortes Douglas, Hernan. "Stabilization Policies in Chile: Inflation, Unemployment, and Depressions, 1975–1982." In *The National Economic Policies of Chile*, edited by Gary M. Walton. Greenwich, Conn.: JAI Press, 1985.

―――――. "Opening Up and Liberalizing the Chilean Economy: The 1970s." In *Export-Oriented Development Strategies: The Success of Five Newly Industrializing Countries*, edited by Vittorio Corbo, Anne O. Krueger, and Fernando Ossa. Boulder, Col.: Westview Press, 1985.

Cotler, Julio. "State and Regime: Comparative Notes on the Southern Cone and the 'Enclave' Societies." In *The New Authoritarianism in Latin America*, edited by David Collier. Princeton: Princeton University Press, 1979.

Crockett, Andrew D. "Stabilization Policies in Developing Countries: Some Policy Considerations." *Staff Papers* 27 (March 1981).

de Janvry, Alain. *The Agrarian Question and Reformism in Latin America*. Baltimore: Johns Hopkins University Press, 1981.

de Melo, Jaime. "Sources of Growth and Structural Change in Korea and Taiwan: Some Comparisons." In *Export-Oriented Development Strategies: The Success of Five Newly Industrializing Countries*, edited by Vittorio Corbo, Anne O. Krueger, and Fernando Ossa. Boulder, Col.: Westview Press, 1985.

de Melo, Jaime, and Sherman Robinson. "Trade Adjustment Policies and Income Distribution in Three Archetype Developing Economies." *Journal of Development Economics* 10 (1982).

Dagnino Pastore, Jose Maria. "Assessment of an Anti-Inflationary Experiment: Argentina in 1979–81." In *Economic Liberalization and Stabilization Policies in Argentina, Chile, and Uruguay*, edited by Nicholas Ardito Barletta, Mario I. Blejer, and Luis Landau. Washington, D.C.: World Bank, 1983.

————. "Progress and Prospects for the Adjustment Program in Argentina." In *Prospects for Adjustment in Argentina, Brazil, and Mexico*, edited by John Williamson. Washington, D.C.: Institute for International Economics, 1983.

Diaz-Alejandro, Carlos F. *Essays on the Economic History of the Argentine Republic*. New Haven: Yale University Press, 1970.

————. "Southern Cone Stabilization Plans." In *Economic Stabilization in Developing Countries*, edited by William R. Cline and Sidney Weintraub. Washington, D.C.: Brookings, 1981.

————. "Exchange Rates and Terms of Trade in the Argentine Republic, 1913–1976" In *Trade, Stability, Technology, and Equity in Latin America*, edited by Moshe Syrquin and Simon Teitel. New York: Academic, 1982.

————. "Stories of the 1930s for the 1980s." In *Financial Policies and the World Capital Market*, edited by P. A. Armella, Rudiger Dornbusch, and M. Obsfeld. Chicago: University of Chicago Press, 1983.

————. "Some Aspects of the 1982–83 Brazilian Payments Crisis" *Brookings Papers on Economic Activity* 2 (1983).

————. "Latin American Debt: I Don't Think We Are in Kansas Anymore." *Brookings Papers on Economic Activity* 2 (1984).

————. "No Less Than One Hundred Years of Argentine Economic History Plus Some Comparisons." In *Comparative Development Perspective*, edited by Gustav Ranis, et al. Boulder, Col.: Westview Press. 1984.

————. "Goodbye Financial Repression, Hello Financial Crash." *Journal of Development Economics* 19 (1985): 1–24.

Dick, Herman, Egbert Gerken, Thomas Mayer, et al. "Stabilization Strategies in Primary Commodity Exporting Countries" *Journal of Development Economics* 15 (1984).

Di Tella, Guido. "The Economic Policies of Argentina's Labour-Based Government, 1973–76." In *Inflation and Stabilization in Latin America*, edited by Rosemary Thorp and Laurence Whitehead. New York: Holms & Meier, 1979.

Dore, Ronald P. "Latin America and Japan Compared." In *Continuity and Change in Latin America*, edited by John J. Johnson. Stanford: Stanford University Press, 1964.

Dornbusch, Rudiger "Stabilization Policies in Developing Countries: What Have We Learned?" *World Development* (September 1982).

————. "A New Chance for Argentina." *Challenge* (January/February 1986).

Edwards, Sebastian. "Stabilization with Liberalization: An Evaluation of Ten Years of Chile's Experiment with Free Market Policies, 1973–1983." *Economic Development and Cultural Change* 33 (1985).

————. "Monetarism in Chile, 1973–1983: Some Economic Puzzles." *Economic Development and Cultural Change* (April 1986).

Elias, Victor Jorge "Sources of Economic Growth in Latin American Countries." *Review of Economics and Statistics* 60 (1978): 363–370.

Epstein, Edward C. "Control and Co-option of the Argentine Labor Movement." *Economic Development and Cultural Change* 27 (1979).

Falabella, Gonzalo. *Labour in Chile Under the Junta, 1973–79*. London: Institute of Latin American Studies, University of London, 1981.

Fei, John C. H., and Lili Chiang. "Inflation in the ROC in the Early Postwar Years (1950–1963)." In *Conference on Inflation in East Asian Countries*. Taipei: Chunghua Institution for Economic Research, undated.

Fei, John C. H., and Gustav Ranis. "A Model of Growth and Employment in the Open Dualistic Economy." *Journal of Development Studies* 11 (1975).

Fei, John C. H., Gustav Ranis, and Shirley W. Y. Kuo. *Growth with Equity: The*

Taiwan Case. London: Oxford University Press, 1979.

Fischer, B., U. Hiemenz, and P. Trapp. "Economic Development, Debt Crisis, and the Importance of Domestic Policies—The Case of Argentina." *Economia Internazionale* (February 1985).

Fishlow, Albert. "Indexing Brazilian Style: Inflation Without Tears?" *Brookings Papers on Economic Activity*(1 (1974).

————. "Lessons from the Past: Capital Markets During the 19th Century and the Interwar Period." In *The Politics of International Debt*, edited by Miles Kahler. Ithaca: Cornell University Press, 1986.

Fitzgerald, E. V. K. *The Political Economy of Peru, 1956–78: Economic Development and the Restructuring of Capital*. Cambridge: Cambridge University Press, 1979.

————. "Stabilization Policy in Mexico: The Fiscal Deficit and Macroeconomic Equilibrium, 1960–77." In *Inflation and Stabilization in Latin America*, edited by Rosemary Thorp and Laurence Whitehead. New York: Holms & Meier, 1979.

Foxley, Alejandro. "Stabilization Policies and Their Effects on Employment and Income Distribution: A Latin American Perspective." In *Economic Stabilization in Developing Countries*, edited by William R. Cline and Sidney Weintraub. Washington, D.C.: Brookings, 1981.

————. "Economic Stabilization and Structural Change: The Chilean Economy After 1973." In *Trade, Stability, Technology, and Equity in Latin America*, edited by Moshe Syrquin and Simon Teitel. New York: Academic Press, 1982.

————. "Towards a Free Market Economy." *Journal of Development Economics* (February 1982).

————. *Latin American Experiments in Neoconservative Economics*. Berkeley, Calif.: University of California Press, 1983.

Frank, Charles R., Kwang Suk Kim, and Larry E. Westphal. *Foreign Trade Regimes and Economic Development: South Korea*. New York: National Bureau of Economic Research, 1975.

French-Davis, Ricardo. "Old and New Forms of External Instability in Latin America." In *Trade, Stability, Technology, and Equity in Latin America*, edited by Moshe Syrquin and Simon Teitel. New York: Academic Press, 1982.

————. "The Monetarist Experiment in Chile: A Critical Survey." *World Development* 11 (1983).

Frenkel, Jacob A. "Economic Liberalization and Stabilization Programs." In *Economic Liberalization and Stabilization Policies in Argentina, Chile, and Uruguay*, edited by Nicholas Ardito Barletta, Mario I. Blejer, and Luis Landau. Washington, D.C.: World Bank, 1983.

Frenkel, Robert, and Guillermo O'Donnell. "The 'Stabilization Programs' of the International Monetary Fund and Their Internal Impacts." In *Capitalism and the State in U.S.-Latin American Relations*, edited by Richard R. Fagen. Stanford: Stanford University Press, 1979.

Friedman, Douglas. *The State and Underdevelopment in Spanish America: The Political Roots of Dependency in Peru and Argentina*. Boulder, Col.: Westview Press, 1984.

Fry, Maxwell J. "Models of Financially Repressed Developing Economies." *World Development* 10 (1982).

Galbis, Vincent "Money, Investment, and Growth in Latin America, 1961–73." *Economic Development and Cultural Change* 27 (1979).

Galenson, Walter, ed. *Economic Growth and Structural Change in Taiwan*. Ithaca: Cornell University Press, 1979.

————. "The Labor Force, Wages, and Living Standards." In *Economic Growth and Structural Change in Taiwan*, edited by Walter Galenson. Ithaca:

Cornell University Press, 1979.

Giersch, Herbert, et al. *Essays on Inflation and Indexation.* Washington, D.C.: American Enterprise Institute, 1974.

Gil Diaz, Francisco. "Mexico's Path from Stability to Inflation." In *World Economic Growth*, edited by Arnold C. Harberger. San Francisco: Institute for Contemporary Studies, 1985.

Harberger, Arnold C. "In Step and Out of Step with the World Inflation." In *Development in an Inflationary World*, edited by M. June Flanders and Assaf Razin. New York: Academic Press, 1981.

————. "The Chilean Economy in the 1970s: Crisis, Stabilization, Liberalization, Reform." In *Economic Policy in a World of Change*, edited by Karl Brunner and Allan H. Meltzer. Amsterdam: North-Holland Publishing Co., Carnegie Rochester Conference Series on Public Policy, 1982.

————. "Observations on the Chilean Economy, 1973–1983." *Economic Development and Cultural Change* (April 1985).

————, ed. *World Economic Growth.* San Francisco: Institute for Contemporary Studies, 1985.

Hirschman, Albert O. "The Political Economy of Import-Substituting Industrialization in Latin America." *Quarterly Journal of Economics* 82 (1968): 1–32.

————. "The Turn to Authoritarianism in Latin America and the Search for Its Economic Determinants." In *The New Authoritarianism in Latin America*, edited by David Collier. Princeton: Princeton University Press, 1979.

————. "Reflections on the Latin American Experience." In *The Politics of Inflation and Economic Stagnation: Theoretical Approaches and International Case Studies*, edited by Leon N. Lindberg and Charles S. Meir. Washington, D.C.: Brookings Institution, 1985.

Ho, Samuel P. S. *Economic Development in Taiwan, 1860–1970.* New Haven: Yale University Press, 1978.

Ho, Yih-Min. *Agricultural Development of Taiwan, 1903–60.* Nashville, Tenn.: Vanderbilt University Press, 1966.

Hofheinz, Roy, and Kent E. Calder. *The East Asia Edge.* New York: Basic Books, 1982.

Hong, Wontack. *Trade, Distortions and Employment Growth in Korea.* Seoul: Korea Development Institute, 1979.

————. "Export Promotion and Employment Growth in South Korea." In *Trade and Employment in Developing Countries. I. Individual Studies*, edited by Anne O. Krueger, et al. Chicago: University of Chicago Press, for National Bureau of Economic Research, 1981.

————. and Lawrence B. Krause, eds. *Trade and Growth of the Advanced Developing Countries in the Pacific Basin.* Seoul: Korea Development Institute, 1981.

International Monetary Fund. *World Economic Outlook.* Washington, D.C.: IMF, 1980 onward.

Jenneret, Teresa. "Structure of Protection in Chile." In *The Structure of Protection in Developing Countries*, edited by Bela Balassa. Baltimore: Johns Hopkins University Press, 1971.

Jud, Gustav Donald. *Inflation and the Use of Indexing in Developing Countries.* New York: Praeger Publishers, 1978.

Kafka, Alexandre. "Indexing for Inflation in Brazil." In *Essays on Inflation and Indexation*, edited by Herbert Giersch, et al. Washington, D.C.: American Enterprise Institute, 1974.

Kaneda, Hiromitsu. "Structural Change and Policy Response in Japanese Agriculture After the Land Reform." *Economic Development and Cultural Change* 23 (1980).

Kaufman, Robert R. "Democratic and Authoritarian Responses to the Debt Issue: Argentina, Brazil, Mexico." In *The Politics of International Debt*, edited by Miles Kahler. Ithaca: Cornell University Press, 1986.

Keesing, Donald B. "Outward-Looking Policies and Economic Development" *Economic Journal* 77 (June 1967).

Khan, Mohsin S. "Monetary Shocks and the Dynamics of Inflation." *Staff Papers* 27 (1980).

————. "Some Theoretical and Empirical Issues Relating to Economic Stabilization in Developing Countries." *World Development* 10 (1982).

Khan, Mohsin S., and Malcolm D. Knight. "Stabilization Programs in Developing Countries: A Formal Framework." *Staff Papers* 28 (March 1981).

Khan, Mohsin S., and Roberto Zahler. "The Macroeconomic Effects of Changes in Barriers to Trade and Capital Flows: A Simulation Analysis.' *Staff Papers* 30 (983).

Killick, Tony, ed. *Adjustment and Financing in the Developing World.* Washington, D.C.: International Monetary Fund, 1982.

————, ed. *The IMF and Stabilization: Developing Country Experiences*. London: Heinemann Educational Books, 1984.

————, ed. *The Quest for Economic Stabilization: The IMF and the Third World*. London: Heinemann Educational Books, 1984.

Kincaid, G. Russell. "Korea's Major Adjustment Effort." *Finance and Development* (December 1983).

King, Timothy. *Mexico: Industrialization and Trade Policies Since 1940*. Paris: Organization for Economic Cooperation and Development, 1970.

Kohsaka, Akira. "The High Interest Rate Policy Under Financial Repression." *The Developing Economies* (December 1984).

Koo, Anthony Y. C. *The Role of Land Reform in Economic Development: A Case Study of Taiwan*. New York: Praeger, 1968.

Kronish, Rich, and Kenneth S. Mericle, eds. *The Political Economy of the Latin American Motor Vehicle Industry*. Cambridge, Mass.: The MIT Press, 1984.

Krueger, Anne O. *Foreign Trade Regimes and Economic Development: Liberalization and Consequences*. New York: National Bureau of Economic Research, 1978.

————. *The Developmental Role of the Foreign Sector and Aid*. Cambridge, Mass.: Harvard University Press, 1982.

————. *Trade and Employment in Developing Countries: 3. Synthesis and Conclusions*. Chicago: University of Chicago Press, for National Bureau of Economic Research, 1983.

————. "The Experience and Lessons of Asia's Super Exporters." In *Export-Oriented Development Strategies: The Success of Five Newly Industrializing Countries*, edited by Vittorio Corbo, Anne O. Krueger, and Fernando Ossa. Boulder, Col.: Westview Press, 1985.

————. et al., eds. *Trade and Employment in Developing Countries: I. Individual Studies*. Chicago: University of Chicago Press, for National Bureau of Economic Research, 1981.

Kuo, Shirley W. Y. *The Taiwan Economy in Transition*. Boulder, Col.: Westview Press, 1983.

————. Gustav Ranis, and John C. H. Fei. *The Taiwan Success Story: Rapid Growth with Improved Distribution in Republic of China, 1952-1979*. Boulder, Col.: Westview Press, 1981.

Kuznets, Paul W. *Economic Growth and Structure in the Republic of Korea*. New Haven: Yale University Press, 1977.

————. "Response to External Shocks: The Experience of Four Countries in 1973-80." In *Economic Notes*, Monte Dei Paschi Di Shiena (1972-1982).

Lal, Deepak. *The Poverty of "Development Economics."* Cambridge, Mass.: Harvard University Press, 1985.

Latorre, Carmen Lux "The Chilean Crisis: A Note on the Consequences of Liberal Policies Towards the Private Sector." *The Developing Countries* 12 (1984).

Lee, Teng-hui. *Intersectoral Capital Flows in the Economic Development of Taiwan, 1889-1960.* Ithaca: Cornell University Press, 1971.

Lee, T. H., and Kuo-shu Liang "Taiwan." In *Development Strategies in Semi-Industrial Economies,* edited by Bela Balassa and Associates Staff. Baltimore: Johns Hopkins University Press, 1982.

Li, Kwoh-ting, and Tzong-shian Yu, eds. *Experiences and Lessons of Economic Development in Taiwan.* Taipei: Academia Sinica, 1982.

Liang, Kuo-shu, and Ching-ing Hou Liang. "Trade and Incentive Policies in Taiwan." In *Experiences and Lessons of Economic Development in Taiwan,* edited by Kwoh-ting Li and Tzong-shian Yu. Taipei: Academia Sinica, 1982.

Lin, Ching-yuan. "Industrial Development and Changes in the Structure of Foreign Trade." *Staff Papers* 15 (1968).

―――. *Industrialization in Taiwan, 1946-72: Trade and Import-Substituting Policies for Developing Countries.* New York: Praeger Publishers, 1973.

―――. *Developing Countries in a Turbulent World: Patterns of Adjustment since the Oil Crisis.* New York: Praeger Publishers, 1981.

―――. *Japanese and U.S. Inflation: A Comparative Analysis.* Lexington, Mass.: Lexington Books, 1984.

Little, Ian, Tibor Scitovsky, and Maurice Scott. *Industry and Trade in Some Developing Countries: A Comparative Study.* Paris: Organization for Economic Cooperation and Development, 1970.

Lopes, Francisco L., and Edmar L. Bacha. "Inflation, Growth, and Wage Policy: A Brazilian Perspective." *Journal of Development Economics* 13 (August-October 1983).

Lowenthal, Abraham F. *The Peruvian Experiment: Continuity and Change Under Military Rule.* Princeton: Princeton University Press, 1975.

Lowenthal, Abraham F., and C. McClintock, eds. *The Peruvian Experiment Reconsidered.* Princeton: Princeton University Press, 1983.

Luedde-Neurath, Richard. *Import Controls and Export-Oriented Development: A Reassessment of the South Korean Case.* Boulder, Col.: Westview Press, 1986.

Macedo, Roberto. "Wage Indexation and Inflation: The Recent Brazilian Experience." In *Inflation, Debt, and Indexation,* edited by Rudiger Dornbusch and Mario Henrique Simonsen. Cambridge, Mass.: The MIT Press, 1983.

Maddison, Angus. *Two Crises: Latin America and Asia, 1929-38 and 1973-83.* Paris: OECD Development Center, 1985.

Malan, Pedro S., and Regis Bonelli. "The Brazilian Economy in the Seventies: Old and New Developments." *World Development* 5 (January/February 1977).

Mamalakis, Markos J. *The Growth and Structure of the Chilean Economy: From Independence to Allende.* New Haven: Yale University Press, 1976.

―――. *Historical Statistics of Chile: Demography and Labor Force, Vol. 2.* Westport, Conn.: Greenwood Press, 1980.

Mamalakis, Markos J., and Clark Winston Reynolds. *Essays on the Chilean Economy.* New Haven: Yale University Press, 1965.

Mann, Arthur J., and Carlos E. Sanchez. "Monetarism, Economic Reform and Socio-Economic Consequences: Argentina, 1976-1982." In *Festschrift in Honour of George F. Rohrlich, II,* edited by J. C. O'Brien. Bradford, West Yorkshire: MCB University Press, 1984.

Marshall, Jorge, Jose Luis Mardones, and Isabel Marshall. "IMF Conditionality: The

Experiences of Argentina, Brazil, and Chile." In *IMF Conditionality*, edited by John Williamson. Washington, D.C.: Institute for International Economics, 1983.

Mathieson, Donald J. "Financial Reform and Capital Flows in a Developing Economy." *Staff Papers* 26 (September 1979).

————. "Financial Reform and Stabilization Policy in a Developing Economy." *Journal of Development Economics* 7 (September 1980).

————. "Inflation, Interest Rates, and the Balance of Payments During a Financial Reform: The Case of Argentina." *World Development* 10 (1982).

————. "Estimating Models of Financial Market Behavior During Periods of Extensive Structural Reform: The Experience of Chile." *Staff Papers* 30 (1983).

McDonald, Dorogh C. "Debt Capacity and Developing Country Borrowing: A Survey of the Literature." *Staff Papers* 29 (1982).

McKinnon, Ronald I. *Money and Capital in Economic Development*. Washington, D.C.: Brookings, 1973.

————. "The Order of Economic Liberalization: Lessons from Chile and Argentina." In *Economic Policy in a World of Change*, edited by Karl Brunner and Allan H. Meltzer. Amsterdam: North-Holland Publishing Co., Carnegie-Rochester Conference Series on Public Policy, 1982.

Morawetz, David. *Twenty-Five Years of Economic Development, 1950–1975*. Baltimore: Johns Hopkins University Press, for the World Bank, 1977.

————. "Manufactured Exports, Labor Productivity, and Employment in Latin America: A Hypothesis Based on the Clothing Industry in Columbia." In *Trade, Stability, Technology, and Equity in Latin America*, edited by Moshe Syrquin and Simon Teitel. New York: Academic Press, 1982.

Nakamura, Takafusa. *The Postwar Japanese Economy: Its Development and Structure*. Tokyo: University of Tokyo Press, 1981.

Nam, Chong Hyun. "Trade and Industrial Policies, and the Structure of Protection in Korea." In *Trade and Growth of the Advanced Developing Countries in the Pacific Basin*, edited by Wontack Hong and Lawrence B. Krause. Seoul: Korea Development Institute, 1981.

Nogues, Julio. "The Nature of Argentina's Policy Reforms During 1976–81." Washington, D.C.: World Bank Staff Working Papers, No. 765, 1986.

Papanek, Gustav F., ed. *Development Policy: Theory and Practice*. Cambridge, Mass.: Harvard University Press, 1968.

Park, Yung Chul. "Inflation and Stabilization Policies in Korea, 1960–1980." In *Conference on Inflation in East Asian Countries*. Taipei: Chung-hua Institution for Economic Research, undated.

————. "Economic Stabilization and Liberalization in Korea, 1980–1984." In *Monetary Policy in a Changing Financial Environment*, by Bank of Korea. Seoul: Bank of Korea, 1985.

————. "Korea's Experience with External Debt Management." In *International Debt and the Developing Countries*, edited by Gordon W. Smith and John T. Cuddington. Washington, D.C.: World Bank, 1985.

Parkin, Vincent. "Economic Liberalism in Chile, 1973–82: A Model for Growth and Development or a Recipe for Stagnation and Impoverishment?" *Cambridge Journal of Economics* 7 (1983).

Patrick, Hugh T. "Financial Development and Economic Growth in Underdeveloped Countries." *Economic Development and Cultural Change* 14 (January 1966).

Pauuw, Douglas S., and John C. Fei. *The Transition in Open Dualistic Economies*. New Haven: Yale University Press, 1973.

Power, John H., Gerardo P. Sicat, and Mo-huan Hsing. *The Philippines/Taiwan*:

Industrialization and Trade Policies. Paris: Organization for Economic Cooperation and Development, 1971.

Ramos, Joseph R. "The Economics of Hyperstagflation: Stabilization Policy in Post–1973 Chile." *Journal of Development Economics* 7 (1980).

Rangel, Carlos. *The Latin Americans: Their Love-Hate Relationship with the United States*. New York: Harcourt Brace Jovanovich, 1977.

Ranis, Gustav. "Industrial Development." In *Economic Growth and Structural Change in Taiwan*, edited by Walter Galenson. Ithaca: Cornell University Press, 1979.

————. "Challenges and Opportunities Posed by Asia's Superexporters: Implications for Manufactured Exports from Latin America." In *Export Diversification and the New Protectionism: The Experiences of Latin America*, edited by Werner Baer and Malcolm Gillis. Champaign, Ill.: University of Illinois, 1981.

Reynolds, Clark W. "Why Mexico's 'Stabilizing Development' Was Actually Destabilizing." *World Development* 6 (1978): 1005–1018.

Rhee, Yung Whee. *Instruments for Export Policy and Administration: Lessons from the East Asian Experience*. Washington, D.C.: World Bank Staff Working Papers, No. 725, 1985.

Rhee, Yung Whee, Bruce Ross-Larson, and Gary Pursell. *Korea's Competitive Edge: Managing the Entry into World Markets*. Baltimore: Johns Hopkins University Press, 1984.

Rodriguez, Carlos Alfredo "The Argentine Stabilization Plan of December 20th." *World Development* 10 (1982).

Sachs, Jeffrey. "LDC Debt in the 1980s: Risk and Reforms." In *Crises in the Economic and Financial Structure*, edited by Paul Wachtel. Lexington, Mass.: Lexington Books, 1982.

————. "External Debt and Macroeconomic Performance in Latin America and East Asia." *Brookings Papers on Economic Activity* 2 (1985).

Saieh, Alvaro, and Larry A. Sjaastad. "Economic Reforms in Chile, 1973–1981." In *Economic Incentives: Proceedings of a Conference Held by the International Economic Association at Kiel, West Germany*, edited by Bela Balassa and Herbert Giersch. London: Macmillan, 1986.

Saini, Krishan G. "The Monetarist Explanation of Inflation: The Experience of Six Asian Countries." *World Development* 10 (1982).

Sargent, Thomas J. "The Ends of Four Big Inflations." In *Inflation: Causes and Effects*, edited by Robert E. Hall. Chicago: University of Chicago Press, 1982.

Scheetz, Thomas. *Peru and the International Monetary Fund*. Pittsburgh: University of Pittsburgh Press, 1986.

Schydrowsky, Daniel M. "The Anatomy of an Economic Failure: Peru, 1968–1978." In *The Peruvian Experiment Reconsidered*, edited by A. Lowenthal and C. McClintock. Princeton: Princeton University Press, 1983.

Scott, Maurice. "Foreign Trade." In *Economic Growth and Structural Change in Taiwan*, edited by Walter Galenson. Ithaca: Cornell University Press, 1979.

Shaw, Edward S. *Financial Deepening in Economic Development*. New York: Oxford University Press, 1973.

Sheahan, John. "Market-Oriented Economic Policies and Political Repression in Latin America." *Economic Development and Cultural Change* 28 (1980).

————. "The Economics of the Peruvian Experiment in Comparative Perspective." In *The Peruvian Experiment Reconsidered*, edited by A. Lowenthal and C. McClintock. Princeton: Princeton University Press, 1983.

Simonsen, Mario Henrique. "Indexation: Current Theory and the Brazilian Experience." In *Inflation, Debt, and Indexation*, edited by Rudiger Dornbusch and Mario

Henrique Simonsen. Cambridge, Mass.: The MIT Press, 1983.

Sjaastad, Larry A. "Liberalization and Stabilization Experiences in the Southern Cone." In *Economic Liberalization and Stabilization Policies in Argentina, Chile, and Uruguay*, edited by Nicholas Ardito Barletta, Mario I. Blejer, and Luis Landau. Washington, D.C.: World Bank, 1983.

Stallings, Barbara. *Class Conflict and Economic Development in Chile, 1958–1973*. Stanford: Stanford University Press, 1978.

Street, James H. "Coping with Energy Shocks in Latin America: Three Responses." *Latin America Research Review* 17 (1982).

Suh, S. C. *Growth and Structural Changes in the Korean Economy, 1910–1940*. Cambridge, Mass.: Harvard University, 1978.

Sutton, Mary "Structurism: The Latin American Record and the New Critique." In *The IMF and Stabilization: Developing Country Experiences*, edited by Tony Killick. London: Heinemann Educational Books, 1984.

Suzuki, Yoshio. *Money, Finance, and Macroeconomic Performance in Japan*. New Haven: Yale University Press, 1986.

Tanzi, Vito, and Mario I. Blejer. "Inflation, Interest Rate Policy, and Currency Substitution in Developing Economies: A Discussion of Some Major Issues." *World Development* 10 (1982).

Taylor, William G. "The Anti-Export Bias in Commercial Policies and Export Performance: Some Evidence from the Recent Brazilian Experience." *Weltwirtschaftliches Archiv* 119 (1983).

Teitel, Simon, and Francisco E. Thoumi. "From Import Substitution to Exports: The Manufacturing Exports Experience of Argentina and Brazil." *Economic Development and Cultural Change* (April 1986).

Thorp, Rosemary. "The Stabilization Crisis in Peru, 1975–78." In *Inflation and Stabilization in Latin America*, edited by Rosemary Thorp and Laurence Whitehead. New York: Holms & Meir, 1979.

Tsiang, S. C. "Exchange Rate, Interest Rate, and Economic Development: The Experience of Taiwan." In *Quantitative Economics and Development: Essays in Memory of Ta-Chung Liu*, edited by L. R. Klein, M. Nerlove, and S. C. Tsiang. New York: Academic Press, 1980.

—————. "Taiwan's Economic Miracle: Lessons in Economic Development." In *World Economic Growth*, edited by Arnold C. Harberger. San Francisco: Institute for Contemporary Studies, 1984.

—————. "Foreign Trade and Investment as Boosters for Take-off: The Experience of Taiwan." In *Export-Oriented Development Strategies: The Success of Five Newly Industrializing Countries*, edited by Vittorio Corbo, Anne O. Krueger, and Fernando Ossa. Boulder, Col.: Westview Press, 1985.

Tsuru, Shigeto. *Essays on Japanese Economy*. Tokyo: Kinokuniya, 1958.

United Nations (CEPAL). *Five Studies on the Situation of Women in Latin America*. Santiago, Chile: United Nations, 1983.

Virmani, Arvind. "Government Policy and the Development of Financial Markets: The Case of Korea." Washington, D.C.: World Bank Staff Working Papers, No. 747, 1985.

Wachter, Susan M. "Structurism vs. Monetarism: Inflation in Chile." In *Short-Term Macroeconomic Policy in Latin America*, edited by Jere Behrman and James A. Hanson. Cambridge, Mass.: Ballinger, for National Bureau of Economic Research, 1979.

Weaver, Frederick Stirton. *Class, State, and Industrial Structure: The Historical Process of South American Industrial Growth*. Westport, Conn.: Greenwood Press, 1980.

Weintraub, Sidney. "Case Study of Economic Stabilization: Mexico." In *Economic Stabilization in Developing Countries*, edited by William R. Cline and Sidney Weintraub. Washington, D.C.: Brookings, 1981.

Wells, John R. "Brazil and the Post-1973 Crisis in the International Economy." In *Inflation and Stabilization in Latin America*, edited by Rosemary Thorp and Laurence Whitehead. New York: Holms & Meir, 1979.

Westphal, Larry E. "The Republic of Korea's Experience with Export-led Industrial Development." *World Development* 6 (March 1978).

Westphal, Larry E., Yung W. Rhee, and Garry G. Pursell. "Korean Industrial Competence: Where It Came From." Washington, D.C.: World Bank Working Paper, No. 469, 1981.

Westphal, Larry E., and Kwang Suk Kim. "Korea." In *Development Strategies in Semi-Industrial Economies*, edited by Bela Balassa and Associates Staff. Baltimore: Johns Hopkins University Press for the World Bank, 1982.

Whitehead, Laurence. "Inflation and Stabilization in Chile, 1970–77." In *Inflation and Stabilization in Latin America*, edited by Rosemary Thorp and Laurence Whitehead. New York: Holms & Meir, 1979.

————. "Mexico from Bust to Boom: A Political Evaluation of the 1976–1979 Stabilization Programme." *World Development* (November 1980).

Wijnbergen, S. van. "Stagflationary Effects of Monetary Stabilization Policies." *Journal of Development Economics* 10 (1982): 133–169.

Williamson, John, ed. *Prospects for Adjustment in Argentina, Brazil, and Mexico: Responding to the Debt Crisis*. Washington, D.C.: Institute for International Economics, 1983.

————, (ed. *IMF Conditionality*. Washington, D.C.: Institute for International Economics, 1983.

————, ed. *Inflation and Indexation: Argentina, Brazil, and Israel*. Washington, D.C.: Institute for International Economics, 1985.

Wisecarver, Daniel L. "Economic Regulation and Deregulation in Chile, 1973–1983." In *The National Economic Policies of Chile*, edited by G. M. Walton. Greenwich, Conn.:JAI Press, 1985.

World Bank *World Development Report* (various issues). Washington, D.C.: World Bank.

————. *Korea: Policy Issues for Long-Term Development*. Washington, D.C.: 1979.

————. *Chile: An Economy in Transition*. Washington, D.C.: World Bank, 1980.

————. *Brazil: Industrial Policies and Manufactured Exports*. Washington, D.C.: World Bank, 1983.

————. *Brazil: Financial Systems Review*. Washington, D.C.: World Bank, 1984.

————. *Brazil: Economic Memorandum*. Washington, D.C.: World Bank, 1984.

————. *Argentina: Economic Memorandum*. Washington, D.C.: World Bank, 1985.

————. *Korea: Development in a Global Context*. Washington, D.C.: World Bank, 1984.

Wynia, Gary W. *Argentina in the Postwar Era: Politics and Economic Policy Making in a Divided Society*. Albuquerque, New Mexico: University of New Mexico, 1978.

Yu, Tzong-shian. "An Analysis of Inflation in Taiwan Since the First Oil Crisis." In *Conference on Inflation in East Asian Countries*. Taipei: Chung-hua Institution for Economic Research, undated.

INDEX

ABOUT THE AUTHOR

Ching-yuan (Ken) Lin (1932–1987) was a senior economist in the Research Department of the International Monetary Fund. He held a B.A. from National Taiwan University, an M.A. from Vanderbilt University, and a M. Phil. and a Ph.D. from The George Washington University—all in economics. In addition, he was a UN Fellow at the Economic Commission for Asia and the Far East (Bangkok) during 1963 and 1964; a Visiting Fellow at the Economic Growth Center, Yale University, during the academic year 1981–1982; and a Visiting Scholar at the Brookings Institution during the summer months of 1982.

Dr. Lin was keenly interested in the policy issues and problems of economic development, and was the author also of *Industrialization in Taiwan, 1946–1972: Trade and Import-Substitution Policies for Developing Countries*; *Developing Countries in a Turbulent World: Patterns of Adjustment since the Oil Crisis*; and *Japanese and U.S. Inflation: A Comparative Analysis*.